A Guide to the National Park Sites

CIVIL WAR

BATTLEFIELDS AND LANDMARKS

With Official National Park Service Maps for Each Site

FRANK E. VANDIVER

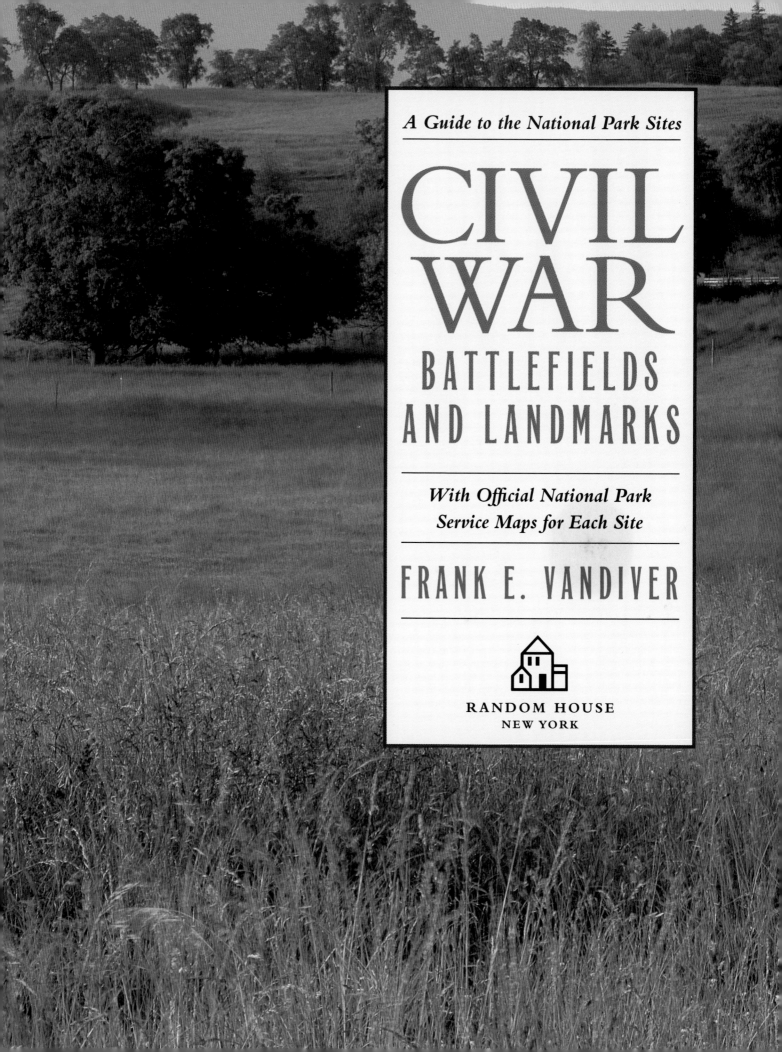

A Guide to the National Park Sites

CIVIL WAR

BATTLEFIELDS AND LANDMARKS

With Official National Park Service Maps for Each Site

FRANK E. VANDIVER

RANDOM HOUSE
NEW YORK

Previous pages: Antietam National Battlefield, Maryland: the scene of the bloodiest single day of the war.

Page 1: Zouaves clashing with the Confederate Black Horse Cavalry in the First Battle of Manassas.

Library of Congress cataloging-in-publication data is available.

ISBN: 0-679-44898-5

Produced by Saraband Inc., PO Box 0032, Rowayton, CT

Design © 1996 by Ziga Design

Manufactured in Slovenia

First Edition

THE EDITOR

Frank E. Vandiver is a scholar of military history whose distinguished work has earned him fellowships and honors at both American and European universities. Dr. Vandiver is Chairman of the Board of the Mosher Institute for International Policy studies and President Emeritus of Texas A&M University. He is also that university's first Distinguished University Professor, a Rockefeller Fellow, a Guggenheim Fellow, a former Harmsworth Professor of American Hsitory at the University of Oxford, England, and visiting professor at the United States Military Academy, West Point. Among his published works of military history are twenty books, including: *Their Tattered Flags: The Epic of the Confederacy* (Harper's Magazine Press, 1970—Jefferson Davis Award of the Confederate Memorial Literary Society; Fletcher Pratt Award), *Mighty Stonewall* (McGraw, 1957—Carr P. Collins Prize, Texas Institute of Letters, 1958), and *Black Jack: The Life and Times of John J. Pershing* (Texas A&M University Press, 1977—Finalist, National Book Awards, 1978). In addition to his academic and writing commitments, he currently serves as Chairman of the Board of the American University in Cairo.

THE CONTRIBUTORS

Michael Golay (MG) is the author of *To Gettysburg and Beyond: The Parallel Lives of Joshua Lawrence Chamberlain and Edward Porter Alexander* (1994). He has also written *The Civil War* (1992), *The Spanish-American War* (1995), and *Reconstruction and Reaction: Black Experience of Freedom: 1861–1913* (forthcoming, 1996). A former newspaper journalist, Michael Golay has an honors degree in American history from Indiana University and a master of arts in history from the State University of New York at Stony Brook. He lives in North Stonington, Connecticut.

Elizabeth Miles Montgomery (EMM) received a degree in history at Hollins College, VA, and has worked in book publishing as an editor and picture researcher since 1974, concentrating on military history and the Civil War. Currently Assistant Curator at the Lockwood-Mathews Mansion Museum in Norwalk, Connecticut, she researched and developed the 1995 Civil War exhibition *Heroines of the Home Front: Life North of the Battlefield.*   •

CONTRIBUTING EDITORS: Susan Bernstein, Robin Langley Sommer

PHOTOGRAPHY: Michael A. Smith

CARTOGRAPHY: Courtesy of the National Park Service

Editorial assistants: Gail Janensch, Emily Head

Project development: Sara Hunt

Picture research: Gillian Speeth

Graphic artist: Chris Berlingo

Contents

The American Civil War

by Frank E. Vandiver

America's Civil War began differently from most insurrections or revolutions. It originated in long arguments between Northern and Southern states about slavery, states' rights, economics, and the nature of democracy. Southern states withdrew from the Union by what they considered constitutional processes: the constitution was a compact among the signatory states, and that compact rested on continuing agreement among the states. When one or more found the Union inimical or repressive, they could withdraw from the compact and resume their independence.

In 1860 several Southern states, fearing the antislavery attitudes of the Republican Party, seceded from the Union when Abraham Lincoln—the Republican presidential nominee—won the presidential election. Once out of the Union, these states coalesced into a new Confederacy. Hoping for peaceful separation, the Confederacy prepared for war. And war came, not as a chaotic revolution, but as a war between two nations, a war following the usual standards of such conflicts. Britain granted belligerent rights to the Confederate States, as did other powers, and so regularized such matters as prisoners of war, recognition of commissions, naval pratique, and accessibility to foreign markets.

No one expected the wrenching changes brought by this first modern war, one that swirled and sprawled across the continent. During its four years, the war exhausted most Southern resources; Northern strength, slightly stretched by war, nonetheless increased as westward expansion continued.

Vast political, social, and economic transformations came from the war: slavery ended, society changed enormously, a new national labor system emerged along with a new national banking system, and the whole political balance shifted from the states toward the Federal government as the Union remained intact.

And all these things are true, but they do not explain the continuing interest in the Civil War. It recruits fervid followers in each generation. "Brother's wars" do cause lasting reaction, but the Civil War has more than usual appeal. Especially does the "Lost Cause" linger in popular imagination—a cause linked to moonlight, magnolias, slaves, and a life style slower, quieter, less crass than the growing frenzy of Northern commerce. In the case of the Civil War, the losing side is clearly holding its historical own.

Courage has something to do with the Civil War's power of attraction. Shocking casualties—greater than in all previous American wars combined—wholesale deaths from shot, shell, and atavistic medicine, a great, consuming conflict that swept civilians into the crush of modern war, combined to tax faith, will, and the far reaches of human endurance.

But there is more. British, French, German, Russian, and other foreign observers watched the American war for lessons. What did this war of the Industrial Revolution teach? It could have taught much—but, as is so often the case, the watchers were trapped by tradition into missing most of what they saw. Wars usually begin with the ideas and tactics of the last combat. Military myopia is fairly generalized, not only in wartime but also in times between conflicts.

General J. F. C. Fuller, in an important article entitled "The Place of the American Civil War in the Evolution of War," suggested that tactical ideas had not advanced beyond Napoleonic concepts of the massed bayonet attack—tactics fostered by the muzzle-loading, short-range muskets (approximately 90 meters), and artillery boasting only case and round shot. When the Civil War began, the Minié cartridge had transformed the musket into a muzzle-loading rifle with a range of about 725 meters and reduced misfires per thousand rounds to less than a half dozen. The rifle became the machine gun of its time and changed everything about the battlefield. Massed infantry and cavalry charges would become almost suicidal, but the mounted arm still retained such important tasks as observation and flanking maneuvers.

Rifled artillery increased range and accuracy dramatically. Though rifled guns were known when the Civil War began, smoothbores dominated action for the first two years. Gradually, rifled guns spread from fixed emplacements to field batteries.

With these changes in weaponry, American lessons began to be noticed, especially as attacks withered in blood. Soldiers in the field quickly realized the need for field entrenchments, and after 1862 hasty works appeared where armies gathered. Field works, combined with increased firepower, gave defenders the advantage over attackers. So the offensive, always the way of winning, lost its punch. Few frontal assaults occurred after mid-1863: longer-ranged ordnance pushed the opposing troops farther apart; bayonet charges became rare. Carnage took precedence over battlefield decisions—wastage, to use a World War I term, replaced quick victory.

Since the North began with all the military baggage of American history, it stuck pretty much to precedent; the South, cut loose from precedent, tried new organizations, weapons, even command concepts.

Circumstances had much to do with the way each side fought the Civil War and certainly complicated command problems. President

Abraham Lincoln, untutored in war, sought a general to organize the Union's strength and hurl it against the Rebels, as Southerners were called. Confederate President Jefferson Davis, an able war minister under President Franklin Pierce, worked to orchestrate operations of his own armies. Both leaders sought capable generals as they struggled to perfect strategies for victory. Lincoln found General Ulysses S. Grant after the Vicksburg campaign in 1863 and within a year made him general-in-chief of Union armies. Davis found Lee in time for the Seven Days' battles of 1862 and kept him in command of the most visible Confederate army—which came to be called Lee's Army. Lincoln groped for and finally developed a fairly centralized command system to implement a comprehensive strategy of pressure. Davis experimented with various command arrangements to implement a strategy of the "offensive-defensive": he tried a departmental system and, finally, a theater system to cope with distance and communication problems.

With superior numbers and resources, Grant sought to crush the South by force. Lee, with fewer men and resources, played a game of maneuver, lightning movement, and dazzling attacks—hewing to the idea that the weaker side must be the most audacious. Davis's other generals, lacking Lee's skill or daring, fought more traditional, often wasteful and inconclusive battles in the west—Albert Sidney Johnston's Shiloh campaign, Braxton Bragg's Kentucky campaign, and his battles at Murfreesboro, Perryville, and Chattanooga are examples.

Clearly, the weaker side could not continue frontal assaults against heavily entrenched forces; weaponry forced a change in tactical philosophy. Some recent studies argue that even Lee's tactics were too costly, that he threw away the flower of his army in assaults from the Seven Days' to Gettysburg; only the entrenchments of the Wilderness in 1864 saved him from even more serious wastage. There is some truth to this argument, but the fact is that Lee's daring partially did negate Union strength in the eastern theater; his daring did produce victories that had a chance to win the war for the Confederacy.

Would other tactics have been better? Did the tactics of the Braggs, the Beauregards, the Joseph E. Johnstons achieve equal or more effective results? Bragg achieved nothing save loss; he squandered his great opportunity after the Battle of Chickamauga in late 1863, and his other battles were marvels of timidity. General Pierre Gustave Toutant Beauregard's strategic euphorias overshadowed his good battle sense and irked President Davis, which resulted in restricting the general's opportunities to defensive operations.

What of Joseph E. Johnston? Wounded at Seven Pines in May 1862, he yielded command of his army to Lee. Never a Davis favorite, Johnston did, nonetheless, receive a daring assignment as theater commander in the west late in 1862—a chance for lasting fame. But he could not rise to the challenges of his satrapy and yearned for traditional army command. Still, his campaign against General William T. Sherman from Dalton to Atlanta in 1864 remains a classic of Fabian tactics. Grudgingly, he retreated and sought to avoid combat save on impregnable ground, to elude a superior enemy and lure him deep into Confederate territory, to retire against his own base at Atlanta and stretch Sherman's communications. President Davis removed him from command in July 1864 when he refused to explain his plans about fighting or holding Atlanta. His replacement, General John B. Hood, fought two fierce battles for the city, lost them, and turned to a ruinous campaign in Tennessee.

Was Johnston right? Should the Confederacy have stood on the defensive, yielded ground and conserved strength? Winning by not losing had the precedent of the American Revolution, but Confederate politics worked against such a strategy. States' rights governors cherished every inch of their states; a national war plan had to be built around that fetish. And Johnston's Fabian tactics would probably not have worked for two overriding reasons: Union strength in men and logistics and matching Southern weaknesses.

Shortages of rail cars, engine works, trackage; vulnerable rivers; drastic weaknesses in ship production—all these fragmented Confederate logistical efforts and hampered effective organization of blockade running.

By the end of the Civil War, fighting around Richmond focused along some thirty-five miles of trenches—trenches much like those to be found fifty years later in Europe. Looked at in long perspective, the Civil War stands a precursor of the First World War—but it is more.

As the first of the modern conflicts, it remains a model of warfare in our time. It boasted the first really new weapons in more than a century, and they brought tactical innovations. It raged over vast distances that forced reliance not only on railroads, but also on the telegraph, on battlefield semaphore signals, and on new command arrangements. Massed casualties induced new methods of medical treatment in the field and in hospitals. As it persisted, the war generated an anger of its own that brought changes unintended at first. War against civilians characterized Sherman's 1864 campaign, some of Grant's operations around Vicksburg, and Confederate general Jubal A. Early's 1864 operations in Pennsylvania. The mere existence of large armies changed both North and South. When numbers of men from across both sections gathered together, the first really national experiences began for most of them. So armies constituted large change agents in themselves.

Other changes? Economic warfare became part of the North's war plan, as exemplified by Sherman's march through Georgia and blockading of the South's internal and external borders. All of these initiatives show the modern nature of the war.

America's conflict of the 1860s stands as a landmark in the rising scope of wars that engulf our present century: because that is true, the Civil War holds a lasting place in the widening history of insurrections.

The Eastern Theater of War

War in the east raged mainly along the hundred-mile corridor between Washington and Richmond—with some expansions into the Shenandoah Valley, Maryland, and Pennsylvania. Two great armies filled the eastern stage—the North's Army of the Potomac and the South's Army of Northern Virginia.

Unlucky army, legend said of the Army of the Potomac, badly officered and slackly run, army of wasted lives and chances, army cast against the fates and Lee—but an army that stuck to its steadfast duty against the odds and finally, as Grant's blunt bludgeon, it would win.

Amazing army, legend said of the Army of Northern Virginia, well officered, led at last by a man who used it like a rapier against a baffled giant, army of romantic rustics who gave their wary hearts to Robert E. Lee and never doubted, never balked, and failed him rarely—though he often asked of it things beyond the gift of mortals.

Blooded at First Bull Run (Manassas) in July 1861, these two armies fought through the Seven Days' battles, through Second Manassas, Antietam, Fredericksburg in 1862, through Chancellorsville, Gettysburg, Bristoe Station, Mine Run in 1863, through the Wilderness, Spotsylvania, Cold Harbor, and entrenched into the siege lines at Richmond and Petersburg in 1864. Lee tried desperately to prevent a crippling siege—whose grim outcome he prophesied—and, after it began, detached Jubal Early's Corps on a Washington raid to loosen Grant's grip. When that failed, Lee's Army burrowed into a labyrinth of trenches south and west of Petersburg to play a Stoic's game of attrition and of holding on. When, at last, Grant's lines extended too far, Lee's lines broke on April 2, 1865, and he began his last retreat toward Appomattox Court House and surrender on April 9th. Lee's surrender marked the effective end of the Civil War, although scattered forces struggled on for several weeks.

Other military activities occurred in the eastern theater—General Beauregard maintained a masterful defense of Charleston Harbor through 1864; Confederates turned back a major Union invasion of Florida at Olustee in February of that same year. And western war edged eastward as Sherman marched to the sea.

Below Richmond on the South Atlantic Coast, important naval and river operations slowly closed most Confederate ports and estuaries to outside commerce. At last only Wilmington, North Carolina; Charleston; Mobile; Galveston; and Matamoros, Mexico, were open to the vital blockade runners that propped the South for the last two years of the war. Wilmington's loss, in January 1865, slammed the last outside door and drove the Rebels to their last supplies.

Naval activities sputtered along the east coast throughout the war, as makeshift Confederate ironclads engaged Union ships at various inlets. Sea mines were used by the Rebels and did considerable damage to Union ships. A Confederate submarine, after a series of deadly tests, managed to sink a Union vessel in February

1864. And such Rebel commerce raiders as the *Florida, Georgia, Alabama,* and *Shenandoah* sparked a "flight from the flag" by U.S. merchantmen.

War ended in the east when Joseph E. Johnston surrendered his remnant of the Army of Tennessee to Sherman on April 26, 1865.

Much of the Confederate war effort centered in Virginia, North Carolina, South Carolina, and Georgia. As the war progressed, the South created surprising industrial complexes around Richmond's huge Tredegar Iron Works and Fayetteville, North Carolina's arsenal, and around Atlanta's important rail connections. A world class powder works at Augusta sustained Southern needs until the end; large arsenals, armories, and laboratories in Macon and Columbus and Charleston provided arms, ammunition, caissons, and cannon.

A small but expanding cattle industry in central Florida, the small ports along the inland waterway on the east coast, and the peripatetic coastal salt works, gave the state logistical importance beyond its size. Florida, too, by population ratio, contributed more men to Rebel ranks than any other state.

Population concentration added importance to the eastern theater. Such wealth as the South boasted, after the loss of New Orleans, centered around Richmond, Atlanta, Charleston, and Mobile.

An important intangible added to eastern importance—morale. South Carolina, "the cradle of secession," boasted the fieriest of fire-eaters, and the state remained a fount of Rebel sentiment. Western Virginia would separate from its Piedmont neighbor because of the war, and Georgia and North Carolina had enclaves of antiwar sentiment, with some mountain areas in virtual rebellion against the Confederacy. Georgia's Governor Joseph E. Brown and North Carolina's Zebulon B. Vance raised state-rights resistance to virtually every Confederate need: Brown commissioned most state militiamen to foil the draft, and Vance kept 92,000 new uniforms in state depots while Lee's army froze in the Petersburg lines. Around Atlanta, though, and especially near the armies, patriotism waxed fairly high.

For the North, the eastern theater seemed the fulcrum of the Union—not only because of Washington, but also because of heavy population, industrial, and financial concentrations in the corridor from Washington through Baltimore, Philadelphia, New York, and Boston.

There were morale problems, too, in that area for the North. Maryland's loyalty wavered occasionally. In New York City, angry, underpaid workers rioted against a discriminatory draft in July 1863, and the pro-Southern mayor suggested that the city secede and join the Confederacy!

Delaware remained a slave state until after the war, but never flagged in support of suppressing the rebellion. Rhode Island, Maine, Massachusetts, Connecticut, all the upper tier, sent large numbers to swell Union ranks while keeping a wary eye on Canada for evidence of English help to the South. Not everyone in those states supported the war, but few supported a Copperhead conspiracy against the Union.

From all standpoints, the eastern theater claimed attention as the power base of war for both sides. Historians would argue—still do—that the war was won and lost in the west. But eastern devotion made the war in the North and sustained it to victory. That same devotion sustained the Rebels through early successes and later defeats, invasion, destruction of resources, and on to total defeat.

—*Frank E. Vandiver*

Fort Sumter

After the war of 1812, Congress allocated funds to construct a series of forts and batteries around Charleston Harbor to defend that important port city. One of those defensive structures, Fort Sumter, was a five-sided brick fort on a manmade granite island four miles out in the harbor.

When South Carolina seceded from the Union on December 20, 1860, Fort Sumter was still unfinished and was armed with only 48 of the 140 cannon that it was designed to mount. The harbor defenses—which included Fort Moultrie on Sullivan's Island, Castle Pinckney on Shute's Folly Island, and Fort Johnson on James Island across from Fort Moultrie—were commanded by Major Robert Anderson, a career artillery officer from Kentucky, with a force of fewer than 100 Federal troops and 43 civilian engineers.

On the night on December 26, 1860, Anderson ordered all his men to transfer secretly to Fort Sumter in the middle of the harbor from the outlying batteries and Fort Moultrie. Southern militia units—which had flocked to Charleston after secession—took possession of the abandoned posts the following day and established a floating battery off Sullivan's Island. Viewing Anderson's action as an act of war, they demanded the surrender of Fort Sumter.

In January 1861, President James Buchanan and Lieutenant General Winfield Scott, in an attempt to reinforce Anderson,

THE CAPTURE OF FORT SUMTER

On **April 12, 1861,** the opening shots of the Civil War were fired on Fort Sumter by the Confederate batteries lining Charleston Harbor. As recently as December 20, 1860, those forts had been in Federal hands, commanded by Major Robert Anderson; news of South Carolina's secession had impelled him to move all his men to Fort Sumter. When the bombardment began, the **April 14** surrender was inevitable. The next day President Lincoln called out 75,000 militia. The Civil War had begun.

 USA Major Robert Anderson; Captain George S. James

 CSA Brigadier General Pierre G.T. Beauregard

Casualties
One Union soldier killed, four others wounded

dispatched a force of 200 men on *Star of the West,* an unarmed merchant ship. However, the vessel was turned back by an attack from the battery on Morris Island. Although Anderson might have brought his guns to bear and returned fire, he did not because he hoped to receive the needed supplies and

Opposite: This cutaway diagram shows the plan of Fort Sumter, which was still unfinished at the outbreak of hostilities. It was designed to mount 140 cannon and house a garrison of 650 men.

Right, above: This cannon was one of only forty-eight mounted and ready for use when the Confederates opened fire on Fort Sumter from Fort Johnson, on nearby James Island.

Right: The damage inflicted by more than 5,000 rounds of cannon fire is apparent in this photograph.

Below: Fort Sumter commanded the main ship channel for the port of Charleston Harbor. Its five-foot-thick brick walls rose some fifty feet above the water.

THE FIRST SHOT OF THE WAR

Artist William Waud made this wash drawing of black workers mounting a Confederate cannon on Morris Island on April 12, 1861. At nearby Fort Johnson, a Virginia zealot named Edmund Ruffin was given the honor of pulling the lanyard on a symbolic first shot of the Civil War. Not until two hours later did the Union defenders open fire.

troops and knew that such a reaction would inflame his opponents. Several Northern periodicals and newspapers saw the Southern reaction as an overt act of war, and they fanned the flames of dissension.

Anderson and his men remained at Fort Sumter as more states seceded: most Federal forces within the new Confederacy surrendered. On March 4, 1861, Abraham Lincoln took the oath of office as the sixteenth president of the United States. He stated in his inaugural address that he considered secession unlawful, but that the Confederacy would have to make the first move. "In your hands, my dissatisfied fellow countrymen, and not in mine, is the momentous issue of civil war.... You can have no conflict without being yourselves the aggressors." The reaction of the South was to authorize enlistment for 100,000 men for a year's service.

The new Confederate president, Jefferson Davis—who had been the U.S. Secretary of War from 1853 to 1857 in the Franklin Pierce administration—ordered General Pierre Gustave Toutant Beauregard of Louisiana to take command of the forces in Charleston, which numbered some 4,000 men. A month after his inauguration, President Lincoln informed Governor Francis Pickens of South Carolina that he wished to resupply the beleaguered garrison at Fort Sumter with food only—no munitions. The governor advised President Davis, who commanded Beauregard to demand the surrender of the fort. Anderson refused, but told Beauregard, whom he had instructed in artillery at West Point, that his low level of supplies would soon make surrender inevitable.

Beauregard wasn't allowed to wait. At 3:30 AM, well before daylight on April 12, 1861, Anderson received notice that if he didn't surrender within the hour, the Confederate forces would shell the fort. The bombardment, and the Civil War, began at 4:30 AM, true to Beauregard's warning, with a mor-

EYEWITNESS

From the journal entry of a Charleston resident, April 12, 1861:

"Yesterday was the merriest, maddest dinner we have had yet....Our peace negotiator—or envoy—came in. That is, Mr. Chesnut returned—his interview with Colonel Anderson had been deeply interesting—but was not inclined to be communicative, wanted his dinner. Felt for Anderson. Had telegraphed to President Davis for instructions. What answer to give Anderson, &c&c. He had gone back to Fort Sumter, with additional instructions....
I do not pretend to go to sleep. How can I? If Anderson does not accept terms—at four—he shall be fired upon.

I count four—St. Michael chimes. I begin to hope. At half-past four, the heavy booming of a cannon.

I sprang out of bed. On my knees—prostrate—I prayed as I never prayed before.

There was a sound of stir all over the house—pattering of feet in the corridor—all seemed hurrying one way.... It was to the housetop.

The shells were bursting. In the dark I heard a man say 'waste of ammunition.'

I knew my husband was rowing about in a boat somewhere in that dark bay. And that the shells were roofing it over—bursting toward the fort. If Anderson was obstinate—he was to order the forts on our side to open fire. Certainly fire had begun. The regular roar of the cannon—there it was. And who could tell what each volley accomplished of death and destruction.

The women were wild, there on the housetop. Prayers from the women and imprecations from the men, and then a shell would light up the scene."

Left: Albert Bierstadt, perhaps the most famous artist of the Hudson River School, painted this scene of the attack on Fort Sumter in 1861.

Opposite, above: Battery B, Fort Sumter, with the Confederate flag flying over it. The Confederates controlled Fort Sumter from 1861 until Sherman's advance necessitated its evacuation in February 1865.

tar-shot signal from Fort Johnson on James Island. According to a member of Beauregard's staff, "that shot was a sound of alarm that brought every man, woman, and child in Charleston from their beds." The Union force within the fort did not return fire for more than two hours; then Anderson's second in command, Captain Abner Doubleday, fired a thirty-two pounder at a battery on Cummings Point.

The Union defenders, partly because of the scarcity and condition of ammunition, and partly because they were extremely short-staffed, continued to return fire only sporadically. They lobbed two shells at the Moultrie House, a well-known hotel, which scattered the crowd of civilian observers. The Federals ceased firing at twilight, while the Confederates continued intermittently throughout the night. Fires burned in the fort, endangering the powder magazine. Anderson's men scrambled to remove as much gunpowder as possible, but they were forced to close the great metal doors of the magazine and insulate them with a pile of earth. Eventually, even the barrels of powder that had been saved at such risk had to be thrown into the water because of the danger of explosion. Another Confederate shell snapped the flagstaff in half, and the Federal flag fell, leading Confederates to wonder if the fort were ready to surrender.

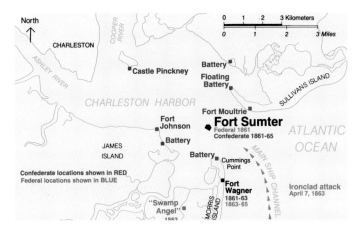

Beauregard's aide, Colonel Louis Wigfall (until recently, a senator from Texas), was rowed across to Fort Sumter, to find out whether the fallen colors signaled that the Federals were ready to surrender. A new flag was raised as he approached the fort, and although he was exposed to the artillery fire of his own side, he reached the island. He brought Anderson honorable terms and granted his request to salute the flag and withdraw with arms and private baggage. Wigfall was not actually authorized to make these terms, but a later emissary brought confirmation from Beauregard that made the terms official. Major Anderson accepted because of the lack of food, supplies, and men. The fear that the damage sustained by the defenses would jeopardize his small force played a part in this decision. Although the Confederates had bombarded the fort for thirty-four hours, setting fire to the barracks and dismounting guns, the Federal garrison had suffered no casualties. During the bombardment, thousands of spectators watched from Charleston rooftops and even from small boats in the harbor.

On April 14 the departing Union force was allowed to fire a fifty-gun salute, during which a pile of ammunition exploded, causing the only Union casualties. Private Daniel Hough became the first soldier killed in the Civil War, and 4 others were wounded at this time, although more than five thousand rounds of cannon fire had been directed at the fort during the engagement. The Confederates, who were unscathed, took possession to applause and shouts from the spectators and gave Anderson and his troops safe conduct to the steamship *Baltic* for the voyage north.

Following the surrender of Fort Sumter, President Lincoln called out 75,000 militiamen to end the insurrection in South Carolina. In response, four more states, Virginia, Arkansas, Tennessee, and North Carolina, joined the Confederacy. Fort Sumter remained in Confederate hands throughout most of the war, guarding the port for many blockade runners, although it was often shelled by the Union Navy. In 1863 eleven members of the Confederate garrison were killed, and forty-one wounded, during one of these bombardments. Eventually, the fort was reduced to little more than rubble.

On April 14, 1865, at the end of the war, Anderson, now a general, but retired because of poor health, returned to Fort Sumter to raise the tattered American flag that had flown over the garrison during the battle exactly four years before.

Left: A map of Charleston Harbor showing its importance as a Confederate stronghold. It provided a breach in the Federal naval blockade through which to receive war supplies and send payment in cotton overseas.

Opposite, above: Residents of Charleston found rooftop vantage points from which to view the cannonade. Some even put out in small boats for a dangerously close look at the proceedings.

Opposite, below: This interior view of the fort shows the damage to the casements from prolonged shelling. The photograph was taken on April 14, 1861, when the Federal garrison surrendered to Confederate troops. The defeated force was given safe conduct to the steamship Baltic *for transport north.*

Below: No one could foresee what the opening guns at Fort Sumter presaged for the newly divided nation.

FORT SUMTER NATIONAL MONUMENT

MAILING ADDRESS
Superintendent, Fort Sumter National Monument, 1214 Middle Street, Sullivan's Island, SC 29482

TELEPHONE
803-883-3123

DIRECTIONS
The fort is located on an island in Charleston Harbor and can be reached only by boat. Tour boats leave from the city boat marina on Lockwood Drive, just south of US 17 in Charleston. For boat schedules call 803-722-1691, or write Fort Sumter Tours, Inc., PO Box 59, Charleston, SC 29402.

VISITOR CENTER
Museum, gift shop, interpretive exhibits, and ten-minute video.

ACTIVITIES
Self-guided walking tours and ranger talks.

HOURS
Open daily from 2 PM to 4 PM, with hours extended to 10 AM to 6 PM in the summer. The fort is closed December 25.

Manassas

The First Battle of Manassas

FIRST MANASSAS/BULL RUN

All of Washington society, it seemed, came out to see the first battle of Bull Run in Manassas, Virginia. On **July 21, 1861,** the Union army under General Irvin McDowell attacked Confederates under P.G.T. Beauregard. However, the resistance offered by General Thomas "Stonewall" Jackson and his men forced the Federals to retreat to Washington.

 USA General Irvin McDowell

 CSA Brigadier General P.G.T. Beauregard; Brigadier General Joseph E. Johnston; Brigadier General Thomas "Stonewall" Jackson

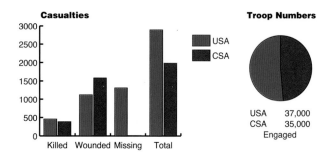

The months after Fort Sumter fell were marked by a few skirmishes and small battles, as both sides strove to consolidate and train their very green troops. Many Union soldiers signed up for only three months, believing that the war would be of short duration. In July 1861, Union General Irvin McDowell, aware that his troops' enlistments were running out, advanced an army of some 37,000 men into northern Virginia from Washington, D.C. It was the largest American force ever assembled, and it outnumbered the opposing Confederate army, commanded by General Pierre G. T. Beauregard, the hero of Fort Sumter, by almost two to one.

McDowell's objective was the important railroad center at Manassas Junction, where the Orange & Alexandria Railroad, which ran north to south, met the Manassas Gap Railroad, the major line to the Shenandoah Valley. If McDowell could take Manassas, he would control a fast route into the Confederate capital at Richmond.

The first day's march carried the force barely five miles into enemy territory, as the raw Union troops broke ranks to hunt for blackberries and fill their canteens with fresh water. They also found some of their equipment too heavy to carry and discarded it by the side of the road. On July 18, they reached Centreville, about thirty miles from Washington, and five miles from the small creek known as Bull Run. The Confederates, with a force of 22,000 commanded by General Beauregard—who was one of McDowell's West Point classmates—were spread out over 8 miles along the southern bank of Bull Run, guarding the fords.

Beauregard, aware of the size of the Union force through his spy network in Washington, requested reinforcements. President Davis sent word to General Joseph E. Johnston to maneuver around the Federal force of General Robert Pat–

Opposite, above: At 5:30 AM on July 21, 1861, Union cannon opened fire on Confederate positions at the Stone Bridge in a diversionary attack.

Right: This sketch by a Confederate officer depicts a Southern battery, complete with cannon drawn by oxen. The Confederates took up positions along the narrow, tree-shaded creek called Bull Run, for which Union forces named the battle. (Southerners usually named battles for the nearest town.)

terson, stationed in the lower Shenandoah Valley, and join Beauregard. Johnston complied, bringing some 10,000 Confederate troops to Manassas by train—the first time the railroad was used to transport troops to the front.

Soon after, there was a skirmish at Blackburn's Ford when a Federal reconnaissance brigade commanded by Colonel I. B. Richardson came upon Confederate troops. After a brief clash, the Federal troops were forced to withdraw, leaving 19 Union soldiers and 15 Confederates dead on the field. This encounter proved that the Confederate center and right were strongly defended, and McDowell changed his plans accordingly; he would make a diversionary flanking movement against the Confederate left at the Stone Bridge.

On July 21, McDowell's main column marched northwest and crossed Bull Run at Sudley Ford to attack the Confederate flank and rear. McDowell also planned a series of diversionary attacks against Beauregard's front at the Warrenton

turnpike and at two other fords, Blackburn's and Mitchell's. It was a good plan, but McDowell's force was too inexperienced to execute it rapidly enough to surprise the enemy.

The Confederates at the Stone Bridge, commanded by General Nathan G. Evans, learned of McDowell's flank march via a semaphore signal and turned to face the Federal attack. This small force, reinforced by troops under Generals Bernard Bee and Francis Barlow, made a gallant stand, but they were overwhelmed and driven back by the Union troops, commanded by Ambrose Burnside, Samuel Heintzelman and William T. Sherman, to new positions on Henry House Hill. McDowell believed he had achieved a great victory.

Confederate General Thomas J. Jackson and his fresh troops arrived at Henry House Hill in time to halt the Federal advance. After Jackson told General Bee to hold the line, Bee shouted to his troops, "There stands Jackson like a stone wall! Rally behind the Virginians!" Thus Jackson received his famous nickname. The Confederate line held and was eventually reinforced by the troops under Johnston's command, arriving by a quick march from Manassas Junction.

At the height of the attack, at about 2:00 PM, McDowell brought up several artillery batteries to fire into Jackson's lines. At this point, the confusion created by uniform colors became a crucial factor. The 33rd Virginia regiment, approaching the Federals from the woods, wore blue uniforms. Federal gunners held their fire, believing these troops to be Union sol-

Above: Fighting during First Manassas, where inexperienced troops on both sides got their first taste of battle. Union soldiers in Zouave uniforms of red and blue added to the confusion caused by various uniform colors among regiments of both sides.

Right: The Stone Church in Centreville, the Confederate outpost captured and recaptured five times in the course of the Civil War.

diers, until they were stunned by a tremendous volley of gunfire and a bayonet charge. During the desperate, sometimes
hand-to-hand, fighting that followed, the cannon were captured and recaptured several times. Eventually, the Confederates were able to take control of Henry House Hill.

With the arrival of more Johnston reinforcements from
Winchester, it was the Confederates' turn to attack. The
Southern attack was aimed at McDowell's right flank and
rear. The Federal line staggered and fell back, slowly at first,
but soon the army was in full retreat. The disorganization
and panic of the retreat was exacerbated by the number of
civilians in carriages who had come out from Washington
to watch the battle. Confederate artillery continued to fire
on the retreating columns, and several shells landed nearby.
This caused a panic that sent the Federal Army literally running back to Washington. The exhausted Confederate force
did not pursue.

Ironically, the loss of the battle proved a greater advantage
to the Union side than the victory was to the Confederates.
The Southerners, now assured that they could "whip the Yankees," still believed the war would be over soon. The Northerners, in contrast, geared up for a long war and became more
determined than ever to put down the rebellion.

Union casualties totaled 2,896 as compared with 1,982 for
the Confederates. Among the civilian dead was Judith Henry,
an 85-year-old bedridden widow, whose house had been
raked by gunfire from both sides as the opposing armies fought
over Henry House Hill.

OFF TO WAR!

Strong sentiment on both sides resulted in such pictures
as this Currier and Ives print of a Union officer's farewell
to his family. It was an era of unabashed and heartfelt
emotion, and the theme of a nation divided against itself
struck a responsive chord in almost every heart. Patriotism
was at a high-water mark in colorful posters like "The
Spirit of '61," in which Liberty brandished a sword and
the American flag in response to Lincoln's first call for
volunteers. Nashville artist Gilbert Gaul painted a touching
farewell between a young Confederate volunteer and his
family, including servants and pets, as his horse stood waiting
at the door. The spirit of the time was idealistic and heroic,
deepening the sad contrast between expectation and the
reality of war, with its carnage, desolation, and waste of
life. Raw recruits on both sides first learned about this
reality on the plains of Manassas, Virginia, where "The
Shadow War" took substance at a cost of more than 800
lives. Hardest hit were New York's 5th and 10th Zouave
Regiments, whose colorful, elegant uniforms made them
easy targets. Much popular art and poetry of the war years
was mawkish and sentimental by today's standards, with "a
farewell group weeping at every cottage," but many artists
and writers captured what was noblest about the Civil War
experience. Oliver Wendell Holmes, the future U.S. Supreme
Court chief justice, was a lieutenant of Massachusetts troops
in 1861 and spoke for a whole generation when he wrote,
"Through our great good fortunes, in our youth our hearts
were touched with fire."

EYEWITNESS

Washington, July 22: Correspondent for the Times *(London)*

"The repulse of the Federalists, decided as it was, might have had no serious effects whatever beyond the mere failure—which politically was of greater consequence than it was in a military sense—but for the disgraceful conduct of the troops. The retreat on their lines at Centreville seems to have ended in a cowardly rout—a miserable, causeless panic. Such scandalous behaviour on the part of soldiers I should have considered impossible, as with some experience of camps and armies I have never even in alarms among camp followers seen the like of it. How far the disorganization of the troops extended I know not; but it was complete in the instance of more than one regiment. Washington this morning is crowded with soldiers without officers, who have fled from Centreville, and with 'three months' men,' who are going home from the face of the enemy on the expiration of their term of enlistment. The streets, in spite of the rain, are crowded by people with anxious faces, and groups of wavering politicians are assembled at the corners, in the hotel passages, and the bars. If in the present state of the troops the Confederates were to make a march across the Potomac above Washington, turning the works at Arlington, the Capital might fall into their hands. "

Opposite: The imposing monument to General Thomas "Stonewall" Jackson, who earned his nickname at First Manassas when he rallied retreating Confederates to hold their ground on Henry Hill.

Above: A sketch by artist-correspondent A. R. Waud of the Rhode Island Brigade on the field at First Manassas.

Below: A contemporary lithograph depicting Zouaves charging against the Confederate Black Horse Cavalry at First Bull Run.

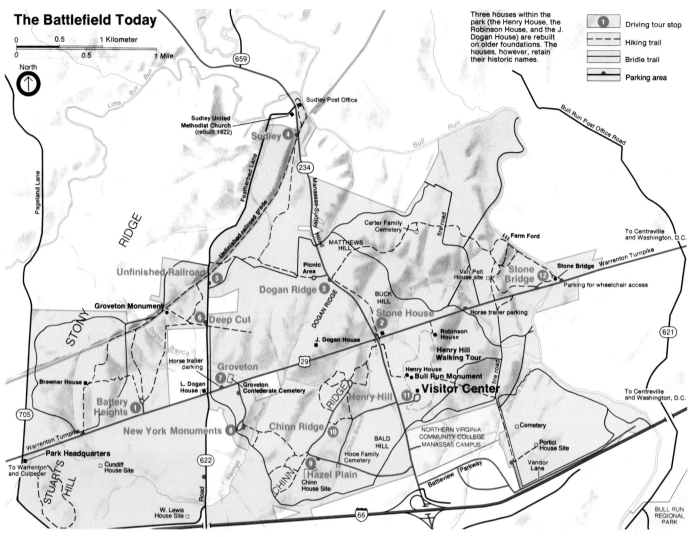

The Battlefield Today

Three houses within the park (the Henry House, the Robinson House, and the J. Dogan House) are rebuilt on older foundations. The houses, however, retain their historic names.

Legend:
- Driving tour stop
- Hiking trail
- Bridle trail
- Parking area

North

0 — 0.5 — 1 Kilometer
0 — 0.5 — 1 Mile

Pageland Lane

RIDGE

Little Bull Run

659

Sudley Post Office

Sudley United Methodist Church (rebuilt 1922)

Sudley 4

Bull Run

Bull Run Post Office Road

234

Featherbed Lane

Manassas-Sudley Road

Unfinished railroad grade

Carter Family Cemetery

Farm Ford

To Centreville and Washington, D.C.

MATTHEWS HILL

Warrenton Turnpike

Unfinished Railroad 5

Picnic Area

Van Pelt House site

Stone Bridge

Stone Bridge 12

Dogan Ridge 3

DOGAN RIDGE

BUCK HILL

Parking for wheelchair access

STONY

Groveton Monument

Deep Cut 6

Stone House 2

Robinson House

Horse trailer parking

621

Young's

Horse trailer parking

J. Dogan House

Henry Hill Walking Tour

Brawner House

Groveton 7

L. Dogan House

Groveton Confederate Cemetery

29

Henry House
Bull Run Monument

Visitor Center 11

fire road

To Centreville and Washington, D.C.

705

Battery Heights 1

RIDGE

Henry Hill

New York Monuments 8

Chinn Ridge

10

Warrenton Turnpike

Park Headquarters

Cundiff House Site

622

BALD HILL

NORTHERN VIRGINIA COMMUNITY COLLEGE MANASSAS CAMPUS

Cemetery

Portici House Site

Vandor Lane

To Warrenton and Culpeper

STUART'S HILL

Hooe Family Cemetery

Hazel Plain 9

Chinn House Site

CHINN

Battleview Parkway

BULL RUN REGIONAL PARK

W. Lewis House Site

66

Many landmarks of both conflicts remain. The one-mile Henry Hill Walking Tour covers the area in which the fighting during **First Manassas** was concentrated. Two further walking tours of First Manassas sites are located at the Stone Bridge and Sudley. Crucial sites in **Second Manassas** are marked on a twelve-mile driving tour keyed to the map above. (Dates refer to the events of August 1862.)

1 Battery Heights On August 28, Jackson's troops attacked from a hidden position north of the turnpike as the Union column marched past.

2 Stone House Pope's head-quarters during the fighting on August 30 (also a field hospital during both conflicts).

3 Dogan Ridge Union artillery position on August 29.

4 Sudley Site of the fighting on Jackson's left flank on August 29.

5 Unfinished Railroad Center of Jackson's line during the fighting on August 29.

6 Deep Cut Confederate troops repulsed the attack ordered by Pope on the morning of August 30.

7 Groveton The cemetery contains the remains of more than 260 Confederate soldiers.

8 New York Monuments 123 men of the 5th New York were killed here on August 30—the greatest loss in any single infantry regiment in a Civil War battle.

9 Hazel Plain Site of the Chinn House, where Longstreet ordered the counterattack on Pope's troops on August 30.

10 Chinn Ridge Union troops held their position here during Longstreet's attack, allowing Pope time to build a defensive position behind them.

11 Henry Hill Site of the final Union stand against Longstreet's troops.

12 Stone Bridge Defeated Union troops withdrew across this bridge over Bull Run after nightfall on August 30.

Opposite: Edwin Forbes' sketch for Leslie's Illustrated *of Confederate batteries shelling the Union position at night during the Battle of Cedar Mountain, August 9, 1862—the prelude to the Second Battle of Manassas. Jackson's troops clashed with a Union corps led by General Nathaniel Banks; the Federals sustained nearly 2,000 casualties as well as a considerable loss of arms and munitions.*

The Second Battle of Manassas

After the failure of General George McClellan's attempt to reach the Confederate capital of Richmond from the Virginia Peninsula, Lincoln created another army, the Army of Virginia, from the scattered forces around the capital. It was commanded by Major General John Pope, who was ordered to join up with McClellan's Army of the Potomac. The force thus created would number more than 175,000, twice the size of any army the Confederacy could field.

General Robert E. Lee, who had replaced Joseph E. Johnston as commander of the Army of Northern Virginia in June, had prevented McClellan from taking Richmond in the series of battles and skirmishes known as the Seven Days'. He was aware that he would have to repulse the new threat of Pope's army before it could meet McClellan's, still on the Peninsula. Assuming that McClellan would not move quickly, Lee took the offensive and sent 12,000 men under General Thomas Jackson north to meet and delay Pope's movement south. Shortly afterward, he sent General A. P. Hill with another 13,000 to join them. When Lee learned that McClellan had withdrawn from the Peninsula by water and was returning to the area near Washington, he hurried

SECOND MANASSAS/BULL RUN

On **August 29–30, 1862**, in the second Battle of Bull Run, the newly formed Union Army of Virginia under General John A. Pope attacked General "Stonewall" Jackson's Confederate troops. Confederate General James Longstreet reinforced Jackson, then counterattacked and pushed the Federals across Bull Run. Robert E. Lee achieved his strategic objective of preventing General George McClellan from joining Pope's Army of Virginia.

 USA: Major General John A. Pope

 CSA: General Robert E. Lee;
Major General Thomas "Stonewall" Jackson;
Major General James Longstreet

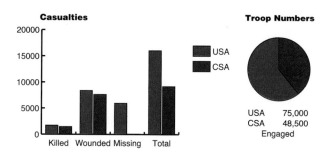

Figures are for entire campaign from August 27 to September 2.

north with another 30,000 men of General Longstreet's Corps to join Jackson. His objective was to defeat Pope's Army of Virginia before it could link up with McClellan's Army of the Potomac.

The Battle of Cedar Mountain on August 9, between Jackson's troops and the Union corps of General Nathaniel Banks, may have given Pope the first indication that a major Confederate force was moving toward him. His reaction was to draw back across the Rappahannock River to a site where he could easily be supplied with munitions and reinforcements from Washington. Lee decided to cut Pope's supply lines, to force his opponent into a battle at the time and place of Lee's own choosing. In a series of skirmishes between the two armies, a party of Confederates under James E. B. (Jeb) Stuart captured Pope's personal baggage and papers. Through

these documents, Lee discovered that the first troops of the Army of the Potomac, the V Corps, commanded by Fitz-John Porter, were close by.

Once again, Lee sent Jackson ahead. By so doing he divided his army, a surprising and audacious maneuver in view of the size of the opposing force. Jackson's orders were to move around the Federal right flank and station his troops in the rear. Any move toward Washington made the Union forces nervous, and Lee was sure that Pope would withdraw toward the capital. Lee and Longstreet's command also began to move north by a similar flanking movement.

Jackson and his "foot-cavalry" marched fifty-four miles in only thirty-six hours, to reach Briscoe Station, on the Federal supply line, where they captured much needed supplies before moving north again to await the arrival of Lee and Longstreet. The subsequent capture of the Union supply base at Manassas Junction gained more equipment for the Confederacy, which was shipped south before the depot was destroyed.

Pope reached Manassas on August 28 to find the depot in ruins. He hoped that Jackson's raid would give him the opportunity to defeat Jackson before Lee could reinforce him. Pope didn't know where Jackson was, but he dispatched troops to several locations where the Confederates had reportedly been sighted. Jackson and his men were still close by, just to the northwest, concealed behind an unfinished railroad embankment north of the Warrenton Turnpike, near the old Manassas battlefield. On the night of August 28, a Union column comprising men from Wisconsin and Indiana (later known as the Iron Brigade) marched east on the Warrenton Turnpike and came upon Jackson's position. Jackson ordered his artillery to open fire, and, after a fierce fight, the outnumbered Federal troops scattered.

After the Union troops re-formed, they counterattacked. The battle, known as Brawner's Farm, continued for two hours of very heavy fighting between forces less than one hundred yards apart in several places. By nightfall, over a third of the combatants were casualties.

Pope, believing he had isolated Jackson, planned a massive attack for the morning of August 29. During the night, Lee and Longstreet moved up to reinforce Jackson's right. Upon receiving reports that Jackson was tightening his lines, Pope surmised that the Confederates were retreating and sent his men forward in a series of waves. Some were momentarily successful in breaching Confederate lines, but all were eventually repulsed.

On the morning of August 30, unaware of the proximity of Longstreet and Lee, Pope ordered another attack. The Federals advanced three lines deep across the open fields and were met by artillery and musket fire. The first two waves were repulsed, but with the third, the Northerners swept up the railroad embankment, straining the Confederate line. As hand-to-hand combat raged along the line, some Confederates ran out of ammunition and were reduced to throwing rocks at the Federals. At last, Longstreet ordered his troops to attack. Jackson also ordered his men forward. Caught between them, Federal units were swept back toward Chinn Ridge.

Heavy fighting on Chinn Ridge bought time for Pope to establish a strong defensive position on Henry Hill. A gallant stand there saved Union forces from total disaster, and they were able to retreat during the night, meeting McClellan's reinforcements as they neared Washington.

As a result of the second Battle of Manassas, the South regained almost all of Virginia and the way was cleared for Lee's first invasion of the North.

Opposite top: This building served as a U.S. Army field hospital for both battles at Manassas. It is now the Sudley Post Office.

Opposite bottom: The Stone House was the site of Union General Pope's headquarters for the August 30 attack on Jackson's troops.

Below: The Henry House family graveyard near the rebuilt home on Henry Hill.

MANASSAS NATIONAL BATTLEFIELD PARK

MAILING ADDRESS
Superintendent, Manassas National Battlefield Park, 12521 Lee Highway, Manassas, Virginia 22110

TELEPHONE
703-361-1339

DIRECTIONS
The park is twenty-six miles southwest of Washington, D.C. Take I-66 southwest from Washington to Virginia Highway 234 Exit. Drive north one mile to the park entrance.

VISITOR CENTER
Museum with Civil War exhibits, a thirteen-minute slide program shown on the hour and half-hour, five-minute battlefield map program continuously shown.

ACTIVITIES
A one-mile self-guided walking tour of first Manassas battlefield and a twelve-mile self-guided auto tour of second Manassas battlefield, which begins at the visitor center. Conducted tours of both battles are available in summer.

HOURS
The visitor center is open daily from 8:30 AM to 5 PM, with hours extended to 6 PM in the summer. The grounds are open from dawn to dusk. The center and grounds are closed December 25.

Harpers Ferry

Left: A sketch of the Federal garrison getting ready to set fire to the armory in Harpers Ferry on April 18, 1861—two years after John Brown's famous raid. The garrison aimed to prevent seceding Virginia from seizing weapons that were manufactured and stored there. Virginians, however, rescued some of the weapons and equipment, which were sent South.

Opposite, below: The U.S. Armory fire house, which John Brown used as his fort during the 1859 raid

The small town of Harpers Ferry (then part of Virginia) is situated at the confluence of the Shenandoah and Potomac Rivers, with Maryland Heights overlooking the town from the north, Loudon Heights from the south, and Bolivar Heights from the west. There the Baltimore and Ohio and the Winchester and Potomac Railroads met. The Chesapeake and Ohio Canal was built away from the town on the opposite side of the Potomac. Eventually, the pro-Union western counties of Virginia seceded from the Confederacy. They were reaccepted into the Union in 1863 as an independent state, first known as Kanawha, and later as West Virginia.

Harpers Ferry became known to most Americans in October 1859, when a radical abolitionist named John Brown captured the Federal arsenal in the town in order to arm the slaves that he hoped to incite to revolt. A force of U.S. Marines, commanded by Colonel Robert E. Lee, quickly recaptured the arsenal. Brown was tried and hanged for treason and conspiracy. However, John Brown's Raid helped focus national attention on the issue of slavery, which was causing a breach between the Northern and Southern states.

When Virginia seceded in April 1861, a Confederate force quickly moved in to take over the armory and arsenal in Harpers Ferry. The Union garrison set fire to the arsenal, but the Southerners were able to rescue much of the contents and, more importantly, the supplies and equipment for making weapons, which were shipped south.

Before First Manassas in July 1861, the town had been the base for a Confederate force under Generals Joseph E. John-

CONDUIT TO THE SHENANDOAH VALLEY

Harpers Ferry first became known for abolitionist John Brown's raid on the U.S. Arsenal here on October 16, 1859 (later it would be called "the rifle barrel pointed at the heart of the Union"). Located at the confluence of the Shenandoah and Potomac Rivers, the town was key to control of the Shenandoah Valley. During the war it changed hands several times, and its arms industry was repeatedly destroyed by both sides. On **September 13–15, 1862,** Stonewall Jackson captured the Union garrison at Harpers Ferry before the Battle of Antietam.

 USA Garrison commander—Colonel Dixon S. Miles (mortally wounded)

 CSA Major General Thomas "Stonewall" Jackson

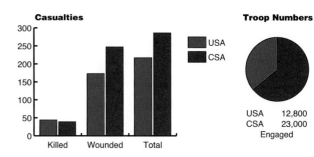

Casualties

USA
CSA

Troop Numbers

USA 12,800
CSA 23,000
Engaged

JOHN BROWN

"I, John Brown, am now quite certain that the crimes of this guilty land will never be purged away but with Blood."

Blood—in the abolitionist cause—is what this controversial historical figure brought. Brown, who had already hacked to death five pro-slavers in Kansas, arrived in tiny Harpers Ferry on October 16, 1859, with thirteen whites and five blacks intent on obtaining weapons from the Federal arsenal established there by President George Washington. The purpose of this act was to arm a slave insurrection that would lead to the establishment of an all-black state as a refuge from slavery.

For two days, Brown's raiders succeeded in holding the repository of 100,000 rifles and muskets. President James Buchanan sent Federal troops, under Col. Robert E. Lee and Lt. J.E.B. Stuart (another future Confederate military hero), and their forces overpowered Brown on October 18th. He was convicted of treason and hanged on December 2 at Charlestown at the age of fifty-nine.

His memory has lasted over the years in part through the lines in the "Battle Hymn of the Republic": "John Brown's body lies a-moldering in the grave, but his truth goes marching on," words written by Julia Ward Howe in 1861 and published in the *Atlantic Monthly* in 1862.

ston and Thomas "Stonewall" Jackson, but when that army moved south, Union troops reoccupied the town. In September 1862, after their success at the Second Battle of Manassas, Lee and the Army of Northern Virginia marched into Maryland. The Union garrison that remained at Harpers Ferry could threaten the invasion, by striking Lee's supply lines from the Shenandoah Valley and the vulnerable rear of the Confederate army.

Because of this threat, the capture of Harpers Ferry became essential to Lee's plan. He sent a force commanded by Stonewall Jackson, who was familiar with the terrain, to take the town. After a brief skirmish on September 13, two divisions under Confederate General Lafayette McLaws moved into position on Maryland Heights, and a wing commanded by Brigadier General John G. Walker crossed the Potomac and occupied Loudon Heights. Jackson planned to complete the encirclement by moving his three divisions in from the west. This would bring the Confederate force up to 23,000 men.

The Union garrison, commanded by Colonel Dixon S. Miles, numbered some 12,800, including the reinforcements by General Julius White's brigade from Martinsburg, which had been pushed back by the approaching Confederates. Superior in rank, White nevertheless surrendered command to Miles, who was a regular army veteran familiar with the area and the disposition of troops. In response to the Confederate attack on the high ground, Miles sent troops onto the lower-lying hills known as Bolivar Heights.

On September 14 a small Union force pushed McLaws's Confederates off Maryland Heights, but the commander did not follow up his advantage, which would have enabled reinforcements to reach Harpers Ferry, or at least allowed the garrison to retreat in order. That night, a force of Union cavalry did manage to escape across the Potomac River and even capture a few Confederate prisoners and some supply wagons. At the same time, under cover of darkness, one of Jackson's divisions took up a position opposite the Union left flank on Bolivar Heights.

The following morning Jackson opened his attack with an artillery barrage that was so devastating that the Federals were forced to capitulate. Colonel Miles was mortally wounded during the bombardment, and General White was compelled to surrender the remaining Union force of 12,520 men to Jackson. Actual casualties were light on both sides. Only 44 Union soldiers were killed and 173 wounded, as compared to Confederate losses of 39 killed and 247 wounded. The victorious Confederates also captured a large quantity of much-needed arms, including 13,000 guns and 78 cannon, from the recently resupplied Federal arsenal.

With this quick victory, Jackson and his divisions were able to rejoin the main body of the Army of Northern Virginia for the battle of Antietam. Later in the war, Harpers Ferry, badly damaged by Jackson's barrage, changed hands several times. It became an important Union supply base, and was used as such by General Philip Sheridan in his campaign into the Shenandoah Valley in 1864.

Harpers Ferry
National Historical Park

MARYLAND

WEST VIRGINIA

VIRGINIA

Visitor Center

North
0   0.5   1 Kilometer
0   0.5   1 Mile

EYEWITNESS

A New York Times *correspondent related some snippets of conversations he held with Lee's men:*

"'We have,' said a South Carolinian captain, '150,000 men on Maryland soil, but we do not come as an army of invasion. You go your way and we will go ours.'

'What do you think about pushing us to the wall, now?' playfully remarked another to me. 'How about that 'Onward to Richmond?' inquired a third. 'Cincinnati is ours, and so will Washington soon be,' said a Georgian....

Lee they considered their most able General; Jackson the best for speedy marches and dashes....

McClellan's strategy no one feared. 'How about that last retreat,' they said, has become a by-word with our soldiers....

[How] I asked of a South Carolinian, are you going to keep your Southern Confederacy together on the States right theory?

'Give us a chance and we will show you,' he retorted. 'If we don't make it work, we may return to the old Union, but not with Abolition Lincoln as President.'"

Opposite, above: *Houses line Shenandoah Street in Harpers Ferry, which in the 1860s was a thriving crossroads for shipping, railroads, and numerous industries.*

Previous pages: *A view over the town from Maryland Heights.*

Opposite, below: *Ruins of the mill on Virginius Island at the confluence of the Shenandoah and Potomac Rivers. This island was also the location of the weapons factory fought over so many times during the Civil War that little remains of it.*

The paths highlighted on the map above follow themes of Harpers Ferry's history and scenic features:

1 Lower Town Restored buildings and exhibits provide a glimpse of the town in the Civil-War era.

2 Virginius Island Vestiges of thriving industries can be traced in the ruins that remain along the river.

3 Camp Hill The former armory buildings, restored for the present site of Storer College.

4 Maryland Heights The trail passes ruined forts and affords spectacular views of the town, the surrounding hills, and rivers below.

5 Loudoun Heights Views of the Blue Ridge on the Appalachian Trail.

6 Bolivar Heights Scenic view of the strategic Harpers Ferry Water Gap.

7 Schoolhouse Ridge "Stonewall" Jackson's troops were positioned here during the siege of 1862.

HARPERS FERRY NATIONAL HISTORICAL PARK

MAILING ADDRESS
Superintendent, Harpers Ferry National Historical Park, PO Box 65, Harpers Ferry, WV 25425

TELEPHONE
304-535-6223

DIRECTIONS
The park is sixty-five miles northwest of Washington, D.C. and twenty miles southwest of Frederick, Maryland, via US 340.

VISITOR CENTER
Exhibits on John Brown, the Civil War, and other themes including industry and natural history. Shuttle buses depart from the Center to the historic town.

ACTIVITIES
Hiking trails, self-guided and ranger-guided walking tours, and interpretive talks.

HOURS
The park is open daily, from 8 AM to 5 PM, with hours extended to 6 PM in the summer. The park is closed December 25.

Antietam

Two Indiana soldiers found the long, bulky envelope in a meadow near Frederick, Maryland, during a brief halt in the pursuit of the Army of Northern Virginia. Inside was a document, wrapped around three cigars. They handed the parcel over to their company commander, who sent it along to regimental headquarters. And so on, until the document, which turned out to be a copy of the orders detailing Robert E. Lee's troop dispositions, perhaps lost through an error by D. H. Hill, reached George B. McClellan, commander of the Army of the Potomac.

The Confederates crossed the Potomac into Maryland in September 1862 with several objectives. Lee wanted to shift the fighting out of war-blighted Virginia, so the autumn harvest could be gathered in undisturbed. He anticipated political and diplomatic gains as well: a battlefield victory on

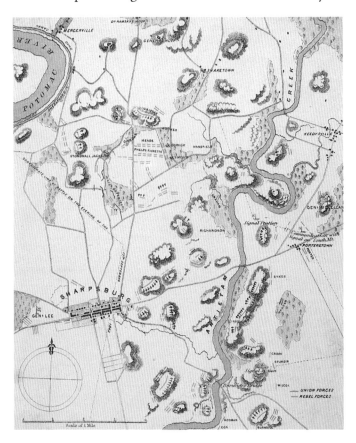

Above: This topographical map, drawn from a Union engineer officer's survey, shows the battlefield, the village of Sharpsburg, and environs.

Opposite: The armies clashed in the meadows, tilled fields and woodlots of the rich valley of the Antietam. The battlefield today looks much as it did in September 1862.

THE BLOODIEST SINGLE-DAY BATTLE

On **September 17, 1862,** General Robert E. Lee's first invasion of the North was halted by the Army of the Potomac, under Major General George B. McClellan, along Antietam Creek near Sharpsburg, Maryland. The battle of Antietam was a Union victory only in that Lee's advance was stopped. In 12 hours of fighting, 23,000 men were killed or wounded, making the battle of Antietam the bloodiest one-day battle of the war.

 USA Major General George B. McClellan; Major General Joseph Hooker; Major General Ambrose Burnside

 CSA General Robert E. Lee; Major General Thomas "Stonewall" Jackson; Major General J. E. B. Stuart

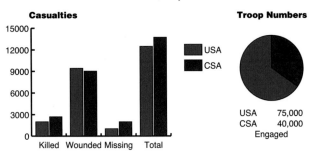

Northern soil would demoralize the loyal states and encourage antiwar opinion there. It might also persuade Britain to recognize Confederate independence.

Lee ran tremendous risks in invading the enemy's country. A summer of hard fighting, from the Virginia Peninsula in June and July to Manassas in August, had bled the army down and left it short of clothing, shoes, and provender. Thousands of men dropped out on the march, too tired, hungry, and weak to keep pace. As they swarmed over Maryland's orchards and fields for ripening apples and green corn, the threadbare Confederates looked as much like mendicants or refugees as soldiers. Still, nobody who saw them doubted that they could, and would, fight.

"They were the dirtiest men I ever saw, a most ragged, lean and hungry set of wolves," one Marylander wrote of his first glimpse of Lee's army. "Yet there was a dash about them that the northern men lacked."

But a Confederate staff officer's careless handling of Lee's Special Orders 191 changed everything. By the evening of September 13, McClellan knew that Lee had divided his army in the face of the superior Federal force. Lee had sent Thomas J. Jackson with more than half the Confederate strength to Harpers Ferry, to capture the Federal garrison there and secure

his line of communications with the Shenandoah Valley. The balance of the army, fewer than 20,000 men, waited behind the screen of South Mountain, the 50-mile-long northern extension of the Blue Ridge.

"Now I know what to do," McClellan said. But he did nothing for sixteen hours.

Meanwhile, Lee learned that McClellan had read Special Orders 191. The strategy had to be revised completely. Even so, Lee decided to stay in western Maryland and fight. He sent word for the army to concentrate behind Antietam Creek near the village of Sharpsburg, a mile or so from the Potomac. By early on the 15th, the Confederates were fanning out over the high ground overlooking the creek: open country, then, as now, tilled fields and meadows, but with plenty of cover for the infantry—ravines and woodlots, expanses of tall corn, rock outcroppings, the Dunker church, and split-rail fences.

"We will make our stand on those hills," Lee announced.

The Army of the Potomac, meantime, came up on the National Road from Frederick to Turner's Gap in South Mountain and, after a day of sharp fighting, broke through the Confederate rearguards there. By the afternoon of September 15, the first Federals had reached the Antietam valley. McClellan would have a chance to destroy Lee's army before the six divisions with Jackson at Harpers Ferry could rejoin it.

In hindsight, Lee's own officers questioned his decision to risk his divided command at Sharpsburg. The destruction of the Army of Northern Virginia could mean the end of the Confederacy. Why did he choose to fight there, with his army

backed up against the Potomac and with only one ford available for retreat in the event of disaster? Lee believed he could win. For one thing, he did not rate McClellan highly as a fighting general. A brilliant organizer, McClellan moved slowly and cautiously in the field. Lee thought he could be counted on to give the scattered Confederates time to reassemble. For another, Lee had perfect confidence in the fighting qualities of his troops. Lee's aggressive temperament doubtless played a part, too.

"He found it hard, the enemy in sight, to withhold his blows," one of his generals, James Longstreet, said later.

Jackson forced the surrender of Harpers Ferry on the morning of the 15th. Within a few hours, he had five of his six divisions in motion for Sharpsburg, seventeen miles away. McClellan let the afternoon of the 15th pass without a fight, failing even to send out cavalry patrols to probe Lee's strength. He held off all through the 16th as well, even though by then he had some 60,000 troops in line, double the number available to Lee.

During the afternoon and evening of the 16th, McClellan massed three of his six corps north of Sharpsburg for an advance the next morning down the Hagerstown Turnpike. To the south, a single corps would launch a diversionary attack over the first of the four bridges that spanned Antietam Creek. The tactical plan left McClellan with two corps in reserve, to be used wherever circumstances looked most promising.

A drizzling rain fell during the night. The Federal I Corps opened the Battle of Antietam in the damp, murky twilight

Above: *The simple white-washed church of the Dunker sect as it appears today.*

Left: *A view of the Miller Farmhouse, the woods, and cornfield where the initial Union attack took place.*

Below: *The shell-pocked meetinghouse in the aftermath of the battle, with the dead laid out in the foreground. More than 4,800 Union and Confederate soldiers were killed at Antietam. Another 20,000 were wounded or missing.*

of dawn on Wednesday, September 17, aiming for the white-washed meetinghouse of a sect of German Baptists—the Dunker church—a half-mile down the turnpike.

Skirmishers led the way, driving the Confederates ahead of them. The fighting spread outward, into a cornfield and the woods that stretched away on either side of the road. The I Corps commander, Joseph Hooker, summoned 36 fieldguns to the front in an attempt to blast a way through the head-high corn. When the guns had done their work, it looked to Hooker as though every stalk had been "cut as closely as could have been done with a knife." Near the edge of the cornfield, the advancing Federals and Jackson's infantry exchanged a series of scorching volleys. "They stood and shot at each other till the lines melted away like wax," a New York rifleman recalled.

Hooker's assault drove the Confederates from the cornfield. Just as Jackson's line seemed about to break, a fresh Confederate division emerged from the West Woods, knelt, and delivered a rapid, accurate fire—"like a scythe running through our line," in the words of one Yankee survivor. Within a few minutes, the attackers were streaming back through the cornfield, up the turnpike, and out of the battle, leaving 2,500 dead and wounded behind.

Meanwhile, Hooker sent word for the XII Corps to take his place. The corps commander, Joseph Mansfield, was killed at the outset, but his leading division pressed on, evicting the Confederates from the cornfield for a second time. The XII Corps advance carried to within 200 yards of the Dunker church before Jackson's troops, with reinforcements from the still-quiet Confederate right flank, was able to stop it.

McClellan now fed a fresh corps, the II Corps under Edwin V. Sumner, into the battle. One of Sumner's divisions, attacking through the West Woods toward the Dunker church, seemed to be on the verge of a breakthrough when yet another Confederate unit arriving from Harpers Ferry struck it in the flanks. Within a quarter-hour, the division lost 2,000 men killed and wounded.

So, one after another, the Confederates had stopped three Federal corps totaling 31,000 men. Sumner re-formed his two trailing divisions and, steering clear of the Dunker meetinghouse, swung them toward the center of the Confeder-

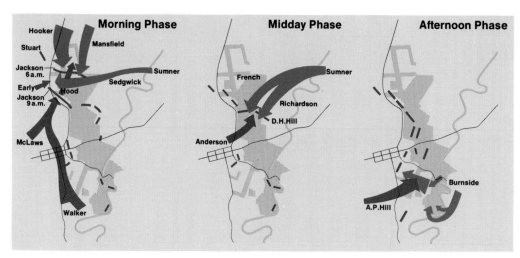

*Left: The Battle of Antietam was fought in three phases: During the **morning**, three Union attacks bent Jackson's line, but did not break it. During the **middle phase**, two Union divisions pierced the Confederate center, but McClellan failed to exploit the opening. In the **afternoon**, A.P. Hill's late-arriving infantry stopped Burnside's attempt to cut off the Confederate line of retreat.*

***Opposite:** The Miller farm.*

ate line, a sunken farm track that ran for about half a mile between split-rail fences.

Sumner's first attack spent itself trying to carry the sunken road, soon to be dubbed Bloody Lane. As his first division fell back, Sumner sent in a second wave. The Confederates, well protected and firing from behind improvised breastworks of stacked fence rails, seemed unassailable here. Then, misinterpreting an order, a Confederate officer pulled his regiment out of the line. The Federals swarmed into the vacated spot, turned, and loosed volley after volley down the lane. The defenders left in a rush, not stopping until they reached the outskirts of Sharpsburg itself.

So ended the firefight along Bloody Lane. The Confederate center had been pierced. The commander there, D.H. Hill, re-formed a thin line at the edge of the village and, with a mere 200 infantrymen, led a futile counterattack. Then he waited for the final Federal push.

"Lee's army was ruined, and the end of the Confederacy was in sight," one of Lee's officers, the artillerist Edward Porter Alexander, wrote later. But Sumner's corps had been badly shot up, and he argued against making another effort. McClellan concurred, and decided against using his reserves to exploit the opening. The battle shifted to the south, to the rising ground on either side of the graceful little three-arched stone bridge over Antietam Creek, known before the battle as Rohrbach Bridge, and ever afterward as Burnside's.

McClellan had instructed Ambrose E. Burnside, the IX Corps commander, to carry the bridge and threaten Lee's right flank. Burnside's efforts had been feeble—so feeble that Lee had been able to shift troops all morning from his right to the threatened positions around the Dunker church and, later, Bloody Lane. A depleted brigade of about 550 Georgians under the former Confederate secretary of state, Robert Toombs, repulsed several attempts to storm the bridge before the Federals finally swept across in a rush an hour or so after noon. By 3:00 PM Burnside had assembled two divisions, around 10,000 men, in the bridgehead.

Here was McClellan's second great chance to destroy the Army of Northern Virginia. As Burnside's troops approached the single road that led to the Potomac ford, Lee's escape route, a dust cloud appeared on the horizon. Gradually, it resolved itself into the van of A.P. Hill's Light Division, which had covered the seventeen miles from Harpers Ferry in eight hours. Hill put his 3,000 infantry into the battle at once. The Light Division pitched into the Federal left flank, bringing Burnside's advance to a standstill.

The entire Federal line recoiled. McClellan, though, still had a fresh corps at hand. For a moment, he thought of committing it. The V Corps commander, Fitz-John Porter, talked him out of so rash an act. "Remember," Porter said, "I command the last reserve of the last army of the Republic."

So evening descended on the valley of the Antietam. The noise of the battle had resounded as far as the hamlet of Sheperdstown, several miles to the west, where residents had "distinctly heard 'the incessant explosions of artillery, the shrieking whistles of the shells, and the sharper, deadlier, more thrilling roll of musketry; while every now and then the echo of some charging cheer would come, borne by the wind, and as the human voice pierced that demoniacal clangor we would catch our breath and listen…'" At the day's end, Lee's lines were intact, the Potomac ford covered. Both armies, in fact, were roughly where they had started at daybreak twelve hours earlier. Some 5,000 men were dead or dying on the battlefield, and another 18,000 were wounded.

Few of the casualties on this most destructive single day of the American Civil War were as fortunate as the Wisconsin officer who had been shot in Hooker's dawn advance into the cornfield. Someone reported that he had been killed, which proved to be an exaggeration. In fact, Edward S. Bragg soon found himself sufficiently recovered to write home to his wife: "I felt faint and went back a few rods, where I met the Gen'l who gave me some whiskey (the first I have tasted since I have been in service) and I revived again and felt as well as ever."

After dark, stretcher bearers of both armies went to work collecting the wounded. "Not a soldier, I venture to say, slept half an hour," recalled Major Henry Douglas of Stonewall Jackson's staff. "Nearly all of them were wandering over the field, looking for their wounded comrades.…Half of Lee's army were hunting the other half."

Right: From the east, a view of Burnside Bridge over Antietam Creek in September 1862. Federal infantry finally carried the bridge late in the battle, after several costly repulses.

Opposite: From the Observation Tower, a look down the sunken farm track known after September 17, 1862, as "Bloody Lane."

Below: In this lithograph, an artist renders a stylized view of Burnside's attack across the stone bridge.

Opposite: The Burnside Bridge as it appears today, from the Confederate side of Antietam Creek.

Right: Civil War photographer Mathew Brady titled this grimly expressive image "Lone Grave on the Battlefield of Antietam."

Below: The Mumma family cemetery lies just north of Mumma Farm. Confederate troops set fire to the house and farm buildings to deny cover to Union sharpshooters.

During the 18th, a bright, hot day, burial details and stretcher parties went out under a flag of truce to collect the dead and wounded. With the expiration of the truce, McClellan might have renewed the battle. He might have overwhelmed Lee's depleted army. But both sides remained at rest. Lee's army went away that night, across the river and home to Virginia.

Tactically, Antietam was a drawn battle. But a drawn battle meant little or nothing to the Confederate cause. Lee's invasion had been turned back; thousands of his best troops would never fight again. "All we can claim," said Longstreet, "is that we got across the Potomac with an organized army."

McClellan claimed much more. Through overcaution, he had missed his opportunity to wreck the Confederacy's main army. Still, Lee had gone. By his own valuation, he had won a great victory. "Those in whose judgment I rely tell me that I fought the battle splendidly and that it is a masterpiece of art," he wrote his wife.

As it happened, Antietam proved to be a turning point of the Civil War. The Federal victory there—or the absence of defeat—gave President Lincoln the opportunity to issue the document that converted the war into a crusade for the destruction of slavery.

On September 22, 1862, five days after the battle, Lincoln issued the preliminary Emancipation Proclamation. After January 1, 1863, the president pledged, people held in slavery would be "then, thenceforward and forever free."

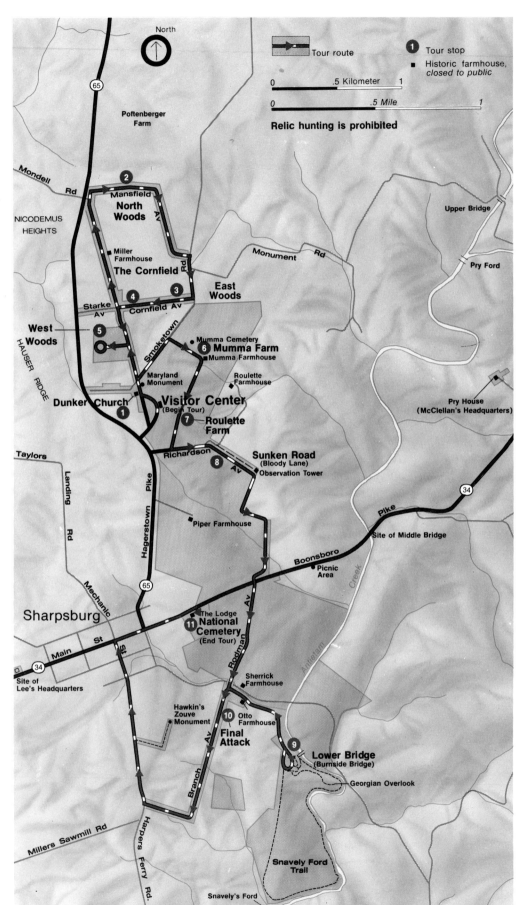

North

Tour route

① Tour stop

■ Historic farmhouse, *closed to public*

0   .5 Kilometer   1

0   .5 Mile   1

Relic hunting is prohibited

Poffenberger Farm

Mondell Rd

NICODEMUS HEIGHTS

Mansfield

North Woods

Upper Bridge

Monument Rd

Pry Ford

Miller Farmhouse

The Cornfield

East Woods

Starke Av

Cornfield Av

West Woods

HAUSER RIDGE

Mumma Cemetery

Mumma Farm

■ Mumma Farmhouse

Roulette Farmhouse

Maryland Monument

Pry House (McClellan's Headquarters)

Dunker Church

Visitor Center (Begin Tour)

Roulette Farm

Taylors

Landing Rd

Hagerstown Pike

Richardson Av

Sunken Road (Bloody Lane)
Observation Tower

Pike

34

■ Piper Farmhouse

Site of Middle Bridge

Boonsboro

Picnic Area

Creek

Mechanic

Sharpsburg

The Lodge
National Cemetery (End Tour)

Rodman Av

Main St

34

Site of Lee's Headquarters

Sherrick Farmhouse

Hawkin's Zouve Monument

Otto Farmhouse

Final Attack

Branch Av

Harpers Ferry Rd.

Lower Bridge (Burnside Bridge)

Georgian Overlook

Millers Sawmill Rd

Antietam

Snavely Ford Trail

Snavely's Ford

The numbered tour stops follow the chronological sequence of the battle.

MORNING PHASE

1 Dunker Church The opening Union attack aimed for the high ground around this meeting-house of the German Baptist Brethren—the Dunkers. Confederates here withstood repeated assaults through the morning. Destroyed by a storm in 1921, the church was rebuilt in 1962.

2 North Woods Gen. Joseph Hooker's corps launched the initial Federal attack from here. Gen. Thomas J. ("Stonewall") Jackson's infantry checked the advance in the Cornfield a half-mile to the south.

3 East Woods Confederate marksmen found the Union Gen. Joseph Mansfield here as he led the XII Corps into battle. He died of his wounds later in the day.

4 The Cornfield The fiercest fighting of the battle occurred here in the ripening corn of the Miller field. The battle surged back and forth over the field for three hours.

5 West Woods A charge here against Jackson's troops cost Union Gen. John Sedgwick's division 2,200 killed, wounded and missing in less than thirty minutes.

6 Mumma Farm The Confederates burned the farmhouse and outbuildings to deny their use to Union sharpshooters. This was the only civilian property destroyed during the battle.

MIDDAY PHASE

7 Roulette Farm Union troops under Gens. William French and Israel Richardson crossed the fields of the Roulette Farm on their way to attack the Confederates in the Sunken Road.

8 Sunken Road (Bloody Lane) For nearly four hours, Union and Confederate troops contested the Sunken Road, a half-mile stretch of country lane so worn over the years by the passage of heavy farm wagons that it formed a natural trench. More than 5,000 men were killed or wounded here in "Bloody Lane."

AFTERNOON PHASE

9 Lower Bridge (Burnside Bridge) A few hundred Georgians held this gracefully arched stone bridge for most of the day against the full weight of Gen. Ambrose Burnside's IX Corps— a key reason for the Union failure to win the battle. It is Antietam's best-known landmark.

10 The Final Attack By late afternoon, Burnside's troops had finally taken the stone bridge and formed for a drive across the hills to Sharpsburg. As the Federals approached Lee's single line of retreat to the Potomac, A.P. Hill's division arrived from Harpers Ferry to halt the advance.

11 Antietam National Cemetery The remains of 4,776 Union soldiers, including 1,836 unknowns, are buried in this hilltop cemetery on the outskirts of Sharpsburg. Most of the Confederate dead lie in Hagerstown and Frederick, Maryland, and in local church and family plots.

Right: President Lincoln with Gen. George B. McClellan and his staff at Antietam shortly after the battle.

THE EMANCIPATION PROCLAMATION

Five days after the bloodshed at Antietam, President Lincoln proclaimed:

"That on the first day of January, in the year of our Lord one thousand eight hundred and sixty-three, all persons held as slaves within any State or designated part of a State, the people whereof shall then be in rebellion against the United States, shall be then, thenceforward, and forever free; and the Executive Government of the United States, including the military and naval authority thereof, will recognize and maintain the freedom of such persons, and will do no act or acts to repress such persons, or any of them, in any efforts they may make for their actual freedom....

And by virtue of the power, and for the purpose aforesaid, I do order and declare that all persons held as slaves within [the rebellious states] are, and henceforward shall be free; and that the executive government of the United States, including the military and naval authorities thereof, will recognize and maintain the freedom of said persons.

And I hereby enjoin upon the people so declared to be free to abstain from all violence, unless in necessary self-defence; and I recommend to them that, in all cases when allowed, they labor faithfully for reasonable wages.

And I further declare and make known, that such persons of suitable condition, will be received into the armed service of the United States to garrison forts, positions, stations, and other places, and to man vessels of all sorts in said service.

And upon this act, sincerely believed to be an act of justice, warranted by the Constitution, upon military necessity, I invoke the considerate judgment of mankind, and the gracious favor of Almighty God.

In witness whereof, I have hereunto set my hand and caused the seal of the United States to be affixed."

ANTIETAM NATIONAL BATTLEFIELD

MAILING ADDRESS
Antietam National Battlefield, PO Box 158, Sharpsburg, MD 21782-0158

TELEPHONE
301-432-5124

DIRECTIONS
The visitor center is one mile north of Sharpsburg, Maryland, on Route 65.

VISITOR CENTER
A twenty-six minute film is shown hourly; museum, bookstore, and observation room.

ACTIVITIES
Ranger-guided programs are offered throughout the summer. Eight-minute self-guided driving tour (rental tapes are available).

HOURS
The visitor center is open daily, from 8:30 AM to 5 PM, with hours extended to 6 PM from June through August. The park is closed Thanksgiving, December 25, and January 1.

Richmond

The Peninsular Campaign

Richmond, the capital of the Commonwealth of Virginia, stands on a series of hills above the James River, barely 110 miles from the Federal capital at Washington, D. C. In 1861 it was also a major industrial center for the South, the site of fourteen iron foundries, six rolling mills, six iron railing plants, and fifty iron and metal works. Among the iron works was the gigantic Tredegar Iron Works, which became known as the "mother arsenal of the Confederacy." Also within the city limits were the Richmond armory; the Confederate States Laboratory, which turned out ammunition, and eight flour mills, including the world's largest, Gallego. The city was also a major transportation center—the terminus of five railroads and the 200-mile Kanawha Canal. When Richmond replaced Montgomery, Alabama, as the capital of the Confederacy on May 21, 1861, it also became a major objective for Federal armies.

After the Union's rout at First Manassas, Lincoln appointed General George B. McClellan commander of the Federal forces in the east. McClellan had become an early hero to the

ON TO RICHMOND!

Because of Richmond's strategic importance as capital of the Confederacy, Union forces made repeated attempts to take the city. There were two major efforts: the Peninsular Campaign of May–July 1862 and the Virginia Campaign of June 1864. The first campaign, the Seven Days' Battle, **June 25–July 1, 1862,** is known for General George McClellan's sluggish progress toward the objective and an opportunity lost.

 USA General George McClellan

 CSA General Joseph E. Johnston; General Robert E. Lee

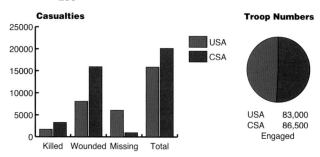

North thanks to his minor victories at Rich Mountain and Philippi, but his real genius lay in organization and training. In the months following Manassas, McClellan turned his green, untutored army into a disciplined force, adept at maneuvers, but still untested in battle.

In late March 1862, after many presidential demands to confront the enemy, McClellan led the Army of the Potomac into the field. His goal was Richmond, but surprisingly, he decided to attack from the southeast. His plan was to move his army by boat to the James and York Rivers, while another Union army, commanded by General Irvin McDowell, marched down from the north. These armies were to be supported by naval batteries from gunboats on the James.

Moving his army down the Potomac by ship, McClellan disembarked at Fort Monroe, at the end of the peninsula, still one hundred miles from Richmond. Once ashore his men built a series of defenses to repel an expected Confederate attack and to allow reinforcements and resupply.

The Confederates, anticipating a Union response to Manassas, had also been training and reorganizing their army, which included many troops who had participated in the victory at Manassas. Moving south to meet the Union threat, they built a line of defenses across the peninsula from Yorktown to the James to gain time and to create a defensive perimeter around

Richmond. McClellan then delayed departure from Fort Monroe for a month, until his entire force was in place—which was very helpful to the Confederates. In addition, McClellan fell short of keeping his agreement to leave enough troops to defend Washington, so Lincoln ordered a large division back to the capital. Inexplicably, McClellan consistently believed that Confederate forces were twice the size they actually were, resulting in his constant requests for vast numbers of reinforcements and his excruciatingly cautious advance.

On May 3 the Confederates began their withdrawal from Yorktown and Newport News, the site of a major naval base. After a small battle near Williamsburg on May 5, which was a victory for McClellan, the Confederates continued to retreat. They reached the outskirts of Richmond by May 15, the same day an attempted attack by a Federal naval force was stopped by a battery at Drewry's Bluff, eight miles below the city.

The Confederate government, which had been undecided up to that point, voted to defend the capital. While McClellan was picking his cautious path up the peninsula, Lincoln ordered McDowell to send 20,000 men to the Shenandoah Valley in the hope of defeating Thomas "Stonewall" Jackson. Lincoln also telegraphed McClellan, ordering him either to attack Richmond or to move back to Washington.

As the Federal force moved up the peninsula, they crossed an area cut by White Oak Swamp and the Chickahominy River, about six miles from Richmond. The very wet spring of 1862, which had turned much of this ground into a morass, forced McClellan to divide his army. He left two corps to protect his left flank on the south side of the river, near the village of Seven Pines, while he marched toward the city on the north bank. General Joseph E. Johnston, commander of the Confederate army, took full advantage of the Federal division and on May 31 repeatedly attacked these two isolated corps, commanded by Generals Erasmus Keyes and Samuel Heintzelman, from three directions. Southern troops were led by Generals James Longstreet, Daniel Harvey Hill, and Benjamin Huger. Despite some confusion, parts of General Edwin V. Sumner's corps were able to cross the river and reinforce Heintzelman's troops. The final Confederate attack was repulsed, with serious losses on both sides. More notably, both the Union troops and McClellan had been awestruck by the ferocity of the Confederate attacks and began to perceive the enemy as invincible.

During this engagement, General Johnston was severely wounded, and his command devolved for a few hours upon General Gustavus Smith, and, on June 1, to General Robert E. Lee. Taking command on the last day of the battle of Seven Pines (or Fair Oaks), Lee tried to bring order to the chaos of the previous day, but by 3:00 PM, he ordered his troops to withdraw. Although the battle ended in a draw, the Confederates were still in a precarious position, with McClellan and his superior force a short distance from Richmond.

To increase his understanding of the situation, Lee detailed General James E. B. "Jeb" Stuart to reconnoiter around the flank of McClellan's army. Beginning on June 12, Stuart went one better and led his 1,200 cavalrymen completely around

Opposite: A Federal mortar battery at the siege of Yorktown near the southeastern tip of the peninsula. General McClellan's cautious advance on Richmond was delayed here for a month by Confederate defenses whose strength McClellan greatly overestimated.

Above: Federal troops re-form along the bluffs of the Chickahominy River after the Battle of Gaines' Mill.

Below: Part of the Confederate defense line at Chickahominy Bluff is still visible today.

EYEWITNESS

From a letter to his family by Georgia cavalryman N. J. Brooks postmarked Richmond, Virginia, July 4, 1862, during the Battles of the Seven Days:

"The route was strewn with a heap of Yankee plunder. Many dead and wounded horses were seen by the wayside and occasionally a dead man. Trees were cut up by cannon balls and the road filled with ambulances, ordnance wagons, worn out soldiers and ordnance and equipment. I went on 'till I came to a mill, where the North Carolinians charged the enemy's entrenchments through brush and an old millpond place and drove them away and lost many a life. This happened the day before. They were lying very thick on both sides of the road. They were lying in every position you could think, some holding up their hands, looking very pitiful, some across their guns.…

After awhile I went on in the direction of the firing, and got in three-fourth miles of where they were bombing each other with all fury.…I was soon on the battlefield and saw the contending parties engaged. It was Yankee infantry fighting our artillery. They were about 100 yards apart and pour into each other a most deadly fire. I could see the men falling. The Yanks fought bravely, keeping a good line and holding their ground very well while I stayed.…

I passed a hospital for wounded, where I heard a woman weeping and wailing like one in deepest despair. I thought that if all the women, North and South, would come upon the hills and valleys around Richmond and could see at once the many slain of their fathers, husbands, sons, brothers and lovers, that their weeping and wailing would be such that it would wring tears from angelic eyes and that there would be a ten-fold greater clamor for peace among them than there ever was for war."

attack against Union troops commanded by Fitz-John Porter. An after-dark attack by troops led by Generals John Bell Hood and George E. Pickett temporarily broke the Union lines, but they recovered. As the Confederates fell back, Porter withdrew his men across the Chickahominy.

McClellan began to retreat toward the safety of Harrison's Landing on the James, and on the fourth and fifth days the Union soldiers were constantly assaulted by Confederate pursuers. On June 30, the Army of Northern Virginia finally made a concerted attack on the Union force at White Oak Swamp, but this was successfully repulsed. Jackson had scarcely reached the main body of the Confederate army by the time the action was called off, and the Federal force settled in at Malvern Hill. The following day, July 1, 1862, Southern troops made another series of attacks, but the Federals were too well entrenched, and their artillery proved superior. Federal gunboats in the James gave added support. By the following day, McClellan had reached the safety of Harrison's Landing.

Although McClellan was not able to engage Lee successfully in a pitched battle, which might have brought a swift end to the war, and despite the high Confederate casualties, he had not achieved his objective of conquering Richmond, His retreat to Harrison's Landing, and ultimately to Washington, spared the Confederate capital until 1864.

The Seven Days' campaign brought home the fact of war to the residents of Richmond, as Confederate wounded poured into private hospitals in the city and military establishments like Chimborazo, just outside it. Richmond had been an army medical center since the return of wounded after the battle of First Manassas; from this point on, the Confederacy would send here most of her casualties from the eastern theater.

THE *MONITOR* AND THE *MERRIMAC*

The 1862 battle between the Union *Monitor* and Confederate *Merrimac* in Hampton Roads off the coast of Virginia revolutionized naval warfare—although their dramatic encounter on March 9 ended in a draw. The Confederates had conceived the ingenious idea of using iron plates to shield against cannonballs; in response, Union forces created their own ironclad and added two additional features. The *Monitor* floated just a few feet above the water and included a revolving gun turret.

the Union army in four days—one of the great exploits of the Civil War. This feat inspired both sides to increase the size of their cavalry regiments.

Learning that Jackson had successfully concluded his Valley Campaign, Lee telegraphed him to return to Richmond and began to reorganize his forces for an assault against McClellan. However, on June 25, before Jackson's troops returned, McClellan ordered General Heintzelman's troops, on his left flank, forward. They came up against the Confederate force of General Huger at Oak Grove. It was the opening of the campaign that became known as the Battle of the Seven Days.

The second day began with fighting around Mechanicsville. Confederate General A. P. Hill, tired of waiting for Jackson, attacked Federal troops in the area and pushed them back into a defensive line, where they were able to repel a subsequent attack. That night, the Federal army withdrew toward Gaines' Mill, and McClellan ordered supplies moved down to the James at Harrison's Landing. Gaines' Mill became the site of combat on the third day, as the Confederates launched an

Cold Harbor

Two years after the Seven Days, Richmond was again the objective of the Army of the Potomac, numbering 114,000 men. In May 1864, the overall commander of Union forces, now Ulysses S. Grant, was moving his troops in a series of flanking movements aimed at cutting off Lee and the 59,000-man Army of Northern Virginia from the city of Richmond. Grant's command to General George Meade in April had been: "Wherever Lee goes, there you will go also." In two months, Grant had achieved the offensive and pinned Lee down—something no other Union commander achieved

Following the costly battles of the Wilderness and Spotsylvania, the Confederates dug massive defenses near two taverns known as Old and New Cold Harbor. The trench warfare that ensued influenced the subsequent siege of Petersburg and would become characteristic of modern war. The battle began on June 1, when Union troops arriving at Cold Harbor, near the 1862 Seven Days' battlefields, were met by well-entrenched Confederates. The Federals, too, entrenched after encountering stiff resistance. Grant planned to attack the next day, but logistical problems delayed this action. The following day saw one of history's bloodiest battles. At 4:30 AM on June 3, Grant launched the first of a series of brutal frontal assaults against the entrenched Confederates, who knew that a Union breakthrough might end the war in Virginia. In one of these attempts, more than 7,000 Union soldiers were either killed or wounded in less than an hour. The survivors dug in where they were, sometimes a mere fifty

ASSAULT ON THE IMPREGNABLE TRENCHES

In the second campaign for Richmond, **June 1–3, 1864,** General Ulysses S. Grant ordered an attack at Cold Harbor, but the Confederate position was well-entrenched. The decisive defeat—7,000 Union casualties in one 30-minute period of the battle—established trench warfare with artillery support as a prime element in future military strategy.

 USA: General Ulysses S. Grant

 CSA: General Robert E. Lee

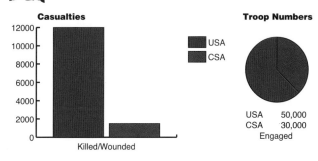

yards from Lee's forces, in hope of surviving the subsequent shelling. The high cost of this battle was to no purpose. Later Grant regretted that it had been attempted. After that day, the opposing sides waited in their trenches for the other to make a move.

In the end, on June 6, Grant requested a truce to collect and care for the wounded and bury the dead who were scat-

Left: The June 1864 Battle of Cold Harbor, in which both sides used a new trench warfare strategy, proved one of the costliest for Grant's army. Lee's forces inflicted 7,000 casualties in 30 minutes—their last major victory in the field. However, Grant's troops held and went on to the siege of Petersburg and the eventual conquest of Richmond.

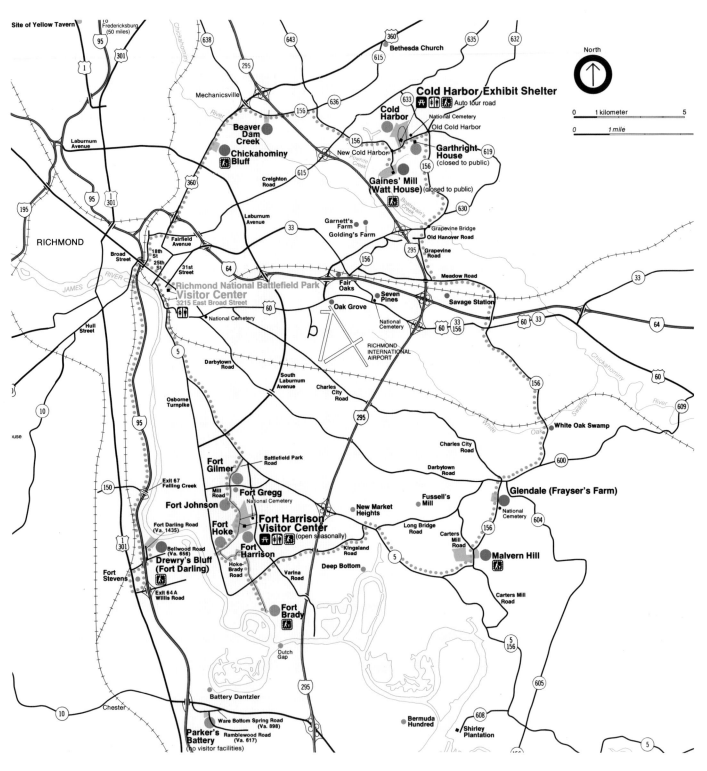

The auto tour of Richmond's battlefields is an 80-mile circuit with ten major sites and a visitor center. Features associated primarily with the 1862 campaign are indicated in red. 1864 campaign sites are shown in in blue.

1862 sites

Chickahominy Bluff On the outer line of Richmond's defenses.

Malvern Hill Area Includes Glendale (Frayser's Farm).

Gaines' Mill (Watt House) Union headquarters.

Drewry's Bluff (Fort Darling) Confederate batteries.

1864 sites

Cold Harbor Confederate field fortifications with an exhibit shelter. Site of Grant's bloody losses and Lee's last field victory.

Fort Harrison and its Visitor Center; several other key forts are in this area.

Fort Brady Built by Union forces to neutralize Fort Darling across the James River.

tered all over the field under a hot June sun. The battle was not resumed, and both sides withdrew. Casualties for the Union army rose to over 12,000, while the smaller Confederate force had lost 1,500 men. Grant moved south to begin the nine-month siege of Petersburg, an important rail center less than thirty miles away.

When Petersburg fell, on April 2, 1865, President Davis, the Confederate cabinet, and other staunch supporters of the cause evacuated Richmond. By order of the Confederate Secretary of the Navy, Stephen R. Mallory, seamen commanded by Admiral Raphael Semmes, late of the commerce raider CSS *Alabama*, destroyed the remaining ships of the James River Squadron. The Richmond Arsenal was blown up, and many military stores, tobacco warehouses, and bridges in the city were also destroyed before it was formally surrendered to the Union. The fire had swept through a large part of the city by the time Federal troops entered the Confederate capital later that day, achieving the goal they had sought for almost four years.

Above: The Union Flag crests the hill at the Confederacy's Fort Harrison as Federal troops pushed into the outskirts of Richmond.

Below: Richmond burned on April 2, 1865—destroyed by Confederate order. President Jefferson Davis and his cabinet evacuated the city. Ships were sunk, bridges destroyed, and the arsenal detonated before Federal troops entered the city.

RICHMOND NATIONAL BATTLEFIELD PARK

MAILING ADDRESS
Superintendent, Richmond National Battlefield Park, 3215 East Broad St., Richmond, VA 23223

TELEPHONE
804-226-1981

DIRECTIONS
Richmond National Battlefield Park consists of nine separate units located south and east of Richmond, Virginia. The Chimborazo Visitor Center, starting point for a tour of the park, is located at 3215 East Broad Street. Take exit 10 off I-95 and drive along 17th Street until it intersects Broad Street. Turn left on Broad and drive sixteen blocks southeast. The visitor center is on the right.

VISITOR CENTER
Civil War exhibits, a twelve-minute slide show and thirty-minute film. Smaller orientation centers with exhibits are located at Cold Harbor and Fort Harrison (staffed seasonally).

ACTIVITIES
Self-guided auto tours (rental tapes are available), hiking trails, and interpretive waysides with audio stations. Additional programs are offered in summer.

HOURS
The visitor center is open from 9 AM to 5 PM, except Thanksgiving, December 25, and January 1.

Fredericksburg and Spotsylvania

The local people knew the 120-square-mile region of briar-choked forest south of the Rapidan River as the Wilderness. The Union and Confederate soldiers who campaigned in and around the second-growth jungle of stunted jack pine and scrub oak knew it as "that repulsive district"—the haunted precincts of some of the fiercest fighting of the Civil War.

From December 1862 to May 1864, the Union Army of the Potomac brought on four great battles in these Virginia killing grounds: Fredericksburg, Chancellorsville, the Wilderness, and Spotsylvania. The first two were clear Confederate tactical victories. The last two, drawn battles both, marked the beginning of the end for the Army of Northern Virginia.

Fredericksburg

General George B. McClellan's failure to pursue the Confederates after the battle of Antietam cost him President Lincoln's support. "He has got the slows," the president complained of McClellan, who lapsed into a state of military somnolence

SLAUGHTER AT FREDERICKSBURG

Four major battles took place in or near the Virginia city of Fredericksburg. The battle of Fredericksburg, **December 11–13, 1862,** was a major Union defeat, as troops attempted a frontal assault on the Confederates' impregnable position.

 USA General Ambrose Burnside

 CSA General Robert E. Lee

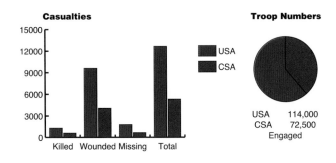

Casualties / Troop Numbers

USA 114,000
CSA 72,500
Engaged

Left: Here on Prospect Hill, Stonewall Jackson's infantry repulsed the Federal assault of December 13, 1862.

Opposite, above: Union engineers, under a harassing fire, laid pontoons across the Rappahannock River at Fredericksburg on December 11, 1862.

Opposite, below: This John Richards painting shows Union columns approaching the battle zone at Fredericksburg in December 1862.

in October 1862. In November, Lincoln replaced him with General Ambrose E. Burnside, a handsome, flamboyantly whiskered, Indiana-born West Pointer of impressive bearing and questionable ability. Still, he had at least one attribute necessary in an army commander: "Burnside could and would fight, even if he did not know how," one of Robert E. Lee's officers remarked.

On taking command, Burnside put the Army of the Potomac in motion for Fredericksburg, an old colonial center of 5,000 on a sharp southward bend of the Rappahannock River midway between Washington and Richmond. Burnside's notion, not a bad one, was to shift the line of operations east to Fredericksburg and make a dash for the Confederate capital from there. Failures of execution doomed the plan. Burnside needed pontoons to cross the 400-foot-wide Rappahannock. Through a mixup, the bridge trains arrived late, giving Lee time to move his army down the right bank and fortify the hills behind the town.

Burnside massed six corps, around 120,000 men, and more than 300 guns opposite Fredericksburg. Lee had 78,000 men, 275 guns, and a nearly unassailable position on the high ground commanding the Fredericksburg plain. The Confederate general James Longstreet, inspecting a section of the line along Marye's Heights, expressed mild doubts about the strength of the position. One of his artillery colonels reassured him. "General," Edward Porter Alexander replied, "we cover that ground now so well that we will comb it as with a fine-tooth comb.

A chicken could not live on that field when we open on it."

On December 9, 1862, troops of the Army of the Potomac were issued three days' cooked rations and sixty rounds of ammunition per man—the essential prelude to a battle. Before dawn on the 11th, Thursday, Burnside's engineers began throwing the pontoons across the river—three bridges at Fredericksburg, another two a couple of miles downstream. Burnside intended to make his main effort from his left, below the town, with two corps under General William B. Franklin. General Edwin Sumner, with another two corps, would make a secondary attack on Marye's Heights.

Lee decided not to contest the crossing, but a brigade of Mississippi sharpshooters harassed the pontoniers. They did it with such élan that Burnside lost a full day trying to evict them so the bridges could be completed. A heavy cannonade set parts of the city on fire. Finally, Federal infantry using pontoons as assault boats crossed and drove away the Mississippians. Their brilliant rearguard action allowed Lee to concentrate the right wing of his army, under General Thomas J. Jackson, on Prospect Hill south of town, opposite Franklin.

The Federals came over in force on December 12th. Burnside spent the balance of the day completing preparations for his two-pronged attack. A thick fog blanketed the plain at first light Saturday, December 13th. As the rising sun burned it off, Franklin's infantry advanced on Jackson's front, aiming to storm the ridge, turn right at the crest, and bowl Lee's entire army off the hills. In Fredericksburg, the first assault brigades spilled out of the town and headed for Marye's Heights.

Franklin scored some initial gains. General George G. Meade's division struck a weak point in Jackson's line and broke through briefly before a Confederate counterattack sealed the breach. In the town, Sumner's troops had no success at all. Confederate riflemen packed three and four deep behind a stone wall at the base of Marye's Heights repulsed a series of brigade-strength frontal assaults, covering the snow-dusted plain with Federal dead and wounded.

In the late afternoon, a lull fell over the battlefield. With the failure of Meade's attack, Franklin suspended the battle on his

Above: The outlines of Jackson's Prospect Hill trench lines can still be traced today.

Right: Deep Run, near Chancellorsville.

Opposite, above: The stone wall at the base of Marye's Heights, Fredericksburg, as it looks today.

Opposite, below: The Confederate line along the stone wall after the futile and costly Union attacks of December 13, 1862.

front. His net gain: nothing, and at a cost of 4,800 casualties. Burnside persisted at Fredericksburg, where the Confederate defenses were even stronger. His infantry launched charge after suicidal charge at the stone wall. The II Corps commander, General Darius Couch, watched the unequal battle unfold from the steeple of the Fredericksburg courthouse. Wrote Couch: "As they charged, the artillery fire would break their formation and they would get mixed; then they would close up, go forward, receive the withering infantry fire, and those who were able would run to the houses and fight as best they could; then the brigade coming up in succession would do its duty and melt like snow coming down on warm ground."

General Winfield S. Hancock's division lost more than 2,000 men—42 percent of its total strength, the heaviest divisional loss of the war. Still the Federals came on, one brigade after another.

"It's only murder now," said Couch.

With nightfall, the fighting sputtered out. The Marye's Heights assaults cost Burnside 7,000 killed, wounded, and missing. His corps commanders talked him out of renewing the battle next day, and the day after. A storm of wind and rain blew through the Rappahannock Valley the night of December 15th–16th. Under its cover, the Federals withdrew across the river, taking up their pontoons behind them.

In Washington, the president was inconsolable. "If there is a worse place than Hell," Lincoln said when word of the disaster reached him, "then I am in it."

NURSING VOLUNTEERS

Illness and battle casualties could overwhelm the medical services of the Civil War armies. To cope, the Union and Confederate services often turned to volunteers.

In mid-1861, the reformer Dorothea Dix organized a corps of Union volunteer women nurses. Eventually, more than 2,000 Northern women served, many of them in the Washington, D.C., hospitals that took in tens of thousands of the wounded from the great Virginia battlefields of 1862–64: Fredericksburg, Chancellorsville, the Wilderness, and Spotsylvania.

Many of the volunteers were untrained in the medical arts. Most knew enough, however, to obey Briton Florence Nightingale's first rule of nursing: "Do the sick no harm." The Massachusetts novelist Louisa May Alcott nursed the wounded from the Battle of Fredericksburg. Her simple prescription for her ward in a Washington hospital involved quantities of fresh air. Her first act of each day was to create the conditions for a health-giving draft. "The men grumble and shiver, but the air is bad enough to breed a pestilence," Alcott wrote in her memoir *Hospital Sketches* (1863). "Poke up the fire, add blankets, joke, coax and command; but continue to open doors and windows as if life depended on it." Harriet Tubman, best known for her prewar abolitionist work as the fearless leader of the Underground Railroad, volunteered as a nurse at a Virginia hospital, having served the Union earlier in the war as a spy.

Southern women came forward in large numbers too, defying convention and strong male prejudices to minister to the Confederate sick and wounded. Such volunteers as Kate Cum-

mings quickly disproved Victorian stereotypes about female frailty. "The foul air from this mass of human beings at first made me giddy, but I soon got over it," Cummings wrote from a Corinth, Mississippi, hospital after the battle of Shiloh. "We have to walk, and when we give the men anything, kneel, in blood and water, but we think nothing of it."

Above: *Clara Barton used the contacts she had developed as the first female employee of the U. S. government (in the Patent Office) to organize relief supplies for troops injured during First Manassas. She went on to become the war's most famous nursing volunteer.*

Left: *Harriet Tubman (extreme left) with a group of slaves she helped escape before the war. She continued her commitment to helping those most vulnerable in a variety of roles, including nursing and relief work, until she died at the age of ninety-three.*

Chancellorsville

General Joseph B. Hooker—"Fighting Joe" to his admirers, "Mr. F. J. Hooker" to a derisive Lee—succeeded Burnside in January 1863. With the arrival of spring, Hooker planned a grand campaign of maneuver that he brashly predicted would accomplish the destruction of the Army of Northern Virginia. "My plans are perfect," Hooker announced, "and when I start to carry them out, may God have mercy on Bobby Lee; for I shall have none." He conceived a wide turning movement that would force Lee to abandon his powerful Fredericksburg defenses and fall back on Richmond.

Three corps of the Army of the Potomac marched north on April 27, 1863, for the Rappahannock and Rapidan fords. Three days later, 70,000 Federals arrived on Lee's flank and rear at the crossroads hamlet of Chancellorsville, nine miles west of Fredericksburg, near the southern edge of the Wilderness. Another two Federal corps crossed the Rappahannock below Fredericksburg, threatening the Confederates there.

Lee, however, caught on to Hooker's scheme in time to counter it. Guessing, correctly, that the main effort would come from the north, he left 10,000 troops in Fredericksburg and sent the balance, around 45,000 men, toward Chancellorsville. Advance elements of the two armies met east of the crossroads just before noon Friday, May 1. The initial firefight seemed to deflate Hooker. He sent word at once for his lead divisions to suspend the advance and pull back to Chancellorsville. His corps commanders were dumbstruck to learn that Hooker, flinching at this first contact, had decided to fight on the defensive and allow the initiative to pass to Lee.

TRAGEDY AT CHANCELLORSVILLE

At Chancellorsville, **May 1–6, 1863,** another Union defeat, the Confederates used a brilliant flank attack. However, they suffered an irreparable loss when General Thomas "Stonewall" Jackson was wounded in the left arm and right hand by friendly fire. After Jackson's arm was amputated, he contracted pneumonia and died.

 USA Major General Joseph Hooker

 CSA General Robert E. Lee, Lt. General Thomas "Stonewall" Jackson (mortally wounded)

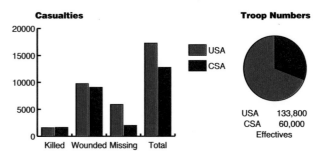

That evening, Lee and Jackson considered the question of how to attack the massive army in their front. "Show me what to do, and we will do it," Jackson offered. A cavalry patrol had reported the Federal right flank "in the air"—that is, unprotected by any natural barrier. Lee decided to divide his army into a third segment, sending Jackson with 26,000 men on a wide swing through the Wilderness with orders to fall on and crush General Oliver O. Howard's XI Corps. The 16-mile

Left: *This lithograph depicts the wounding of Stonewall Jackson in a "friendly fire" incident at Chancellorsville the evening of May 2, 1863. Jackson died of complications of the wound on May 10. "I know not how to replace him," Lee said when he learned of Jackson's passing.*

approach march consumed most of the day on May 2nd. It was mid-afternoon before Jackson had his first view of the target—Howard's line, facing south and wholly vulnerable to an attack from the west. Years later, the cavalry general Fitzhugh Lee described what he and Jackson could see that afternoon from a thicket overlooking the XI Corps' flank: "The soldiers were in groups in the rear, laughing, smoking, probably engaged, here and there, in games of cards and other amusements indulged in while feeling safe and comfortable, awaiting orders. In the rear of them were other parties driving up and butchering beeves."

A little before 6:00 PM, the relaxed Yankees caught sight of large numbers of deer and smaller wildlife bounding out of the woods to the west. A moment later, and close behind the startled deer, long lines of Confederate infantry emerged. They were Jackson's men, advancing at a trot and shrieking the Rebel yell.

The Federal line disintegrated. Within a few minutes, the rout was on. Howard found himself powerless to stem it. Jackson's infantry surged forward unchecked. "Push right ahead," Jackson called out to his brigade and regimental commanders. "Press them, press them!" By nightfall, the advance had carried to within a mile or so of Chancellorsville and a reunion of two of the three wings of Lee's divided army.

Then, for Jackson, calamity: In the darkness and confusion, as he rode among the jumbled units to organize a night attack that would cut off the enemy retreat to the Rappahannock, his own troops opened fire on him. Gravely wounded, Jackson turned over command to General A.P. Hill. Then Hill, too, fell wounded. By the time the cavalry general J.E.B. "Jeb" Stuart arrived to take charge, the moment had passed.

Next day, May 3, Sunday, the battle flared on two fronts.

EYEWITNESS

Excerpt from a message to President Lincoln from Union general Joseph Hooker, in the field at Chancellorsville, May 1863:

We have had a desperate fight yesterday and to-day, which has resulted in no success to us, having lost a position of two lines, which had been selected for our defense. It is now 1:30 o'clock, and there is still some firing of artillery. We may have another turn at it this p.m. I do not despair of success. If Sedgwick could have gotten up, there could have been but one result. As it is impossible for me to know the exact position of Sedgwick as regards his ability to advance and take part in the engagement, I cannot tell when it will end. We will endeavor to do our best. My troops are in good spirits. We have fought desperately to-day. No general ever commanded a more devoted army.

Above: Confederate guns firing from Hazel Grove on May 3, 1863, dominated the Chancellorsville clearing.

Opposite, above: Federal fire destroyed this Confederate caisson at Marye's Heights, Fredericksburg, on May 3, 1863. The photograph is credited to Mathew Brady.

Opposite, left: This stone marks the site of the field hospital where a Confederate surgeon treated the mortally wounded Stonewall Jackson the night of May 2, 1863.

Opposite, Right: The Confederates used the Old Salem Church as a field hospital during the Chancellorsville campaign.

Stuart launched a dawn attack that drove the Federals out of Chancellorsville and into a defensive arc guarding United States Ford on the Rappahannock. At Hooker's order, General John Sedgwick went into action at Fredericksburg. Sedgwick's infantry stormed Marye's Heights and set out down the Orange Turnpike toward Lee's rear. "You will hurry up your column," a rattled Hooker told him. "You will attack at once." Stuart's early morning success allowed Lee to turn and deal with Sedgwick. The Confederates stopped his advance late in the afternoon of May 3 at Salem Church, six miles short of Chancellorsville.

All day on the 4th, Lee searched for an opening to attack and destroy the Sedgwick component of the Union army, while Stuart held off the inert Hooker's much larger force. But the late-day assaults were uncoordinated and, in consequence, unsuccessful. That night, Sedgwick withdrew across the river.

Hooker, too, prepared to retreat. As at Fredericksburg six months earlier, a storm covered the rearward movement. Rain began falling around noon on Tuesday, May 5th. By midnight, the Rappahannock had risen six feet, a freshet that threatened to tear the two pontoon bridges loose from their moorings and sweep them away. They held, though. By midday of the 6th, the army had safely recrossed.

So ended Hooker's attempt, begun with such promise, to wreck the Army of Northern Virginia. He had been thoroughly outgeneralled in what is regarded as Lee's masterpiece battle. Although the Federals suffered 17,000 casualties, Hooker failed to bring a large part of his force to bear—thousands of bluecoats had hardly been engaged at all. "How had one half of the army been defeated while the other half had not fought?" one baffled Yankee wondered. For his part, Hooker offered no excuses. He had simply bungled the job. "For once I lost confidence in Joe Hooker, and that is all there is to it," he said.

The Confederates lost heavily as well—13,000 killed, wounded and missing, including the incomparable Stonewall, who died of complications of his Chancellorsville wound on May 10th. Lee recognized, too, that for all the brilliance of his victory, the Army of the Potomac had escaped largely intact. At the time, it seemed part of a pattern of Yankee failure—the Seven Days', Bull Run, Fredericksburg, now Chancellorsville. Still, in the long reach, the Confederate triumphs would prove barren.

"However badly beaten he never relaxed," the Confederate artillerist Alexander said of his enemy, "& he always came back again."

The Wilderness and Spotsylvania

With the blooming of the dogwoods, the armies returned to the old Wilderness battlefields. Grant's spring campaign of 1864 opened with the crossing of the Rapidan on May 4th and 5th. Grant, now commander-in-chief of all the Union land forces, had given precise instructions to General George Meade, commanding the Army of the Potomac. "Lee's army will be your objective point," he told him. "Wherever Lee goes, there you will go also."

So the leading elements of the 120,000-strong Federal army advanced south from the Rapidan fords into the Wilderness. Lee, with barely half Grant's numerical strength, resolved at once to attack. Two of his three corps came in on parallel routes from the west, aiming to strike the Federals in flank before they could clear the Wilderness tangle. The battle opened around 7:00 AM Thursday morning, May 5, 1864, when the II Corps under General Richard S. Ewell bumped into General Gouverneur Warren's V Corps in the thickets near Wilderness Tavern. The collision touched off a full day's blind, confused, and inconclusive struggle.

"As for fighting," one veteran recalled, "it was simply bushwhacking on a grand scale, in brush where all formation

THE WILDERNESS AND SPOTSYLVANIA

The battles of both the Wilderness, **May 5–6, 1864,** and Spotsylvania, **May 8–21, 1864,** ended in costly stalemates for both sides. It was the beginning of the last long year—one of ceaseless fighting from Cold Harbor to Appomattox.

 USA General Ulysses S. Grant

 CSA General Robert E. Lee

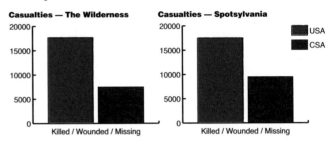

Troop numbers—The Wilderness: USA 120,000; CSA 60,000 (Engaged)
Troop numbers—Spotsylvania: USA 110,000; CSA 50,000 (Engaged)

Below: *A Civil War view of the second-growth forest tangle known as the Wilderness.*

Opposite: *The Federal IX Corps attacked Confederate positions near the Widow Tapp farm on May 6, 1864.*

beyond that of regiments or companies was soon lost and where such a thing as a consistent line of battle on either side was impossible."

Ewell's battle died out around 3:00 PM. As soon as the guns fell silent, his infantry began digging fieldworks along both sides of the Orange Turnpike. To the south, the Federal II Corps under Hancock struck A.P. Hill's corps athwart the Orange Plank Road. Here, as the long day waned, the Yankees pressed the Confederates nearly to the breaking point. Only the coming of darkness saved Hill's outnumbered, outgunned corps from collapse.

That night, Grant sent orders for Hancock to renew the attack at first light Friday. For his part, Lee passed word to Longstreet, whose I Corps was still on the way to the battlefield, to be ready to pitch into Hancock as soon as he arrived. Hill, meantime, granted his frazzled troops a full night's rest, ignoring a recommendation from one of his division commanders to keep the men awake and at work entrenching.

When Hancock struck, Hill's unfortified line gave way almost at once. Only the timely arrival of the first of Longstreet's infantry double-timing down the Plank Road prevented a rout. Longstreet's lead brigades drove the Federals back to their startlines and allowed Hill time to regroup. During the lull, Longstreet prepared his counterstroke.

Earlier, a Confederate staff officer discovered an unfinished, overgrown railroad cut through which a flanking column could approach unobserved. Longstreet assembled four brigades, some 5,000 infantry, and assigned them the task of moving up through the cut and pouncing on Hancock's unsupported left. The idea was to crumple the flank, then make a great left wheel with the rest of the corps, and in turn with the rest of the army, that would hurl Grant back across the Rapidan.

The initial assault overwhelmed Hancock's left. His end brigade broke, then the next in line, and so on. "They had fought all they meant to fight," one of Hancock's officers observed, "and there was an end to it." But Longstreet's great wheel never got rolling. As he pushed up to the front, jittery Confederate infantry opened fire on him. The wounding of Longstreet brought the attack to an abrupt standstill, much as Stonewall Jackson's wounding under similar circumstances had done at Chancellorsville the year before.

Fighting broke out again late in the afternoon, with Confederate lunges at both Union flanks. On Ewell's front, a brigade-sized attack managed a limited breakthrough and had the added effect of spreading alarm and despondency as far back as Grant's field headquarters. The first reports sounded dire; one unstrung officer claimed breathlessly that Lee had turned the Union right and soon would sweep up the entire army. For once, the usually imperturbable Grant lost his temper.

"I am heartily tired of hearing what *Lee* is going to do," he said. "Some of you always seem to think he is going to turn a double somersault and land in our rear and on both flanks at the same time. Go back to your command and try to think what we are going to do ourselves instead of what *Lee* is going to do."

With darkness coming on, both sides returned to work on their trenches. The exhausted armies rested on the 7th, Saturday, and tallied their losses. The Federal totals were staggering—more than 17,000 killed, wounded, and missing over the three days. The Confederates lost 7,700 men. With brush fires spreading through the woods, stretcher parties fanned out trying to save as many of the wounded as possible. Some 200 men were burned or suffocated to death in the smoking woods. During the night of the 7th, Grant began to disengage. For many in the ranks, the order to break contact came as no surprise: in the Army of the Potomac tradition, the generals would mismanage a battle, then retreat.

"We had expected so much from General Grant," one private wrote, recording the prevailing view, "and now he was to be defeated as other generals before him had been." This time, though, there would be no turning back. Grant pulled away from Lee not to retreat, but to continue the southward

march. He put the army on the road for Spotsylvania Courthouse twelve miles away—and on the shortest and most direct route to Richmond.

Cavalry reconnaissance tipped Lee to the move, and advance units of the Army of Northern Virginia managed to reach Spotsylvania just ahead—literally, only a few minutes ahead—of the Federals. The Confederates withstood a series of piecemeal attacks on May 8th. With the arrival of the rest of the army, they hunkered down in a strongly entrenched semicircle, with a prominent bulge (dubbed the "Mule Shoe" for its shape) in the center. From these fieldworks, they repulsed a series of full-scale assaults on May 10, inflicting heavy casualties on the attackers.

Grant took a day off to plan an all-out effort at the Mule Shoe for Thursday, May 12, with Hancock's II Corps leading the way. Rain fell in torrents during the night, then slackened to drizzle before dawn. A little after 4:30 AM, 20,000 Yankees came ghosting through the murk. The initial advance overwhelmed the defenders. Hancock's assault troops took 2,500 prisoners and 20 cannon in the first rush.

The Confederates regrouped and launched a furious counterattack that stopped the advance before it could cut Lee's army in half. The Yankee infantry settled into the enemy's trenches and thwarted all efforts to retake the salient, soon to be known

as the "Bloody Angle." The battle took on aspects of a night-mare, one from which thousands would never awake. Bodies lay eight deep in some trenches. Much of the fighting took place at arm's length, and in a cold, numbing rain. The volume of fire rose to an intensity never before experienced in war. Toward midnight an oak tree, twenty-two inches in diameter crashed into the Confederate lines, cut in two by gunfire.

Around midnight, some twenty hours after the II Corps assault brigades loomed out of the fog, the Confederates finally abandoned the salient, falling back to a shorter line a few hundred yards to the rear. The combined casualties of the Mule Shoe fighting approached 13,000 men. "The world has never seen so bloody and protracted a battle as the one being fought," Grant wrote his wife, "and I hope never will." For the next three days, the armies lay quiet, as though in shock. A final set of attacks on May 18 and 19 failed to break the stalemate.

The Federals, on the attack nearly all the time, lost 35,000 men killed, wounded, and missing in the Wilderness and at Spotsylvania, nearly twice the Confederate total. "I propose to fight it out on this line if it takes all summer," Grant had wired Lincoln on the eve of the Mule Shoe operation. And although the line shifted, the fighting never ceased. The armies were to remain under each other's fire every day for nearly a year—until the end, in fact. On May 20 Grant pulled out of Spotsylvania and resumed the march south, along roads that would lead to Cold Harbor, Petersburg, and, finally, Appomattox.

EYE-WITNESS

Melville's poem recalls the Battle of Chancellorsville. It was inspired by the Battle of the Wilderness a year later, when the opposing armies re-entered Virginia's Wilderness they found grim relics of the bitter fight that resulted in the death of Thomas J. "Stonewall" Jackson.

"The Wilderness"
In glades they meet skull after skull
Where pine cones lay—the rusted gun.
Green shoes full of bones, the mouldering coat
And cuddled-up skeleton;
And scores of such. Some start as in dreams.
And comrades lost bemoan:
By the edge of those wilds Stonewall had charged—
But the year and the Man were gone.
— *Herman Melville*

Above: *The Bloody Angle at Spotsylvania as it appears today.*

Opposite: *An artist's conception of a Union assault on the Confederate works at Spotsylvania, May 1864.*

The self-guided tour begins in Fredericksburg, moves west to Chancellorsville, west again to the Wilderness, then southeast to Spotsylvania Court House.

The Fredericksburg and Spotsylvania National Military Park Headquarters is at Chatham, an antebellum mansion on the north bank of the Rappahannock that once was a Union military hospital. Visitor centers are in Fredericksburg and at Chancellorsville. A seven-mile hiking trail connects important sites at Spotsylvania.

FREDERICKSBURG

1 Visitor Center A path leads from the center to the Sunken Road, where Confederate infantry poured a devastating fire into the attacking Federals. Some 7,000 Union soldiers fell here at the base of Marye's Heights.

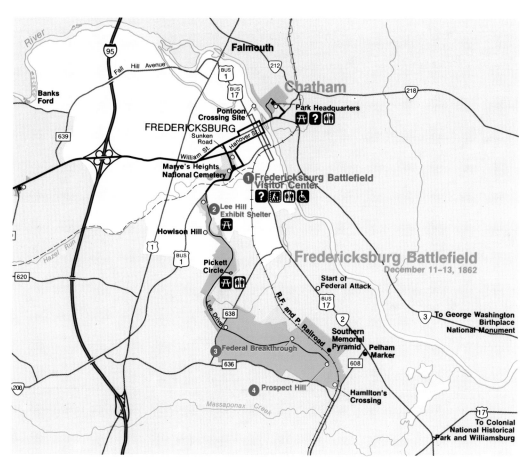

2 Lee Hill Exhibit Shelter Lee's tactical headquarters were here during the three-day battle. The height afforded him a panoramic view. "It is well war is so terrible,"

Lee remarked as he watched the Federals advance across the plain, "or we would become too fond it."

3 Federal Breakthrough Here Pennsylvania troops under Gen. George Meade pierced Jackson's line. A savage counterattack sealed the breach.

4 Prospect Hill This was the anchor of Lee's right wing, entrusted to the II Corps of Gen. Thomas "Stonewall" Jackson.

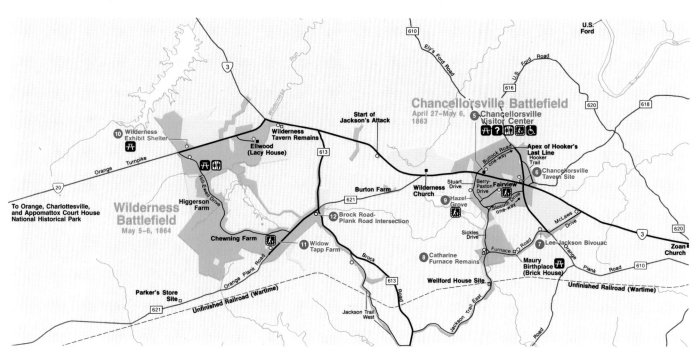

CHANCELLORSVILLE

5 Visitor Center The Orange Turnpike, a key route through the tangle of second-growth forest known as the Wilderness, runs past the center.

6 Chancellorsville Tavern Site Union Gen. Joseph B. Hooker made this his headquarters during the battle. Jubilant Confederate troops celebrated their victory here on May 3. Set alight during the battle, the building burned down.

7 Lee-Jackson Bivouac Lee and Jackson met here the night of May 1 to plan the flank attack that crushed the Federal XI Corps and led to Lee's greatest victory.

8 Catherine Furnace Remains Jackson led his 26,000-strong column past this forge on his circuitous march of May 2 toward the unsupported right flank of the Union army.

9 Hazel Grove Early on May 3, Federal troops abandoned this position, one of the few clearings in which artillery could be used effectively—"a gratuitous gift of a battlefield," said a Confederate cannoneer. From here, Confederate guns dominated Chancellorsville at the critical point of the battle.

THE WILDERNESS

10 Wilderness Exhibit Shelter The armies made first contact near here on May 5 when Confederate troops of Ewell's II Corps bumped into V Corps infantry under Warren. Fighting continued inconclusively for most of the day.

11 Widow Tapp Farm Near this site on the Orange Plank Road, Longstreet's arriving infantry checked the advance of the Federal II Corps under Hancock early on May 6 and gave Hill's battered III Corps a chance to regroup.

12 Brock Road-Plank Road Intersection A Confederate flank attack at midday on May 6 overwhelmed the Union left. Longstreet's wounding here may have cost the Confederates a decisive victory. The resulting confusion and delay allowed Hancock time to strengthen his defenses and cover this critical road junction.

SPOTSYLVANIA

13 Spotsylvania Exhibit Shelter The Confederates won the race to Spotsylvania, but only just. At nearby Laurel Hill, Confederates withstood a series of assaults from Warren's V Corps.

14 Bloody Angle In a cold rain on May 12, the armies fought hand-to-hand in the Mule Shoe Salient for nearly 20 hours. The dead were piled several deep in the trenches after one of the war's bloodiest days.

15 East Angle Burnside's IX Corps attacked this face of the Mule Shoe at 4:30 AM on May 12. His assault forces were thrown back with heavy losses.

16 McCoull House Site The house sat just inside the Confederate lines at the Mule Shoe Salient. Like everything else in the immediate vicinity, it suffered badly during the Spotsylvania fighting.

FREDERICKSBURG AND SPOTSYLVANIA COUNTY BATTLEFIELDS MEMORIAL NATIONAL MILITARY PARK

MAILING ADDRESS
Fredericksburg and Spotsylvania County Battlefields Memorial National Military Park, 120 Chatham Lane, Fredericksburg, VA 22405

TELEPHONE
703-373-4461

DIRECTIONS
The Fredericksburg Visitor Center is located on US 1, at the foot of Marye's Heights , at 1013 Lafayette Blvd., in Fredericksburg, Virginia. The Chancellorsville Visitor Center is located ten miles west of Fredericksburg on VA 22. The Wilderness Battlefield Unit is located approximately fifteen miles west of Fredericksburg on VA 3. The Spotsylvania Court House Battlefield Unit is located approximately seven miles southeast of the Wilderness Unit on VA 613.

VISITOR CENTERS
Slide presentations and exhibits.

ACTIVITIES
Chatham Manor, an eighteenth-century plantation house used as a Union Army headquarters and field hospital, is open daily. Jackson Shrine, the house where Stonewall Jackson died, is open seasonally. Ranger-guided walking tours in summer.

HOURS
Open daily from 9 AM to 5 PM, with hours extended to 8:30 AM to 6:30 PM in summer.

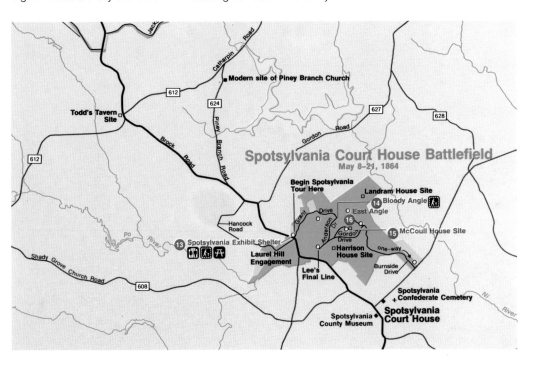

Fort Pulaski

Fort Pulaski stands on Cockspur Island, a group of low-lying grassy hummocks in the salt marsh near Tybee Island, fifteen miles downriver from the city of Savannah, at the mouth of the Savannah River. Named for the Revolutionary War hero Count Casimir Pulaski, the fort was part of a series of coastal fortifications designed in 1816 by the French general Simon Bernard, formerly of Napoleon's staff. Construction on the fort began in 1829, and one of the engineer officers involved in the drainage of Cockspur Island was Lieutenant Robert E. Lee, a recent graduate of West Point. When it was completed in 1847, Fort Pulaski boasted masonry walls thirty-five feet high and seven-and-a-half feet thick, surrounded by a moat thirty-five feet wide and seven feet deep. Most artillery officers believed that the walls could not be penetrated by existing weapons.

Fort Pulaski was seized by the Georgia Volunteer Militia as early as January 3, 1861, sixteen days before Georgia seceded from the Union. It was the Confederates who completed its armament, increasing the number of cannon on the upper level, or terreplein, to forty-eight, including two of the new rifled cannon developed in Great Britain. Many of the guns faced north, over the Savannah River.

By November 1861, the Port Royal Expedition—a Federal campaign to recapture the sea islands of Georgia and South Carolina—began. After establishing a beachhead on Hilton

NEW WEAPONS SHOW THEIR POWER

The **April 10–11, 1862,** attack on Fort Pulaski by Union batteries is best remembered for the devastating effect of newly developed rifled artillery. Located on Cockspur Island, near the entrance to the harbor of Savannah, Georgia, Fort Pulaski, with its thick masonry walls, was considered impregnable. However, the fort, which had taken decades to build, was partially reduced to rubble in a well-planned and -executed bombardment.

 USA Brigadier General Quincy Adams Gillmore

 CSA Colonel Charles Olmstead, commander of the garrison (385)

Below: Although the Confederates thought Fort Pulaski, strategically located at the mouth of the Savannah River, impregnable, it fell to Union forces after bombardment by a new instrument of warfare—the rifled cannon.

Opposite, above: The fort was designed to mount 110 cannon.

Opposite, below: More than 5,000 rounds of fire destroyed walls believed to be rock-solid. The surrender of Fort Pulaski made the port of Savannah useless to the South.

Head Island, on the north side of the mouth of the Savannah, Federal forces landed on Tybee Island in February 1862. The Confederates had abandoned the island in the face of the Union incursion, leaving Cockspur Island and its fort vulnerable. Federal troops commanded by Chief Engineer Quincy A. Gillmore, an enthusiastic believer in the power of rifled cannon, began to construct artillery batteries on the firm ground of northern Tybee Island. The work involved building two-and-a-half miles of road through sand and marsh grass, and as they approached Cockspur Island, they worked at night to conceal the extent of their efforts.

By April 9, preparations were complete. Facing Fort Pulaski at distances ranging from 1,650 to 3,400 yards stood 11 artillery batteries named for President Lincoln, members of his cabinet, and Union generals, including McClellan, Grant, and Sherman. The 36 artillery pieces, a combination of mortars and smoothbore and rifled cannon, had been landed in heavy surf and dragged silently across the sand by night. Five of the 10 rifled pieces were 30-pound Parrots, which, it was later established, had an effective range of 8,453 yards. The spiral, or rifled, grooves within the barrel put a spin on the shell that increased its range, accuracy, and penetration. Most of these were placed in Batteries Sigel and McClellan, nearest the fort.

Early on April 10, Union forces formally requested the surrender of Fort Pulaski. The Confederate commander, Colonel Charles Olmstead, refused. He believed, as did many others, that the fort was impregnable. At the time, it was thought that even rifled cannon were not accurate at distances over 1,000 yards. If besieged, Olmstead was well supplied with arms and food, and the fort's cisterns could hold 200,000 gallons of water. He had also made defensive preparations, digging pits

and ditches within the fort to catch rolling shot and building wooden shields and barricades to deflect shell fragments.

At 8:15 AM on April 10, a mortar shell from Battery Halleck signaled the beginning of the bombardment. At first, the rate of fire from Union guns seemed slow, but it gradually increased. Only 20 of Olmstead's guns were positioned to return fire, and those were also the most vulnerable. The Confederate cannon fire diminished as a number of guns were dismounted or destroyed by accurate fire from Union artillery,

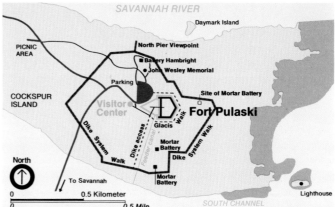

Top: *The moat surrounding the fort as seen through a cannon port.*

Left: *The Union's rifled cannon delivered blows that toppled the fort's mounted cannon, pierced the walls, and eventually threatened the magazine, with its 20 tons of gunpowder.*

Above: *The self-guided tour of Fort Pulaski begins at the Visitor Center, and includes audio-taped information at locations including the Northwest Magazine, surrender room, and prison. The defenses—the moat, gorge wall, drawbridge, and cannon—are well preserved and provide a vivid picture of the fort as it was during the battle.*

Left: A typical casement, wherein nearly 400 Confederate prisoners were housed in the northeast, southeast, and south walls of the fort during the winter of 1864 under particularly harsh conditions.

FORT PULASKI NATIONAL MONUMENT

MAILING ADDRESS
Fort Pulaski National Monument, PO Box 30757, Savannah, GA 31410-0757

TELEPHONE
912-786-5787

DIRECTIONS
The fort is located on US 80, fifteen miles east of Savannah, Georgia.

VISITOR CENTER
Museum and audiovisual program.

ACTIVITIES
Ranger talks and demonstrations are conducted on weekends throughout the year and daily during the summer. The monument encompasses more than 5,000 acres; there is a one-quarter-mile marked nature trail and other trails allow for further exploration of the island.

HOURS
The monument is open daily except December 25, from 8:30 AM to 5:15 PM, with hours extended to 6:45 PM in the summer.

while heavier Union guns hammered at the walls of the fort, particularly the southeast corner. By evening, although the fort appeared intact from the outside, the results of the barrage were apparent within. The southeast wall was damaged heavily, and several gun embrasures had been opened up by Union fire. Throughout the night, the Union artillery kept up a sporadic barrage, which prevented the Confederates from making repairs and righting their dismounted guns.

In the morning, the Union cannonade resumed. Confederate guns that had been repaired were silenced again. As the morning progressed, the damage became more obvious, and the Federal artillery continued to lob shells at the most vulnerable locations. By noon, they were aiming directly at the doors of the magazine, which contained more than 40,000 pounds of gunpowder. Threatened by the explosion of his own munitions, Olmstead surrendered at 2:15 PM. During the 30-hour barrage, Federal batteries had fired 5,275 rounds against Fort Pulaski.

Although a Confederate force of only 385 had managed to hold off a Union force nearly three times its size for a day and a half, the result of the battle was in little doubt from the outset. Only one man on each side was killed, and thirteen Confederates were wounded. The Savannah River was closed to Confederate raiders and blockade runners, and a transit base for the Federal Navy was established nearby. For the rest of the war, Fort Pulaski would remain in Federal hands. In the long run, the importance of the battle for Fort Pulaski was the discovery that masonry forts, hitherto the main defensive structures of warfare, had become obsolete in the face of rifled cannon, a critical advance in military technology.

Below: This drawbridge over the moat, which was thirty-five feet wide in some places, was one of the many defenses that made Fort Pulaski appear impenetrable. But bullet-shaped projectiles from 30-pounder Parrott guns sailed easily over these obstacles.

Gettysburg

The two forces met by chance at Gettysburg. The Confederates came for shoes. Federal cavalry troops were already on the scene.

In early June 1863, a month after his brilliant victory at Chancellorsville, Robert E. Lee put the Army of Northern Virginia in motion for the Potomac fords. Pressures elsewhere had rubbed some of the luster off the Virginia triumph. In the West, Union forces had closed on Vicksburg on the Mississippi and were on the march in Middle Tennessee.

General James Longstreet and others suggested shifting forces west to meet the Federal threats. Lee countered with a proposal for a second invasion of the North. (The first had ended 10 months earlier in the drawn battle of Antietam.) Confederate resources were limited and, in Lee's view, Virginia remained always the decisive theater.

"It becomes a question between Virginia and Mississippi," he said.

So Lee's army marched north, through the Blue Ridge passes and up the Shenandoah Valley to the Potomac and beyond, rekindling the old dream of winning the great battle on enemy soil that would fuel Northern antiwar sentiment and encourage the British and French to intervene for the Confederacy.

TURNING POINT OF THE WAR

General Robert E. Lee's second invasion of the North was met and repulsed by General George Meade's Army of the Potomac in the three-day battle of Gettysburg, Pennsylvania, July 1–3, 1863. This proved to be the turning point of the war; never again would Lee be able to mount such an offensive. The Confederates withdrew on July 4, 1863, the same day that Vicksburg surrendered to Union forces in the West.

 USA General George Gordon Meade

 CSA General Robert E. Lee

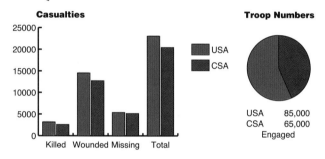

Left: *This view looks from the observation tower on Culp's Hill to the southwest toward Seminary Ridge.*

Opposite: *This monument on Little Round Top is a memorial to the 155th Pennsylvania Volunteers. A sturdy Union defense of the hill on July 2, 1863, preserved the vulnerable left flank of Meade's army.*

The army, 75,000 strong, organized in 3 infantry corps and with 6 brigades of cavalry and 270 great guns, had never been stronger. Lee had limitless faith in his troops. "There never were such men in an army before," Lee said. "They will go anywhere and do anything if properly led." And the troops had an almost religious reverence for Lee.

The Army of the Potomac, with 90,000 men of all arms, followed Lee, although its commander, General Joseph Hooker, seemed to give chase with reluctance, doubtless recalling the pain Lee had inflicted on him at Chancellorsville in May. First Hooker proposed attacking the tail of the advancing Confederates; then he turned about and suggested marching south, toward Richmond, while his adversary marched in the opposite direction, toward Washington, Baltimore, and Philadelphia.

Sensing that Hooker had lost his nerve, President Lincoln replaced him on June 28 with General George Gordon Meade. On that day, the Army of the Potomac lay in and around Frederick, Maryland. Lee, characteristically, had divided his army. Longstreet's and A.P. Hill's corps were near Chambersburg, Pennsylvania. Forty miles and more to the northeast, Richard Ewell had split his corps too, sending part to Carlisle and part to York.

For nearly a week, Lee had been advancing into the unknown. With General J. E. B. "Jeb" Stuart and his three cavalry brigades away on an ill-advised sweep to the east, Lee had lost the "eyes and ears" of his army—his chief source of news of the enemy's movements. Lee actually believed the Federals were still in Virginia. One of Longstreet's scouts finally caught up with him on the night of June 28 to report that the Federals were across the Potomac and only two days' march to the south. Within a few hours, Lee had dispatched orders for the army to concentrate at the crossroads town of Gettysburg.

The First Day

The Confederates found the high-summer Pennsylvania countryside a perpetual feast. The troops, a Louisiana soldier wrote, were living "on the very fat of the land—milk, butter, eggs, chickens, turkeys, apple butter, pear butter, cheese, honey, fresh pork, mutton and every other imaginable thing that was good to eat." Shops and storehouses were full of clothing and other goods. Rumor reached one of Hill's division commanders, Henry Heth, of a warehouse full of shoes at Gettysburg. When Heth went off to collect the shoes, he touched off the greatest battle of the Civil War.

Three brigades of Federal cavalry awaited the Confederates just west of Gettysburg. "They will come booming—skirmishers three-deep," the Yankee commander, John Buford, told one of his brigadiers. "You will have to fight like the devil until supports arrive." At 8:00 AM on Wednesday, July 1, 1863, they came. Fighting dismounted, blazing away from behind trees and rocks with rapid-fire Spencer carbines, Buford's troopers held off the Confederates for more than two hours, barely time enough for the I Corps infantry of John Reynolds to reach the battlefield.

Reynolds sent word of the developing battle to Meade, still in Maryland fifteen miles to the southeast. He called for the two nearest Federal corps, the XI under Oliver Otis Howard and the III under Daniel Sickles, to double-time to Gettysburg. Then Reynolds turned to the task of deploying his own corps. A Confederate marksman shot him dead as he directed the arriving infantry into line on a spur of high ground known as McPherson's Ridge.

The Federals held fast for several hours, but at great cost. One of the hardest-hitting formations in the Army of the

Left: A Confederate sharpshooter lies dead in the Devil's Den in this famous Mathew Brady photograph. This was fiercely contested ground on the afternoon of July 2nd.

Opposite: Field guns in a row on Cemetery Hill. Federal forces formed a new line here after their repulse north of Gettysburg on July 1st. On succeeding days, heavy fighting took place on Cemetery Hill and on Culp's Hill to the east.

Potomac, the Iron Brigade of 5 Midwestern regiments, lost a full two-thirds of its strength, 1,200 men killed and wounded, in the fighting there and on a parallel rise to the southeast, Seminary Ridge. Meantime, both sides fed fresh forces into the battle. Howard's corps took up a position north of Gettysburg and prepared to meet the leading elements of Ewell's Confederates coming down from Carlisle and York. By midafternoon, some 24,000 Confederates faced some 19,000 Yankees in a line curving from Seminary Ridge to Oak Ridge, north of the town.

Lee reached the battlefield just as Ewell's assault brigades were driving a wedge into Howard's front. He ordered a general advance at once. Howard's line swiftly collapsed, and his troops fell back through the streets of Gettysburg in a panic. Howard's failure unhinged the right flank of the I Corps, which also began to withdraw. The remnants of both corps, about 7,000 men, kept going until they cleared the outskirts of town and reached the commanding high ground to the south.

There, on Cemetery and Culp's Hills, the Federals threw up rough defensive works and awaited a renewed attack. A senior general, Winfield Scott Hancock, arrived to bring order out of chaos. His mere presence seemed to steady the troops. "One felt safe near him," one of his officers said of the imposing Hancock. Three more Federal corps reached Gettysburg during the night. Meade rode in an hour or so before daybreak. By then, Hancock had fashioned a strong line, since likened to a fishhook: the barb at Culp's Hill, then the hook curving westward to Cemetery Hill, the shank running southward down Cemetery Ridge to the eye, a rocky eminence called Little Round Top. The Confederates were arrayed just opposite, beyond the Emmitsburg Road a mile to the west on Seminary Ridge.

By midnight, it had become clear that Lee had lost the initiative. If he renewed the battle here, it would be on the enemy's terms. Longstreet proposed an alternative—a wide flanking movement to the left that would land the Confederates between the Army of the Potomac and Washington. But Lee resolved to fight at Gettysburg.

"The enemy is there," he told Longstreet, gesturing toward Cemetery Ridge, "and I am going to fight him there."

Left: *Gettysburg yielded a hellish harvest of more than 50,000 killed, wounded and missing. Here are Union dead in the declivity aptly known as the Devil's Den.*

Below: *This lithograph depicts scenes in the Union artillery lines at Gettysburg.*

The Second Day

Lee assigned Longstreet to carry out the attack of Thursday, July 2, to be aimed at the left of Meade's fishhook line. During the day, the Federal III Corps commander, Sickles, created an outward bulge in the lower portion of the shank when he moved the corps a half-mile forward onto higher ground west of a little stream called Plum Run. The Sickles salient, as it would be called, ran from the Emmitsburg Road near the Cordori Farm south through a peach orchard,

where it bent back at an acute angle through a wheatfield to a jumble of boulders known as the Devil's Den. Behind the Devil's Den rose Little Round Top, a craggy hillock that commanded the entire length of Meade's line. By an oversight, Little Round Top had been left undefended for most of the day.

Longstreet was slow to move to the attack. Lee had hoped to bring off the battle early in the morning, or at least well before noon; as it happened, Longstreet was not ready until

4:00 PM. By then one of his brigade commanders had reported Little Round Top free of the enemy and proposed a flanking move to occupy it. Longstreet, who had already tried twice and failed twice to persuade Lee to alter his plans, rejected the proposal. The attack went forward as Lee had ordered.

Over the next few hours, some of the war's hardest fighting boiled up in the peach orchard, the wheatfield, and the Devil's Den. Longstreet's 15,000 infantry overran the so-called Sickles Salient and knocked the III Corps out of the battle.

And Longstreet's right-hand brigades came agonizingly close to capturing Little Round Top.

Just in time, one of Meade's staff officers recognized the danger and quick-marched a brigade to Little Round Top. The brigade's left-hand regiment, the 20th Maine, had barely settled into position before the first enemy infantry came charging up the slope. The 20th Maine, under a 34-year-old former Bowdoin College professor named Joshua Lawrence Chamberlain, repulsed five successive Confederate assaults.

Above: Looking down into the Devil's Den from Little Round Top. Union Brig. Gen. Gouverneur K. Warren (statue, left), Meade's chief engineer, regarded Little Round Top as the "key of the battlefield" on July 2nd.

Left: In this scene sketched by Edwin Forbes, Meade's extreme left holds during the evening of July 2nd.

"The blood," Confederate Colonel William Oates recalled, "stood in puddles in some places on the rocks."

The Maine regiment not only held its ground but, with more than a third of its complement killed and wounded and running low on ammunition, swept the attackers away for the last time in a bayonet charge. Quiet descended on Little Round Top, but down the line the fighting continued unabated. Only the desperate charge of the half-sized 1st Minnesota regiment prevented the Confederates from achieving a breakthrough on Cemetery Ridge. The charge blunted a division-strength assault for just long enough to give Hancock time to rush reinforcements to the front. The 1st Minnesota lost all but 47 of its 262 officers and men.

Toward sunset, the three-hour battle flared out. Two days of fighting had left a total of 35,000 men killed and wounded. The Union commanders agreed at a council of war Thursday night to stay on for a third day at Gettysburg. And Lee, who still believed he could achieve a victory there, laid plans for the Confederate debacle that would be known as Pickett's Charge.

The Third Day

The Confederates had tested the Union right and the Union left. On the third day, July 3, Friday, Lee decided to test the center, using the Virginia division of George E. Pickett, which had reached the battlefield only the evening before, and two other divisions. Lee called for a massive opening bombardment that would stun Meade's infantry and disrupt his artillery long

EYEWITNESS

From the diary of a Union soldier who fought at Gettysburg with the 6th Corps, Army of the Potomac:

"July 3rd 1863—This morning the troops were under arms before light and ready for the great battle that we knew must be fought. The firing began, and our Brigade was hurried to the right of the line to reinforce it. While not in the front line yet we were constantly exposed to the fire of the Rebel Artillery, while bullets fell around us. ...Our Brigade marched down the road until we reached the house used by General Meade as Headquarters. The road ran between ledges of rocks while the fields were strewn with boulders. More than two hundred guns were belching forth their thunder, and most of the shells that came over the hill struck in the road on which our Brigade was moving. The flying iron and pieces of stone struck men down in every direction. ... Soon the Rebel yell was heard, and we have found since that the Rebel General Pickett made a charge with his Division and was repulsed after reaching some of our batteries. Our lines of Infantry in front of us rose up and poured in a terrible fire. As we were only a few yards in rear of our lines we saw all the fight. The firing gradually died away, and but for an occasional shot all was still. But what a scene it was. Oh the dead and the dying on this bloody field."

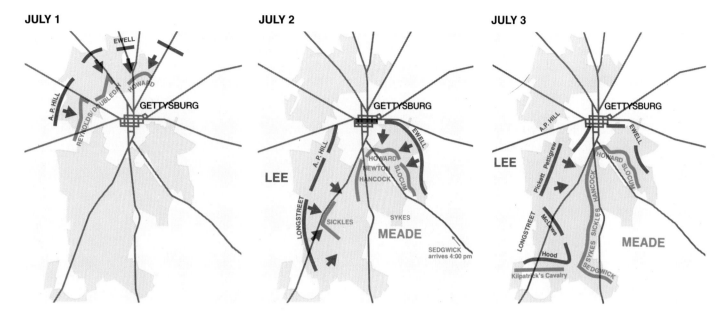

JULY 1

JULY 2

JULY 3

THE GETTYSBURG ADDRESS

President Lincoln delivered this tribute to the Union dead of Gettysburg at the dedication of the National Cemetery on November 19, 1863. The chief orator, Edward Everett of Massachusetts, spoke for two hours; no one remembers his words today. Lincoln's five-minute address, which offered eloquent comfort to the bereaved and gave a deeper, larger meaning to the great sacrifice of Gettysburg, has come to be regarded as one of the finest in the American annals.

"Four score and seven years ago our fathers brought forth on this continent, a new nation, conceived in liberty, and dedicated to the proposition that all men are created equal.

Now we are engaged in a great civil war, testing whether that nation, or any nation so conceived and so dedicated, can long endure. We are met on a great battlefield of that war. We have come to dedicate a portion of that field, as a final resting place for those who here gave their lives that that nation might live. It is altogether fitting and proper that we should do this.

But, in a larger sense, we cannot dedicate—we cannot consecrate—we cannot hallow—this ground. The brave men, living and dead, who struggled here, have consecrated it, far above our poor power to add or detract. The world will little note, nor long remember what we say here, but it can never forget what they did here. It is for us the living, rather, to be dedicated here to the unfinished work which they who fought here have thus far so nobly advanced. It is rather for us to be here dedicated to the great task remaining before us—that from these honored dead we take increased devotion to that cause for which they gave the last full measure of devotion—that we here highly resolve that these dead shall not have died in vain—that this nation, under God, shall have a new birth of freedom—and that government of the people, by the people, for the people, shall not perish from the earth."

The maps above represent the positions of the armies at the start of each of the three days of battle.

JULY 1
Elements of both armies collided just north of Gettysburg at 8:00 AM. As more troops arrived on both sides, the fighting spread along McPherson Ridge. Late in the afternoon, attacking Confederates broke the Union line north of town. The Federals retreated through Gettysburg and occupied the high ground to the south.

JULY 2
During the night, the armies completed their concentration at Gettysburg and Lee prepared to attack the Federal "fishhook" line that curved from Culp's Hill to Cemetery Hill and then ran south along Cemetery Ridge to the Round Tops. Longstreet's late-afternoon assaults on Meade's left made gains, but the Union lines held. On the right, Union defenders withstood Ewell's attacks toward Culp's Hill.

JULY 3
In the morning, Ewell renewed his effort to take Culp's Hill. Lee planned his main blow against the Union center on Cemetery Ridge. After a heavy cannonade, 12,000 Confederate infantry set out across the open fields for the "umbrella-shaped clump of trees" on the ridge. The defenders repulsed Pickett's Charge with ease. On July 4, Lee disengaged and began his retreat to Virginia.

Opposite: *Based on a wartime sketch, Edwin Forbes' painting shows the fighting on Cemetery Hill.*

enough to give the 14,000-strong storming column a chance to cover the mile-long distance and break the Federal line.

As the sun climbed, the day became hot and sultry. Near the objective point of the Confederate assault, an umbrella-shaped clump of trees on Cemetery Ridge, the Union troops lay as though in a daze, stunned by the heat. There had been fighting earlier, on Ewell's front. But by midday all had become still. Then, at a few minutes past 1:00 PM, the Confederate great guns opened fire, delivering the heaviest cannonade of the war. Union gunners returned fire in a roaring artillery duel that could be heard as far away as Pittsburg, 150 miles distant.

It went on for nearly two hours, causing havoc in the Federal rear, damaging some guns, but barely disturbing the front-line infantry. At 3:00 PM, Longstreet reluctantly signaled the advance. "I don't want to make this attack," he told one of his officers. "I believe it will fail. I do not see how it can succeed. I would not make it even now, but General Lee has ordered & expects it."

So the Confederates set out for the clump of trees, advancing on a mile-wide front at the stately pace of a hundred yards a minute. They made an easy target. The Federal artillery tore great gaps in the slow-moving line. "We could not help hitting them at every shot," one of the Yankee gunners recalled. Federal infantry swung out on either flank to rake the attackers as they struggled on upslope through the high grass.

"Home, boys, home!" a Confederate officer shouted. "Remember, home is beyond those hills." It was soon over. A few hundred Virginians managed to breach the Union line; within minutes, all were either dead or captive. Everyone else—around half of those who had started out had been killed or wounded in the charge—streamed back toward Seminary Ridge.

Lee met them there. "It is all my fault," he called out as he rode in among the survivors. "It is I who have lost this fight."

Above: *Monument to the 7th New Jersey Volunteers in Excelsior Field, with the Trostle house in the background.*

Below: *A memorial to Confederates who fought at Gettysburg.*

Opposite: *A row of grave markers in Gettysburg's National Cemetery. President Lincoln dedicated the burial ground on the damp, chilly day of November 19, 1863.*

The Aftermath

The three-day battle left the Army of the Potomac too weak and shaken to mount a counterattack. The casualty totals were staggering: 23,000 Union and 20,000 Confederate killed, wounded, and missing. "We have done well enough," Meade told one of his officers. A hard rain fell during July 4th. That night, Lee began his retreat south to the Potomac.

Meade gave a half-hearted chase. "The enemy pursued us as a mule goes on the chase of a grizzly bear—as if catching up to us was the last thing he wanted to do," the Confederate artillery commander Edward Porter Alexander observed. Yankee cavalry wrecked Lee's pontoon bridge, and heavy rains filled the Potomac and left it too deep for fording. The Army of Northern Virginia went into line near Williamsport on the river and awaited Meade's attack.

It did not come. Lee's engineers built a new bridge and the army crossed safely to the Virginia bank during the night of July 13. Lincoln was disconsolate at the escape. "Our army held the war in the hollow of their hand & they would not close it," he lamented.

Gettysburg, coupled with the great Union victory at Vicksburg on July 4, seemed to leave the Confederacy at the edge of ruin. The invincible Lee had been beaten. The Northern Copperheads, too, toned down their calls for a negotiated peace that would leave Southern slavery intact. And after Gettysburg, the chances of foreign intervention seemed virtually nil.

Still, the South fought on. Lee's escape gave the rebellion nearly two more years of life. From Virginia west to Arkansas, Louisiana, and Texas, from Tennessee to Georgia and the Carolinas, tens of thousands more Americans would be killed and maimed before the Confederacy could be crushed at last.

REPORTING THE WAR

Photographic pioneer Mathew Brady devised a mobile darkroom from which his assistants (he rarely left his New York City and Washington studios) could develop wet-plate negatives of Civil War scenes. Brady's photographers roamed the battlefield after an action, sometimes posing, rearranging or even moving bodies for artistic effect. Altogether, Brady and his associates compiled a documentary record of some 3,500 photographs. The photo above has been attributed to Alexander Gardner or Timothy Sullivan, two of Brady's most skilled associates.

EYEWITNESS

A. L. Long and Marcus J. Wright, memoirs of Gettysburg

I was at the battle of Gettysburg myself, and an incident occurred there which largely changed my views of the Southern people. I had been a most bitter anti-Southman, and fought and cursed the Confederates desperately....The last day of the fight I was badly wounded. A ball shattered my left leg. I lay on the ground not far from Cemetery Ridge, and as General Lee ordered his retreat, he and his officers rode near me. As they came along I recognized him, and, though faint from exposure and loss of blood, I raised up my hands, looked Lee in the face, and shouted as loud as I could, "Hurrah for the Union!"

The General heard me, looked, stopped his horse, dismounted, and came toward me. I confess that I at first thought he meant to kill me. But as he came up he looked down at me with such a sad expression upon his face that all fear left me, and I wondered what he was about. He extended his hand to me, and grasping mine firmly and looking right into my eyes, said, "My son, I hope you will soon be well."

If I live a thousand years I shall never forget the expression on General Lee's face. There he was, defeated, retiring from a field that had cost him and his cause almost their last hope, and yet he stopped to say words like those to a wounded soldier of the opposition who had taunted him as he passed by! As soon as the General had left me I cried myself to sleep there upon the bloody ground!

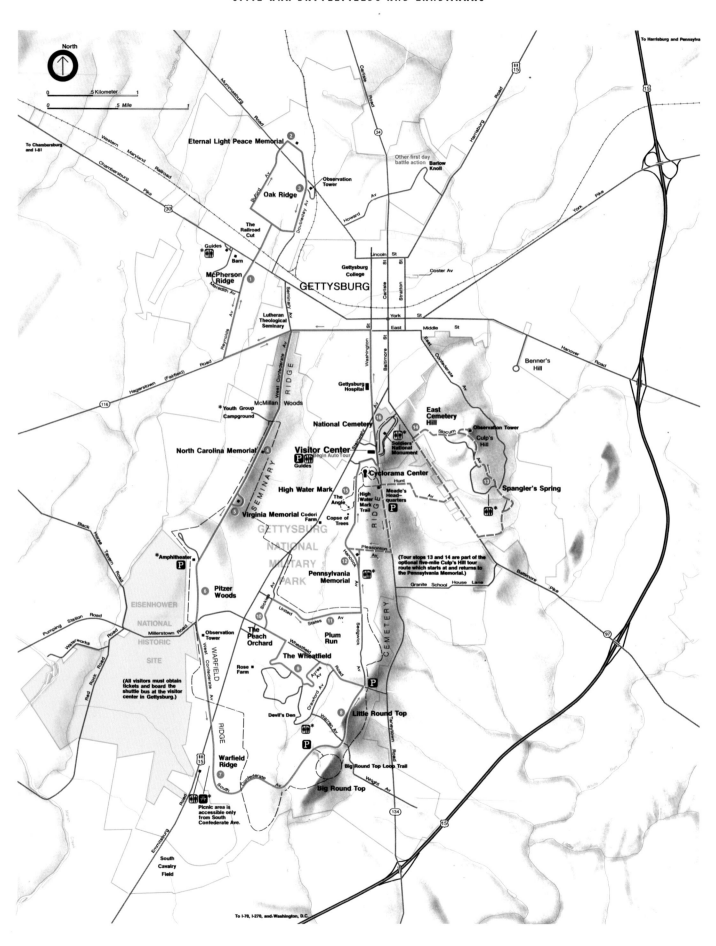

North

0 .5 Kilometer 1
0 .5 Mile 1

To Harrisburg and Pennsylva

To Chambersburg
and I-81

Western Maryland Railroad

Chambersburg Pike

Eternal Light Peace Memorial ②

③ Oak Ridge

Observation Tower

Other first day battle action   Barlow Knoll

The Railroad Cut

Coster Av

*Guides
Barn

McPherson Ridge ①

Meredith Av

Reynolds Av

Gettysburg College

GETTYSBURG

Lincoln St

Carlisle St

Stratton St

York St

East St

Middle St

Hanover Road

Lutheran Theological Seminary

Benner's Hill

Hagerstown (Fairfield) Road

SEMINARY RIDGE

Gettysburg Hospital

East Confederate Av

McMillan Woods

McMillan

*Youth Group Campground

National Cemetery ⑯

East Cemetery Hill

⑭

Observation Tower
Culp's Hill

Slocum Av

North Carolina Memorial ④

Visitor Center
Begin Auto Tour
Guides

Soldiers' National Monument

⑬

Spangler's Spring

High Water Mark

The Angie

High Water Mark Trail

Meade's Head-quarters

Virginia Memorial ⑤

Codori Farm

Copse of Trees

CEMETERY RIDGE

Hunt

GETTYSBURG NATIONAL MILITARY PARK

Pleasonton Av

Hancock Av

(Tour stops 13 and 14 are part of the optional five-mile Culp's Hill tour route which starts at and returns to the Pennsylvania Memorial.)

*Amphitheater

⑫

EISENHOWER NATIONAL HISTORIC SITE

Pitzer Woods ⑥

Pennsylvania Memorial

Granite School House Lane

Baltimore Pike

Pumping Station Road

Millerstown Road

West Confederate Av

Stoke Av

⑩ United States Av

⑪ Av

Sedgwick Av

Observation Tower

The Peach Orchard

Plum Run

Wheatfield Road

Waterworks Road

Red Rock Road

(All visitors must obtain tickets and board the shuttle bus at the visitor center in Gettysburg.)

The Wheatfield

Rose Farm

⑨

Ayres Av

Crawford Av

Warren Av

Hancock Av

Taneytown Road

Devil's Den

⑧ Little Round Top

WARFIELD RIDGE

Warfield Ridge ⑦

South Confederate Av

Big Round Top Loop Trail

Wright Av

Big Round Top

Picnic area is accessible only from South Confederate Ave.

Emmitsburg Road

South Cavalry Field

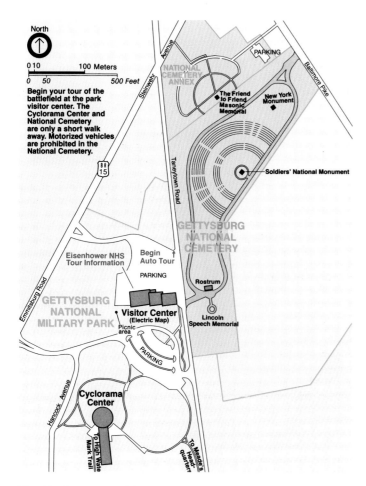

Begin your tour of the battlefield at the park visitor center. The Cyclorama Center and National Cemetery are only a short walk away. Motorized vehicles are prohibited in the National Cemetery.

The 18-mile auto tour follows the battle chronologically.

JULY 1, 1863

1 McPherson Ridge An early-morning clash between Union cavalry and Confederate infantry advancing along the Chambersburg Pike touched off the Battle of Gettysburg.

2 Eternal Light Peace Memorial At 1:00 PM, Gen. Robert Rodes's Confederate division attacked from this hill, threatening Union positions on McPherson and Oak Ridges.

3 Oak Ridge Union defenders temporarily checked Rodes's advance, but the entire line from here to Cemetery Ridge began to give way around 3:30 PM.

JULY 2, 1863

4 North Carolina Memorial The Confederate line was positioned on Seminary Ridge, while Union forces occupied the facing high ground as far south as the Round Tops.

5 Virginia Memorial Confederate infantry massed near here on July 3 for the battle's final assault, known as Pickett's Charge.

6 Pitzer Woods On July 2, Gen. James Longstreet posted troops along Warfield Ridge and anchored his left in these woods.

7 Warfield Ridge Longstreet's assaults jumped off from here around 4:00 PM, aimed at Union positions to the northeast.

8 Little Round Top Brig. Gen. Gouverneur K. Warren, Meade's chief engineer, recognized the Confederate threat to this critical position and rushed an infantry brigade here.

9 The Wheatfield More than 4,000 men were killed or wounded in savage fighting in this area.

10 The Peach Orchard From here Federal artillery raked Longstreet's infantry. The Confederates overran the Peach Orchard around 6:30 PM.

11 Plum Run Union forces falling back from the Peach Orchard traversed this boggy ground.

12 Pennsylvania Memorial Union artillery posted here helped hold the threatened Union center late in the afternoon as the Confederate echelon attack moved down the line from the Wheatfield.

13 Spangler's Spring Around 7:00 PM, Confederates attacked the Union right here and occupied the lower slopes of Culp's Hill.

14 East Cemetery Hill Union forces repulsed a twilight attack at the crest of this hill.

JULY 3, 1863

15 High Water Mark After an intensive two-hour cannonade, 12,000 Confederate infantry set out from Seminary Ridge to deliver Pickett's Charge. The defenders inflicted grievous casualties on the attacking troops.

16 National Cemetery On November 19, 1863, President Lincoln delivered the Gettysburg Address.

GETTYSBURG NATIONAL MILITARY PARK

MAILING ADDRESS
Superintendent, Gettysburg National Military Park, PO Box 1080, Gettysburg, PA 17325

TELEPHONE
717-334-1124

DIRECTIONS
The park is located thirty-seven miles southwest of Harrisburg, Pennsylvania, off US 15. Begin tour of the park at the visitor center on PA 134 (Taneytown Road) near its intersection with Business US 15 (Emmitsburg Road).

VISITOR CENTER
Museum, cyclorama center, and electric map.

ACTIVITIES
Auto tours, ranger-conducted walks and talks, living history and campfire programs.

HOURS
The visitor center is open from 8 AM to 5 PM, with extended hours to 6 PM from mid-June to mid-August. The cyclorama center is open from 9 AM to 5 PM Both centers are closed Thanksgiving, December 25, and January 1.

Above, left: detail map showing the Visitor Center, Cyclorama Center, and the Gettysburg National Cemetery.

Petersburg

The Confederates had fought Grant to a draw in the Wilderness, at Spotsylvania, along the North Anna River, and at Cold Harbor. Still, the Federals kept coming. During the second week in June, in what General Edward Porter Alexander, one of Lee's officers, later called "the most brilliant stroke in all the Federal campaigns of the whole war," Grant moved around Lee, got the army across the water barrier of the James and closed in on Petersburg, which he called "the key to taking Richmond."

Robert E. Lee concurred. Four vital rail lines ran through Petersburg. With these communications severed, the army could not be supplied. Richmond, the Confederacy's political, industrial, and psychological heart, would have to be abandoned. Lee recognized the portents. "We must destroy this army of Grant's before he gets to the James River," he had said at the outset of the spring campaign. "If he gets there it will become a siege, and then it will be a mere question of time."

The Confederate commander at Petersburg, General P. G. T. Beauregard, had the advantage of stout physical defenses, although he could call on only the scantiest of forces to man them. When the Federal van, the XVIII Corps of William F. Smith, with Winfield Scott Hancock's II Corps close behind, approached on June 15, 1864, Beauregard had but 2,500 old men and boys of the Home Guard and a few scattered cavalry units in line. The defenders were drawn up behind fieldworks in a 10-mile arc covering Petersburg. Beauregard's first test came early in the evening of the 15th, when Smith sent a full division—consisting of black troops here seeing their first combat—against two strongpoints along the eastern curve of the arc.

The Yankees swiftly overran more than a mile of the Confederate entrenchments, capturing 7 bastions and 16 guns

LEE'S SUPPLY LINE UNDER SIEGE

After the ruinous battle of Cold Harbor, General Ulysses S. Grant decided to take Richmond by attacking its source of supplies, the railroad and communications center of Petersburg, Virginia. On **June 15, 1864,** Union forces attacked but did not penetrate the city's defenses. The Federals besieged Petersburg for the next ten months, which cut off almost all supplies to the Army of Northern Virginia. General Lee evacuated the city on **April 2, 1865,** and ordered the evacuation of Richmond as well. It was the end of active campaigning for the Army of Northern Virginia.

 USA General Ulysses S. Grant

 CSA General Robert E. Lee

Total casualties for the entire campaign estimated at 42,000 USA and 28,000 CSA. The 1st Maine Heavy Artillery sustained the highest casualties of any Union regiment in the war, losing 632 of 900 troops engaged in less than half an hour.

within an hour or so. Then Smith, turning cautious, broke off the battle. That turned out to be a fatal mistake. According to Beauregard, Smith and Hancock, who arrived later in the evening, could have marched into Petersburg practically unopposed that night.

The missed opportunity did not greatly trouble Grant. "I think it is pretty well," he said, "to get across a great river and come up here and attack Lee in the rear before he is ready

Left: The Union siege line at Fort Sedgwick shows the strength of the Federal fieldworks and the ingenuity of the engineers and troops who built them. The opposing lines were only 1,500 feet apart here at Fort Sedgwick, also known as "Fort Hell."

Opposite: *This lithograph depicts the Union assault on Fort Gregg, April 2, 1865. A desperate Confederate defense gave Lee's army a several-hour head start on the roads leading west.*

for us." Indeed, Lee hesitated for several days, unwilling to believe the Federals were across the James in force. As a consequence, he starved Beauregard of troops. On June 16, two more Union corps reached Petersburg, along with the Army of the Potomac's commander, General George Gordon Meade. The new arrivals brought Grant's strength there to some 75,000 against Beauregard's 14,000.

The Federals launched a series of uncoordinated assaults against the beleaguered Confederates on the 17th. Toward evening, the attacking Federals captured a mile or so of Beauregard's outer works. Meade, in immediate command, failed to follow up this success, opting instead to order a full-scale assault along the entire line for dawn the next day.

With increasing urgency, Beauregard repeated his appeals for reinforcements. By the night of the 17th there could no longer be any doubt that Petersburg was the Union objective. "Prisoners report Grant on the field with his whole army," he wrote Lee shortly after midnight June 18. Persuaded at last, Lee put the main body of the Army of Northern Virginia on the road for Petersburg. Overnight, Petersburg's defenders quietly withdrew to a second, shorter line a mile to the rear.

The Federal advance stepped off at dawn, on schedule. The assault troops found only empty entrenchments in their front. Beauregard's nimble step backward confused Meade's officers. Hours were lost while they reconnoitered the new line and prepared new schemes of attack. Frustrated by the delay, Meade finally ordered his corps commanders to cease making plans

and "attack at all hazards without reference to each other."

In most cases, the troops merely went through the motions. They had learned all they needed to know about the Confederates' skill in building fortifications. "The men feel at present a great horror of attacking earthworks again," one of Meade's division commanders reported. In one sector, a Federal cannoneer called out to an infantry column trudging toward the front to ask whether the men were about to attack. "No, we are not going to charge," came the reply. "We are going to run toward the Confederate earthworks and then we are going to run back. We have had enough of assaulting earthworks."

Theodore Lyman, a Union staff officer, thought all the attacking troops went in grudgingly that day—the cumulative effect, he believed, of the Wilderness, Spotsylvania, and Cold Harbor. "You can't strike a blow with a wounded hand," Lyman said.

All along the line, the defenders easily repulsed the Federal attacks. The fighting of June 15–18 added another 12,000 names to Grant's lengthening casualty lists, which now totaled a heartbreaking 66,000 killed, wounded, and missing since the opening of the campaign on the Rapidan in early May. "For thirty days it has been one funeral procession past me, and it has been too much," the V Corps commander, General Gouverneur K. Warren, lamented.

Grant could see that further attacks would be profitless. "Now we will rest the men, and use the spade for their protection until a new vein can be struck," he told Meade.

Left: *The grass-grown outline of the Crater today. On July 30, 1864, a Union mine blew an enormous hole in the Confederate line here, but the followup assault proved a bloody failure.*

The Crater

So the two armies settled in for a siege. Toward the end of June, a Pennsylvania officer floated an unorthodox idea for breaking the deadlock. Lt. Col. Henry Pleasants of the 48th Pennsylvania proposed tunneling under the Confederates, rigging a mine, and blowing a hole in the works through which infantry could pour. He offered his troops, mostly volunteers from the Schuylkill Valley coalfields, for the job.

General Ambrose E. Burnside, commander of the Federal IX Corps, endorsed the project. Within a month, the industrious Pennsylvanians had burrowed a tunnel more than 500 feet long. Some 8,000 pounds of explosive powder were packed into lateral galleries 20 feet below the Confederate bastion at Elliott's Salient. Burnside planned a four-division advance into the expected breach and assigned a division of black troops specially trained for the work to lead it.

Grant and Meade overruled Burnside's decision to give the starring role to the black troops. The interference demoralized Burnside, who seemed to lose all interest in the operation. Still, the Pennsylvanians held up their end. The mine detonated at 4:44 AM on July 30 with a thunderous roar, obliterating Elliott's Salient and blasting a 400-foot-wide gap in the Confederate line.

The assault troops moved out before the dust had settled. But things went awry from the start. The explosion created a rubble-filled crater 60 feet across, 200 feet wide, and 10 to 30 feet deep. The awestruck attackers paused to gaze into the chasm; hundreds actually descended into it for a close look, or to tend the enemy wounded buried in the debris.

The Confederates acted decisively to seal the breach. Survivors of the blast met the oncoming Federal infantry with a murderous fire. The pit rapidly filled with a milling mass of confused, panicked Yankees seeking cover from the enemy volleys. Counterattacking Confederates surged up to the rim of the crater and poured a point-blank fire into the crowd.

At 9:30 AM, after nearly four hours of pointless bloodshed, Meade ordered the distracted Burnside to suspend the attack. The cost: nearly 4,000 killed, wounded, and missing. Grant regretted the missed opportunity and the wasted lives. It was, he said, "the saddest affair I have witnessed in this war."

Beginning of the End

Through the summer and autumn, Grant carried out large-scale attacks on both flanks of the long Richmond-Petersburg line, costing Lee casualties he could not afford and forcing him to thin his defenses by extending the works westward to protect the vital railroads. By late autumn, a greatly weakened Army of Northern Virginia held a nearly continuous thirty-seven-mile front curving from the White Oak Swamp east of Richmond to Hatcher's Run southwest of Petersburg.

It was a cold, wet, hungry winter for Lee's army. The troops subsisted on a daily diet of a pint of corn meal and an ounce or two of rusty bacon—"a peculiarly scaly color," one veteran recalled, "spotted like a half-well case of smallpox, full of rancid odor, and utterly devoid of grease." Attrition and desertions drained away the Confederate strength. By the New Year, Lee had fewer than 60,000 undernourished, ill-clad troops to face Grant's well-fed, lavishly equipped army of 124,000.

A WAR OF ATTRITION

As the Union siege lines from Richmond south to Petersburg grew tighter, Confederate soldiers and civilians grew hungrier. Meager rations, illness, battle attrition and desertions wore down Lee's army. By early 1864, the war had become far removed from its original Napoleonic character, complete with chivalry and gallant charges. Under the auspices of Grant and Sherman, it had taken on the features of modern total warfare. They used the superior resources of the North—financial, technological, agricultural, and numerical—to wear down the South's will to fight. Destruction by both sides extended to railroads, factories, crops, and cities. Short set-piece battles were being replaced by enervating sieges like that of Petersburg, which denied the necessities of life to civilians there and in nearby Richmond. Confederate soldiers were deserting in great numbers. Food and warm clothing grew increasingly scarce. In Richmond, the Confederate capital, the combination of shortages and extortionate prices had driven many ordinary people to desperation, even before the siege took hold. On April 2, 1863, a mob of several hundred women stormed Richmond's bakeries, demanding "Bread, bread!" Only the threat of troops to fire into the crowd persuaded the rioters to disperse.

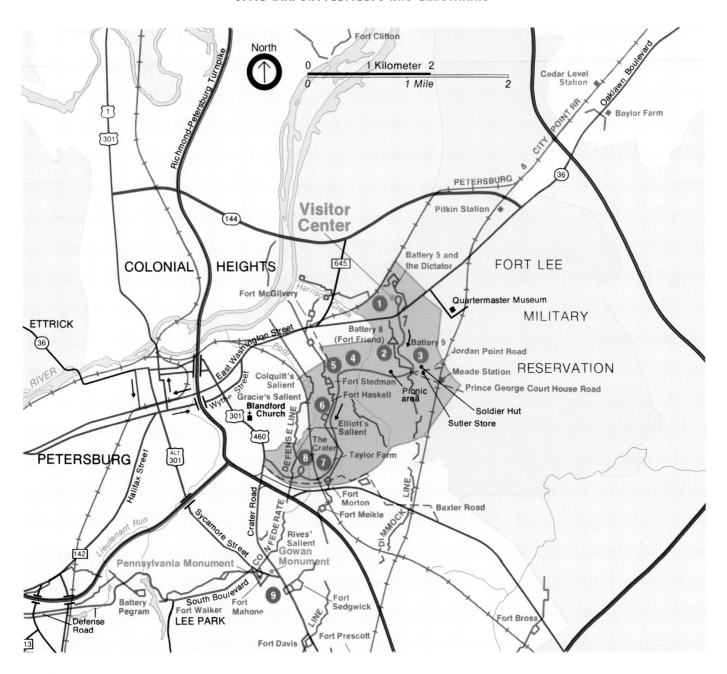

The 2,600-acre Petersburg National Battlefield contains six major units. The recommended starting point for the tour is the Visitor Center east of the city off Virginia Route 36.

The extended driving tour, 16 miles long, includes park areas south and west of Petersburg. U.S. 301, a main road leading into the city from the southeast, is the Jerusalem Plank Road of the war period.

SIEGE LINE TOUR

1 Visitor Center A map program here details the operations of the siege. A trail leads to Battery 5 on the original Confederate line (the Dimmock Line), where Union forces sited the enormous mortar known as "The Dictator."

2 Battery 8 U.S. black troops captured this strongpoint and renamed it Fort Friend for the large Friend House nearby.

3 Battery 9 Hinks's troops captured this work during the first day's fighting.

4 Harrison Creek Driven from their original line in the opening phase of the battle, Confederate forces fell back and dug in along this watercourse. Two days later, they withdrew to a new line closer to Petersburg. In March 1865, the Federals checked Lee's final offensive operation, the attack on Fort Stedman, near here.

5 Fort Stedman Lee struck this strongpoint on March 25, 1865, to relieve Union pressure west of Petersburg. A loop trail leads from Fort Stedman to Colquitt's Salient, from where Lee attacked.

6 Fort Haskell Here Union infantry and artillery stopped the Confederate advance southward from Fort Stedman. So many retreating Federals jammed into this work that most could only load rifles and pass them to the front to be fired.

7 Taylor Farm (Site) All the original farm buildings were destroyed early in the siege. Nearly 200 pieces of artillery were concentrated here during the Battle of the Crater.

8 The Crater A Union mine here blew a huge gap in the Confederate line, but the poorly led assault brigades failed to exploit the opening. Grant called the debacle "one of the saddest affairs" he had witnessed during the war. A trail follows the rim of the Crater.

9 Fort Sedgwick (Site) Union troops built this fort in July-August, 1864, to command the Jerusalem Plank Road. Heavy Confederate sniper and artillery fire aimed at the work earned it the nickname "Fort Hell." The Federal IX Corps launched a major assault on the Confederate line from here on April 2, 1865.

Other sites on the extended driving tour include several forts and the Poplar Grove Cemetery.

Above: Union troops at Petersburg awaiting the order to attack.

With the approach of spring, Lee decided to gamble on a breakout. His March 25 attack on the Federal strongpoint of Fort Stedman turned out to be the Army of Northern Virginia's last offensive operation. A Federal counterattack wiped out all Lee's initial gains. Four days later, Grant sent cavalry and infantry on a wide swing around Lee's right in an operation designed to pry the Confederates out of their defenses, bring them to battle in open country, and settle the issue for good.

Heavy rains slowed the initial advance. Then, on April 1, General Philip H. Sheridan's cavalry and the V Corps infantry routed the Confederates at Five Forks, an important road junction covering the South Side Railroad. As the attackers overwhelmed the Five Forks defenses, the Confederates surrendered in droves. "We are coming back into the Union, boys," one announced to his captors. Sheridan bagged some 5,000 prisoners. More to the point, he turned Lee's right and made the Petersburg lines untenable. When news of Five Forks reached Grant, he ordered a general assault all along the line for first light April 2nd.

Lee barely brought the Army of Northern Virginia out alive. A heroic defense of the outpost of Fort Gregg, in which a few hundred Confederates held off 5,000 Union attackers for more than two hours, bought just enough time for the army to escape. The withdrawal westward, toward a hoped-for junction with Confederate forces in North Carolina, began at nightfall.

At the same time, the Confederate government evacuated Richmond. Retreating Confederates set fire to warehouses and arsenals. Looters helped themselves to such luxuries as remained in the shops. A brisk south wind spread the fires through the heart of the capital. "The old war-scarred city seemed to prefer annihilation to conquest," one Confederate witness thought.

Around seven o'clock the next morning, April 3, the first Federals entered Richmond—among the early arrivals, a regiment of black cavalry. The eighty-year-old mayor of Richmond met the Union troopers with the white flag of surrender.

PETERSBURG NATIONAL BATTLEFIELD

MAILING ADDRESS
Superintendent, Petersburg National Battlefield, PO Box 549, Petersburg, VA 23804

TELEPHONE
804-732-3531

DIRECTIONS
The park's main visitor center is located two-and-one-half miles east of Petersburg on VA 36. The Five Forks Unit is in Dinwiddie County; from I-85, take the Dinwiddie Courthouse Exit, follow signs to Courthouse Road, turn right on Courthouse Road (VA 627) and proceed five miles to Five Forks.

VISITOR CENTER
Museum, interpretive exhibits, and a seventeen-minute map presentation shown every half hour.

ACTIVITIES
Demonstrations of mortar and cannon firings and soldier life in summer; ranger-guided walking tours, cycling, hiking, and self-guided auto tours.

HOURS
The battlefield is open from 8 AM to dusk year-round. The main visitor center is open from 8 AM to 5 PM, with hours extended to 7 PM, in the summer. The visitor center is closed December 25 and January 1.

Appomattox Court House

The beaten Confederates streamed west from Petersburg and Richmond during the first days of April 1865, the Union forces in relentless pursuit. The Army of Northern Virginia sought to push on to the Danville railroad, then turn south for a junction with Confederate forces in North Carolina. The Federals sought to overtake Robert E. Lee's army, block its escape route, and bring the war to a close.

Three separate Confederate columns trudged on toward Amelia Court House, situated thirty-five miles southwest of Richmond, where Lee had arranged for rations to be delivered. The main column, consisting of 20,000 men of all arms, had withdrawn from Petersburg during the night of April 2nd. Some 6,000 miscellaneous troops marched out of the abandoned, burning capital the same night. The third column consisted of a few thousand survivors of the rout at Five Forks—the debacle that unhinged the Petersburg defenses,

SURRENDER!

On **April 9, 1865,** General Lee and the Army of Northern Virginia surrendered to General Grant in the little town of Appomattox Court House. Lee yielded when his army, pursued by Grant's Army of the Potomac since fleeing Petersburg, was cut off at Appomattox by General Philip Sheridan and his forces. This surrender is generally considered the end of the war, although more than 200,000 Confederates remained in the field. The generous terms Grant offered Lee eased the way for surrender of the remaining Confederate forces.

 USA General Ulysses S. Grant

 CSA General Robert E. Lee

forced the evacuation of Richmond, and put Lee's army on the road to Appomattox.

From a distance, the Confederates shuffling westward might have been mistaken for a refugee swarm. The troops were ragged, hungry, inexpressibly weary. The litter of retreat—broken-down wagons and exhausted mules, knapsacks, cooking implements, even arms and ammunition—lay in piles along the road, evidence of an army in disintegration.

"We moved on in disorder, keeping no regular column, no regular pace," a South Carolina officer wrote later. "When a soldier became weary he fell out, ate his scanty rations—if, indeed, he had any to eat—rested, rose and resumed the march when his inclination dictated. There were not many words spoken. An indescribable sadness weighed on us. The men were very gentle toward each other, very liberal in bestowing the little of food that remained to them."

By some bureaucratic misadventure, Lee found a trainload of ammunition at Amelia Court House on Tuesday, April 4, but no rations. He sent forage parties fanning out over the countryside in search of provisions. The delay allowed Grant's pursuing Federals to cut into the Confederate head start from Petersburg. A large force of cavalry and infantry under General Philip H. Sheridan raced in parallel and just to the south of Lee's army, straining to outrun the Confederates, turn, and confront them head on astride their line of retreat.

Sensing the end, Sheridan—the guiding spirit of the pursuit—abandoned all caution. "Sheridan does not entrench," wrote the Union general Joshua Lawrence Chamberlain. "He pushes on, carrying his flank and rear with him—rushing,

flashing, smashing." By April 5 Sheridan had caught and passed his quarry, cut the Danville railroad, and blocked the Confederate escape route to the south. Lee changed direction, heading now for Farmville on the upper Appomattox River. If anything, the Federals stepped up the pace. "There was no pause, no hesitancy, no doubt what to do," one of Grant's staff officers said of him. "He commanded Lee's army as much as he did ours." With forced marches at night, the Confederates maintained a slight lead. But the chase seemed to invigorate the Yankees. "They began to see the end of what they had been fighting four years for," said Grant. "Nothing seemed to fatigue them. They were ready to move without rations and travel without rest until the end."

On April 6, "Black Thursday" to the Confederates, Sheridan's cavalry with heavy infantry support isolated and destroyed General Richard S. Ewell's corps near Sayler's Creek, removing at a stroke a full third of Lee's remaining strength. As the Federal infantry pressed Ewell's front, the cavalry tore into his flanks and rear. After a feeble effort, the line collapsed. The Confederate casualty total for the day reached 8,000—including as many as 6,000 men taken captive, among them, Ewell himself.

"I am still pressing on with both cavalry and infantry," Sheridan wrote Grant that night. "If the thing is pressed I think Lee might surrender." Grant forwarded a copy of Sheridan's message to President Lincoln. "Let the thing be pressed," Lincoln wired back.

As it turned out, Lee had been driven into an all but escape-proof trap. The Confederate general Edward Porter Alexan-

TOURING THE VILLAGE

The Visitor Center introduces the village of Appomattox Court House, rebuilt and restored to reflect its appearance in April 1865. The village roads are closed to motor vehicles. All the buildings shown on the map are within walking distance; the McLean House lies about 1,000 feet from the Surrender Triangle.

McLean House The house, built in 1848, passed into Wilmer McLean's hands in 1863. The slave quarters and kitchen are behind the main house. Robert E. Lee surrendered the Army of Northern Virginia to Ulysses S. Grant in the McLean parlor on the afternoon of April 9, 1865.

Meeks Store Built in 1852, the structure served as a store, a private residence, and a Presbyterian Manse. Francis Meeks was postmaster and druggist as well as storekeeper.

Woodson Law Office
John Woodson bought this building in 1856 and practiced law here until his death eight years later.

Clover Hill Tavern This brick tavern, built in 1819, is the oldest structure in the village. Behind the tavern are the kitchen, now a bookstore, and slave quarters, which now contain restrooms. The guest house accommodated the overflow from the main building.

Courthouse Built in 1846, the original structure burned in 1892; the existing courthouse is a reconstruction.

Jail Finished around 1870, the jail held the county's miscreants for two decades and later served as a polling place.

Kelly House The occupants doubtless watched the formal surrender of the Confederate infantry on April 12, 1865, from the porch of this house.

Mariah Wright House This frame house was built in the mid-1820s. The stone and brick chimneys are typical of the region.

Surrender Triangle Confederate troops here stacked their arms and surrendered their battleflags to an honor guard of Union troops. Lee did not take part in the April 12 ceremony; Grant had already left for Washington.

Isbell House Thomas S. Bocock, the speaker of the Confederate Congress, and his brother built this house (not open to the public).

Peers House George Peers, clerk of the court of Appomattox County for forty years, lived here (not open to the public).

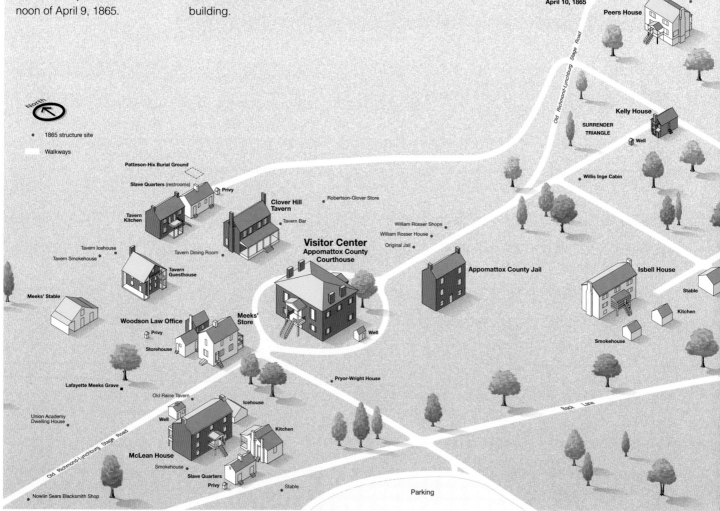

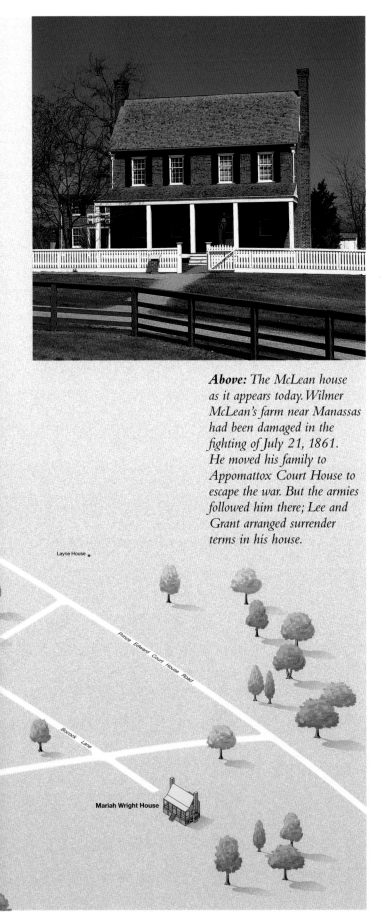

Above: The McLean house as it appears today. Wilmer McLean's farm near Manassas had been damaged in the fighting of July 21, 1861. He moved his family to Appomattox Court House to escape the war. But the armies followed him there; Lee and Grant arranged surrender terms in his house.

Layne House

Prince Edward Court House Road

Bocock Lane

Mariah Wright House

der grasped the situation with one glance at a map. The two armies, Alexander saw, were moving down the jug-shaped peninsula between the Appomattox and James Rivers. "There was but one outlet, the neck of the jug at Appomattox Court House," he wrote, "and to that Grant had the shortest road." If nothing occurred to slow him, Grant would soon be in position to cork the jug.

The retreat continued after dark April 6, a cold night with a biting wind and flurries of snow. Lee intended to cross the Appomattox at Farmville, burn the bridges there, and put the river between himself and Grant. But Federal infantry managed to cross over the partially burned High Bridge a few miles downstream. By dawn on the 7th, Friday, two separate Union columns, each larger than the remnant of the Army of Northern Virginia, were marching alongside Lee: one north of the river, the other south, and both rushing to head off the Confederates at Appomattox Station, just beyond the mouth of the jug. Late that afternoon, Grant sent a note through the lines calling on Lee to surrender.

Lee replied vaguely. "It looks as if Lee meant to fight," Grant thought. The pursuit continued unabated on April 8th. The pressure of it, the nearness of the goal, Lee's evasiveness: all conspired to bring on in Grant what he described as a "sick headache"—a migraine. It tormented him through the night of the 8th and into the morning of April 9, Palm Sunday. Another note arrived from Lee, asking more explicitly for surrender terms. "There is but one condition I would insist upon—namely, that the men and officers surrendered shall be disqualified from taking up arms against the Government of the United States until properly exchanged," Grant responded. These were generous terms, perhaps more than Lee had expected. He answered with a proposal to continue the discussion, this time face to face, at ten o'clock Sunday morning "on the old stage road to Richmond, between the picket lines of the two armies."

Sheridan's cavalry, meantime, had reached Appomattox Station and broken up a small enemy force there, capturing twenty-four guns and, worse, four trainloads of rations and other supplies. By nightfall of the 8th, the Federals held the place in strength. The troopers, with infantry on the way, blocked the Lynchburg road, Lee's last line of retreat.

During the night, Lee issued orders for a final, desperate effort to clear the road to the west. The assault, launched at dawn on Palm Sunday, broke through the light crust of the cavalry lines, then ran headlong into advancing Federal infantry, which had come up during the night in obedience to an urgent summons from Sheridan. "If you can possibly push your infantry up here tonight," he had written from Appomattox Court House to the trailing V Corps, "we will have great results in the morning."

And so it happened. An aide carried word of the failure of the breakout attack to Lee. "Then there is nothing for me to do but go and see General Grant," he said, "and I would rather die a thousand deaths."

Grant did not show up for the ten o'clock appointment. Lee sent another note through the lines, this time expressly offering to surrender. Meantime, an informal one-hour truce went into effect. An aide galloped off to deliver Lee's message to Grant. The commanding general's migraine vanished as though it had never been. "The minute I saw Lee's note, I was cured," he said. Grant pushed his way up to the front. He met Sheridan on the road to the courthouse village.

"Is Lee up there?" Grant wanted to know.

Sheridan thought he was.

"Very well," Grant replied. "Let's go up."

They met at 1:00 PM in the parlor of the house of Wilmer McLean. Lee had turned out in full dress uniform, complete with sash and sword. Grant, saying he had lost touch with his baggage wagon, apologized for his mud-caked boots, spattered trousers, and unadorned coat. There was an awkward silence. As he reported in his *Memoirs*, Grant tried to guess at what must have been going through his adversary's mind.

Grant wrote out his terms—easy ones, as he had indicated earlier. They guaranteed that ordinary soldiers would be immune from prosecution for treason. In the Confederate army, cavalrymen and cannoneers supplied their own horses. At Lee's request, Grant allowed these troops to keep their mounts. The animals would be useful, Grant acknowledged, for spring plowing. "This will have the best possible effect upon the men," Lee told him. "It will be very gratifying and will do much toward conciliating our people." Grant also offered to send over three days' rations to feed the hungry Confederates.

Fair copies of the documents were drawn up and signed. At a few minutes before 4:00 PM, the Army of Northern Virginia passed into history. Lee left the McLean house, mounted his horse Traveller, and rode slowly back to the Confederate lines. As he approached, hundreds of troops surged toward him. The cheering built to a roar, then gradually faded away. "We have fought the war together," Lee began. Then his voice thickened. "I have done the best I could for you," he managed. "My heart is too full to say more." The telegraph flashed word of the surrender to Washington. The capital marked the occasion with the firing of a 500-gun salute. At Appomattox, though, Grant forbade such ostentatious celebration.

"The war is over," he declared. "The rebels are our countrymen again."

EYEWITNESS

From the memoirs of Ulysses S. Grant, on his appointment with Robert E. Lee at Appomattox Court House, April 9, 1865:

"I had known General Lee in the old army, and had served with him in the Mexican War; I did not suppose, owing to the difference in our age and rank, that he would remember me....

When I had left camp that morning I had not expected so soon the result that was then taking place, and consequently was in rough garb. I was without a sword, as I usually was when on horseback on the field, and wore a soldier's blouse for a coat... When I went into the house I found General Lee. We greeted each other, and after shaking hands took our seats. I had my staff with me, a good portion of whom were in the room during the whole of the interview.

What General Lee's feelings were I do not know. As he was a man of much dignity, with an impassable face, it was impossible to say whether he felt inwardly glad that the end had finally come, or felt sad over the result, and was too manly to show it. Whatever his feelings, they were entirely concealed from my observation; but my own feelings, which had been quite jubilant on the receipt of his letter, were sad and depressed. I felt like anything rather than rejoicing at the downfall of a foe who had fought so long and gallantly, and had suffered so much for a cause, though that cause was, I believe, one of the worst for which a people ever fought....

General Lee was dressed in a full uniform which was entirely new, and was wearing a sword of considerable value, very likely the sword which had been presented by the State of Virginia; at all events, it was an entirely different sword from the one that would ordinarily be worn in the field. In my rough traveling suit, the uniform of a private with the straps of a lieutenant-general, I must have contrasted very strangely with a man so handsomely dressed, six feet high and of faultless form. But this was not a matter that I thought of until afterwards."

Left: Union soldiers pose outside Appomattox courthouse after the surrender of the Army of Northern Virginia. The Confederates laid down their arms and gave up their battle flags in a formal march-past on April 12, 1865.

APPOMATTOX COURT HOUSE NATIONAL HISTORICAL PARK

MAILING ADDRESS
Superintendent, Appomattox Court House National Historical Park, PO Box 218, Appomattox, VA 24522

TELEPHONE
804-352-8987

DIRECTIONS
The visitor center is in the reconstructed Court House building on VA 23, three miles northeast of the town of Appomattox, Virginia.

VISITOR CENTER
Audiovisual programs, interpretive exhibits, displays, and a bookstore.

ACTIVITIES
Living history and ranger talks in the summer.

HOURS
The visitor center is open daily in winter from 8:30 AM to 5 PM, and in summer from 9 AM to 5:30 PM The Visitor Center and Park are closed on Federal holidays from November through February.

PRESIDENT LINCOLN'S LAST DAYS

The president told Grant and others of the dream: he had gone aboard some "singular, indescribable vessel…floating, floating away on some indistinct expanse, toward an unknown shore." Lincoln wondered what the dream foretold. At around 10 o'clock in the evening of April 14, 1865, John Wilkes Booth shot the president as he watched an English comedy, *Our American Cousin*, at Ford's Theater (pictured right). Lincoln died around 7:30 next morning in a seedy boardinghouse across the street from the theater. His second inaugural had taken place less than six weeks earlier. Pursuing troops shot and killed Booth. Four of the assassin's co-conspirators were hanged on July 7, 1865.

The Western Theater of War

In the west an amazing drama of strategy, tactics, logistics, and carnage unfolded on a huge and baffling stage. Numbers of Northern and Southern armies contended in sweeping maneuvers from the Alleghenies to the Mississippi and from the Ohio to the Gulf of Mexico. On that grand tableau, Northern strategy evolved into an application of General Winfield Scott's old Anaconda plan, and Davis's offensive-defensive strategy evolved into a new concept of command and control.

This whole area offered great opportunities for maneuver, but opportunities tempered by mountain ranges, rivers, different-gauged rail lines, and poor roads. Still, the very vastness beckoned war. Jefferson Davis saw that the west, if held, could offer natural boundaries to his country; Lincoln grasped early the importance of holding Kentucky in the Union.

Davis sent Albert Sidney Johnston—the man he thought the best general in the country—to organize defenses of the South's heartland. Various forces were available and Davis sent more in a novel use of railroads, rivers, and highways, until Johnston could muster more than 80,000 men against more than 130,000 Federals. Johnston failed the president. Slow to concentrate, he lost two important forts, Henry and Donelson on the Tennessee and Cumberland Rivers, that propped his intended northern line of defense. Then he dawdled while General Henry W. Halleck pulled forces under U. S. Grant and Don Carlos Buell toward a junction between Johnston's scattered Confederate units. Goaded by General Beauregard, Johnston moved at last, concentrated, and took Grant by surprise at the bloody battle of Shiloh, April 6–7, 1862. Johnston was killed in the midst of early success; command passed to General Beauregard, who retreated on the second day and soon took sick leave.

Confederate forces coalesced into the Army of Tennessee under one of the war's most puzzling characters, General Braxton Bragg. Union forces divided into several armies (each named for a river) and Grant finally emerged as the best fighter Lincoln could find in that distant western domain.

Davis, with resources surprisingly permitting, planned a joint offensive in late summer 1862, with Bragg moving into Kentucky and Tennessee and Lee invading Maryland. Bragg's campaign foundered on his indecision at two important battles—Murfreesboro and Perryville—while Lee lost at Antietam. So Davis's bold venture fizzled, but something had been accomplished: the Confederates seized the initiative, and, for a time, stalled Union advances in the central sector.

Davis, realizing the difficulty of controlling operations so far away, came to a theater command arrangement and put General Joseph E. Johnston in charge of all the forces and areas from the Chattahoochie to the Mississippi Rivers. Sadly for Davis, Johnston never understood the satrapy that was his, never rose to the opportunity.

In 1863 Grant's various attempts to take Vicksburg—the South's most important bastion on the Mississippi—succeeded at last. He had his troubles. One advance had been thwarted by General Earl Van Dorn's daring cavalry raid on Grant's base at Holly Springs. And an attempt to dig a canal across an ox bow around Vicksburg failed in a welter of mud and frustration. In May 1863, Grant crossed the river below Vicksburg and ran a swift campaign of maneuver and battle until he forced General John C. Pemberton's defenders into a siege. Johnston failed to help and Vicksburg fell on July 4, the day after Lee's defeat at Gettysburg. Cut in twain, the Confederacy began a precarious dual existence—and the Anaconda began to squeeze.

On that fateful July 4, Bragg found himself maneuvered into the strategic city of Chattanooga by General William S. Rosecrans. Bragg had to hold the city—it covered interior avenues to the Deep South.

Lincoln gave Grant larger western responsibilities while Bragg and Johnston tried to patch up the Army of Tennessee. Rosecrans outmaneuvered Bragg again in early September and pushed him out of Chattanooga. But Bragg counterattacked, won the big battle of Chickamauga, then threw away his victory at Lookout Mountain and Missionary Ridge in November.

With Grant in overall command of the Union's armies in March 1864, General William T. Sherman took charge of several armies rolled into a 100,000-man juggernaut that moved from Chattanooga southeastward along the railroad toward Atlanta. Joe Johnston and the revamped Army of Tennessee blocked the way. Johnston's masterful, grudging retreat toward Atlanta frustrated Sherman in several battles—especially at Kennesaw Mountain in late June 1864. Davis replaced Johnston in July when he received no promise of an intent to hold Atlanta. General John B. Hood fought hard for Atlanta, even tried to lure Sherman up into Tennessee by hitting his communications—but Sherman left him to others and marched on to the sea.

Hood wrecked his army at the battles of Franklin and Nashville, Tennessee, in November and December 1864. Remnants of the Army of Tennessee, back under Joe Johnston, could not halt Sherman's march in the Carolinas, and Johnston surrendered his army at Durham Station, North Carolina, on April 26, 1865.

Increasingly, historians have come to the conclusion that the war was won and lost in the crucial center. Operations in the Trans-Mississippi were peripheral, but when the main Southern positions on the Mississippi and in Tennessee were taken, the way opened for Sherman and others to raid not only the industrial center of the Confederacy but also—and perhaps most importantly—the agricultural heartland. As Confederate forces were progressively defeated, shrank in numbers and morale, gave up vital logistical territory, they lost the heart of their country and the wherewithal of war. While Lee's costly battles did offer some chance of victory in the eastern theater, Grant's, Rosecrans's, and Sherman's successes at Vicksburg, Chattanooga, Atlanta, and on to the sea, ripped the vitals out of the Confederacy and won the war.

—*Frank E. Vandiver*

Wilson's Creek

After the disastrous defeat at First Manassas, the Union Army took time to regroup and develop a plan to reconquer the states that had seceded. Part of the new Union strategy concerned the importance of holding the border states of Delaware, Maryland, Kentucky, and Missouri in the Union. Missouri, a state rich in natural resources, with a large population, was vital to both sides because of its position as the gateway to the West, and the three major river systems—the Mississippi, Missouri, and Ohio—that flowed within or along its boundaries. Control of any river system would give considerable advantage to the side that held it, since it could be used as a conduit to send troops and supplies deep into enemy territory.

The state of Missouri had been divided politically even before its admission to the Union as a slave state in 1820. In 1861 the state had a pro-Confederate governor in Claiborne Jackson, but thanks to Missouri's legislators, who were adamantly antislavery, the state remained loyal to the Union. In fact, Missouri was asked by the Federal government to supply four regiments after the fall of Fort Sumter. Governor Jackson had wanted to take over the arsenal at St. Louis, but was prevented by its commander, Captain Nathaniel Lyon, an ardent Unionist who had secretly dispatched the weapons and ammunition to Illinois. In May, a force led by Lyon captured a number of Confederate militiamen near St. Louis, and, subsequently, the state capitol at Jefferson City. Jackson and the pro-secession members of the State Guard moved south.

A Union force of 6,000 men commanded by Lyon, who had been promoted to brigadier general, set off for the southwestern part of the state in July to push Confederate forces across the Missouri border. However, Lyon retreated to Spring-

SURPRISE ATTACK AT WILSON'S CREEK

On **August 10, 1861,** in a battle for control of Missouri, a Union army under Brigadier General Nathaniel Lyon met Confederate Major General Sterling Price's forces on the banks of Wilson's Creek. Although the Confederates won the battle, their failure to pursue the retreating Federals allowed them to regroup and, ultimately, to secure control of Missouri.

 USA Brigadier General Nathaniel Lyon (killed); Colonel Franz Sigel

 CSA Brigadier General Benjamin McCulloch; Major General Sterling Price

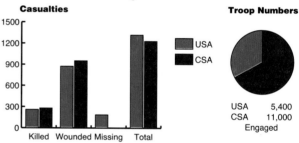

field when he learned that Confederate troops commanded by Brigadier General Benjamin McCulloch, and the Missouri State Guard, led by Major General Sterling Price, had twice as many men in the field and were moving toward the Union army. This force pursued Lyon's and took up a position along Wilson's Creek some ten miles from Springfield, on August 6.

Left: This sketch by newspaper artist Henri Lovie depicts General Nathaniel Lyon falling from his horse after being mortally wounded at Wilson's Creek.

Left: *A view of Bloody Hill from the south. Union troops drove the Confederates from the crest of this ridge and fought off attacks—many at close quarters—for more than five hours.*

Below: *Wilson's Creek, the scene of the battle fought ten miles southwest of Springfield, Missouri, in the struggle for this important western state.*

Although he was more than one hundred miles from his supply depot and greatly outnumbered, Lyon was unwilling to give up his position without a fight. Under cover of darkness on the night of August 9, he sent a flanking detachment of 1,200 men, including artillery, under the command of Colonel Franz Sigel, to approach the creekside encampment from the rear.

On August 10, at 5:00 PM, the remaining Union force made a successful surprise attack on the Confederate front, pushing them down the banks of the creek. As the main body of the Union force swept down on the enemy, Sigel's artillery opened fire, shelling the Southern encampment. After the initial assault, the Confederates were pushed back, and within the hour, General Lyon took possession of some high ground, soon to be known as Bloody Hill.

One Union battalion, under Captain Joseph Plummer, was detached to clear the east bank of the creek, but it met a solid defense that included artillery, and the fight became a stalemate. Aided by an Arkansas artillery battery, Southern infantry reorganized, turned to the front, and stopped the Federal advance.

Colonel Sigel crossed Wilson's Creek, attacked the other end of the Confederate camp, and drove the enemy toward the fighting on Bloody Hill. Then a Louisiana regiment approached, wearing a uniform similar to that of an Iowa unit under Lyon's command, and Sigel held his fire, believing the soldiers to be Federals. The strength of the Southern attack at close range forced him to retreat and abandon five cannon. This mistake may have cost the Union a victory.

With Sigel's artillery silenced, the Confederates turned all their forces on Lyon's position on Bloody Hill. Both armies made a series of attacks and counterattacks over the southern slope, none of which achieved a victory. In some parts of the field, the combatants fought at extremely close quarters,

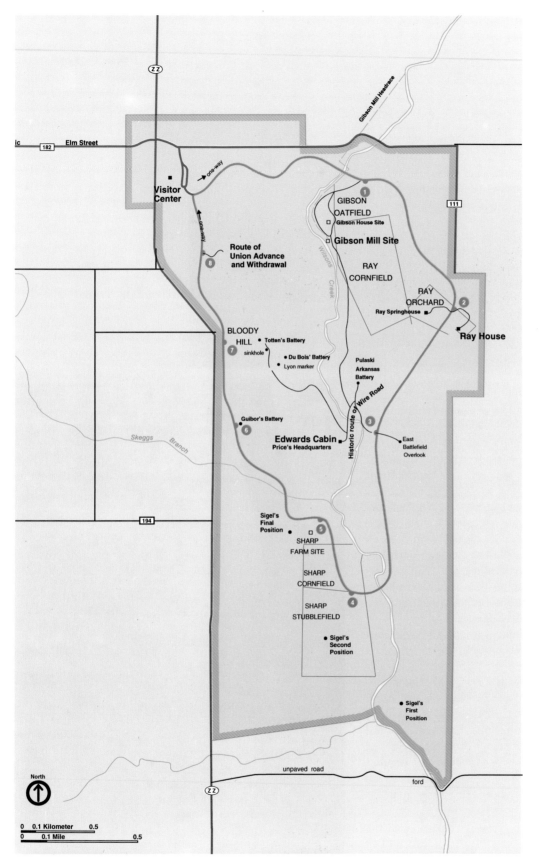

The auto tour of the Wilson's Creek battlefield is a 4.9 mile, one-way loop road with stops at all points of interest:

1 Gibson's Mill. This marks the northern end of the Confederate camps, from which Union General Nathaniel Lyon's assault drove Missouri State Guard troops down to Wilson's Creek.

2 Ray House and Cornfield. The Ray House served as a Confederate field hospital during and after the battle. The only major fighting in this area took place on the hill northwest of here, in the cornfield.

3 Pulaski Arkansas Battery and Price's Headquarters. The cannon of the Pulaski Arkansas Battery opened fire on Bloody Hill, stopping the Union advance and buying time for the Rebel infantry to regroup.

4 Sigel' s Second Position. On the ridge across Wilson's Creek, Colonel Sigel's Union artillery, upon hearing Lyon's attack to the north, opened fire on the Rebel cavalry camped in the field.

5 Sigel's Final Position. Here Sigel was attacked and defeated by Confederate troops he mistook for Federals.

6 Guibor's Battery. Here Confederate Captain Henry Guibor fired at Union positions on Bloody Hill.

7 Bloody Hill. Throughout the battle, General Lyon's 4,000 troops held this high ground.

8 Historic Overlook. The Union army passed through this field on its way to and from Bloody Hill. The Confederate failure to pursue the defeated Federals was a costly error.

EYEWITNESS

Chicago Tribune *correspondent G. C. Clark, who observed the battle of Wilson's Creek, was moved to write:*

"I think by this time the idea of the inhumanity of the enemy must have been exploded. They have been represented as utterly heartless and barbarous, but from all I can hear the [Confederate] forces in Missouri have displayed as much courtesy and humanity as the Union men....They have carried on a mean and tricky warfare at times and used dishonorable deceit, such as displaying Union flags...but...on the whole, I think their character and actions have been misrepresented."

firing at an enemy unseen because of the smoke. In one of these attacks Lyon, already twice wounded, was shot in the chest and killed, the first Union general to die in combat. The Union command devolved upon Major Samuel Sturgis, who managed to hold off another attack. But by 11:00 AM, recognizing that his army was exhausted, short of ammunition and bewildered by Sigel's failure to exert pressure on the Confederate rear, Sturgis gave the command to withdraw toward Springfield. The equally exhausted Southern force, low on ammunition and disorganized, did not pursue.

The Battle of Wilson's Creek, known to the South as Oak Hills, was one of the most vicious engagements of the war. In fact, 15 percent of the troops involved became casualties. Although the two armies were unevenly matched, casualties on both sides were remarkably similar—258 Union dead and 873 wounded as compared to Confederate losses of 279 dead and 951 wounded. The loss of General Lyon was a major moral blow to the Union, but several dozen other officers who fought at Wilson's Creek would become brigadier or major generals during the course of the war. Although it was a Confederate victory, Wilson's Creek ultimately aided the Federal cause. The South's failure to pursue and push Union troops out of Missouri kept the state in Northern hands until the more decisive battle of Pea Ridge secured it for the duration.

Above: This marker memorializes the fall of General Lyon as he led his men up Bloody Hill. It was erected in 1928 by the University Club of Springfield, Missouri.

Left: The Ray house served as a Confederate field hospital during the battle; it is the only surviving structure in the 1,750-acre park associated with the engagement.

WILSON'S CREEK NATIONAL BATTLEFIELD

MAILING ADDRESS
Superintendent, Wilson's Creek National Battlefield, Route 2, Box 75, Republic, MO 65738

TELEPHONE
417-732-2662

DIRECTIONS
Wilson's Creek National Battlefield is located ten miles southwest of Springfield, Missouri. Take I-44 to Exit 77 and drive five miles south on MO 13 (Kansas Expressway) to US 60. Turn right on US 60 and drive seven miles west to Route ZZ. The park is three miles south on Route ZZ. From US 65 at Ozark, drive west fourteen miles on MO 14 to Route ZZ, then turn right; the park is seven miles north on Route ZZ.

VISITOR CENTER
Museum, thirteen-minute film, an electric troop movement map, exhibits, and a bookstore.

ACTIVITIES
A five-mile self-guided tour road contains eight stops, including historic Ray House and Bloody Hill; interpretive programs include tours of Ray House and Bloody Hill, weapons firing demonstrations, and living history demonstrations.

HOURS
The visitor center is open from 8 a.m to 5 PM, except December 25 and January 1. Tour road is open from 8 AM to 9 PM in the summer; 8 AM to 7 PM after Labor Day.

Fort Donelson

Early in the war, the Confederacy recognized the importance of protecting its western reaches from Union assault. Confederate general Albert Sidney Johnston developed a defensive barrier in the west by building a series of forts along several rivers that flowed into the Mississippi. Among them were two forts in Tennessee, just south of the Kentucky border: Fort Henry, on the Tennessee River, and Fort Donelson, on the Cumberland. They were barely twelve miles apart.

Early in 1862, a Union reconnaissance determined that these two forts were probably the most vulnerable. If the Union could capture them, its gunboats would be able to penetrate Alabama and attack Nashville. Ten gunboats commanded by Flag Officer Andrew Foote, and 17,000 Federal soldiers led by Brigadier General Ulysses S. Grant, were sent against these key positions in the Confederate line for the Mississippi Valley.

Foote's ironclads made short work of low-lying Fort Henry. After an artillery barrage of a few hours, on February 6, the Confederate commander, Brigadier General Lloyd Tilghman, surrendered the earthwork fort and its token garrison of some 100 soldiers. Most of his 2,500 men had escaped to Fort Donelson. The battle was so short that Grant's force, marching overland, arrived after the surrender. Several days later, Grant and his men made their way east to Fort Donelson, while Foote descended the Tennessee to reach the Cumberland River with six gunboats and reinforcements.

General Johnston had concentrated a large Confederate force at Fort Donelson—almost 21,000 men commanded by Brigadier General John B. Floyd. His military experience was limited to his tenure as secretary of war in the Buchanan

THE BOMBARDMENT OF FORT DONELSON

The Confederate surrender of Fort Donelson, Tennessee, on **February 16, 1862,** gave the Union its first major victory and its first real hero in Union Brigadier General Ulysses S. Grant, who earned the nickname "Unconditional Surrender." When Confederate Brigadier General Simon Buckner asked for terms of surrender, Grant responded with the now-famous phrase, "No terms except an unconditional and immediate surrender can be accepted." This victory opened the way to Nashville and an invasion of the South.

 USA Brigadier General Ulysses S. Grant; Brigadier General John A. McClernand; Brigadier General Lewis "Lew" Wallace

 CSA Brigadier General John B. Floyd; Brigadier General Gideon Pillow; General Albert Sidney Johnston; Brigadier General Simon Bolivar Buckner

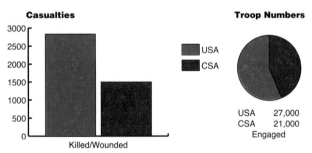

Casualties	Troop Numbers
USA / CSA (Killed/Wounded)	USA 27,000 / CSA 21,000 Engaged

Almost half the Confederate defenders were taken prisoner.

administration. His second-in-command was Brigadier General Gideon Pillow, another inexperienced leader. The only seasoned military professional was General Simon Bolivar Buckner, an old friend of Grant's.

On February 12, Grant reached Fort Donelson and deployed his men south and west of the Confederate fort. They were soon joined by the additional 10,000 on Foote's gunboats, for a combined force of some 27,000 Union troops. On February 14, Foote's gunboats opened fire, returned at once by the eleven Confederate shore batteries. After approximately an hour and a half, Foote was forced to withdraw. Every one of his gunboats had received at least one direct hit, and many were seriously damaged. Foote himself was wounded.

Just after dawn the following day, as Grant and Foote were discussing the possibility of a siege, a Confederate force of 15,500 made a surprise attack on the Federal right, which was commanded by General John McClernand, in an attempt to break the Union encirclement. After heavy fighting, McClernand was forced to withdraw a mile, until reinforced by troops commanded by General Lewis "Lew" Wallace.

EYEWITNESS

A Chicago Tribune *reporter described the bravery of Union soldiers during their advance on the fort in glowing detail:*

"They moved across the meadow through a little belt of woods, came to the base of the hill, and met the leaden rain. But they paused not a moment.... Without firing a shot, without flinching a moment or faltering as their ranks were thinned, they rushed up the hill, regardless of the fire in front or on their flank, jumped upon the rifle pits and drove the rebels down the eastern slope."

Opposite: *Several of the heavy guns used for the defense of Fort Donelson.*

Right: *General Grant (left) points the way to the fort's earthwork embankments.*

Below: *Henri Lovie's sketch of Union General Wallace's charge on Fort Donelson.*

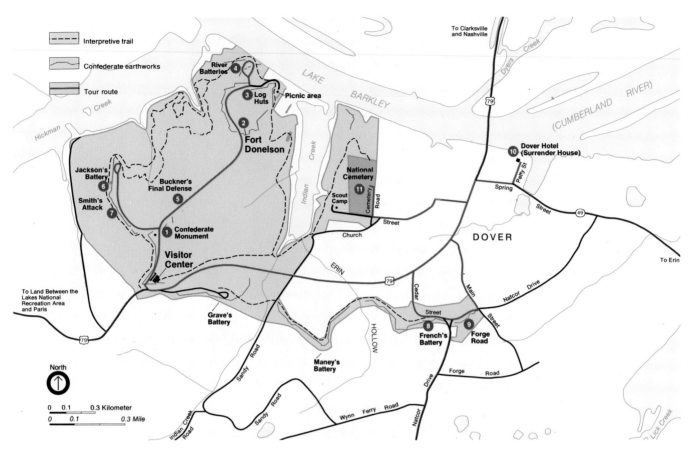

THE RIVER HIGHWAYS

Inland waterways played a vital role for both sides, not only for troop and supply transport, but for attack and defense. Gunboats plied the rivers to support land attacks on such sites as Fort Donelson, Vicksburg, and Fort Pulaski. Union mortar scows shelled Confederate outposts along the Mississippi, and sixty Union ironclads were put into service early in the war. The *Carondelet,* one of eight ironclads built in only one hundred days by James B. Eads, saw action at Forts Henry and Donelson. Especially effective for riverine warfare was the Union ironclad of the "Pook Turtle" type (for designer Samuel Pook). With a draft of only six feet, it could go where few ships of comparable size and weight could follow. The Confederacy was at a disadvantage in commissioning only twenty-two ironclads during the war years.

1 Confederate Monument. The monument, pictured opposite, was erected in 1933.

2 Fort Donelson. The fifteen-acre fort was built by soldiers and slaves, with a ten-foot protective wall of logs and earth.

3 Log Huts. The site of some 100 huts serving as Confederate winter quarters. After the surrender of the fort, they were burned down in an attempt to contain a measles outbreak.

4 River Batteries. Confederate gunners repelled a Union gunboat attack from this position.

5 Buckner's Final Defense. The position of the Confederates' last stand before the fort was surrendered.

6 Jackson's Battery. Jackson placed a four-gun battery at this site on the night of February 13, 1862.

7 Smith's Attack. General C.F. Smith's troops charged up these snow-covered slopes on February 15.

8 French's Battery. A four-gun battery was positioned here to protect against attack through Erin Hollow.

9 Forge Road. The Confederates planned to escape through this route, but succeeded in opening it only briefly on February 15.

10 Dover Hotel (Surrender House). This building served as General Buckner's headquarters during the battle, and was the site of his surrender to General Grant.

11 National Cemetery. In 1867, this site became the Fort Donelson National Cemetery; 655 Union soldiers were reinterred here.

This opened the way for execution of the Confederates' plan to evacuate the fort and seek the safety of Nashville, where they could join the major force under General Johnston. However, the Confederates neither escaped as planned, nor pressed their advantage to defeat the Federals. Instead, they drew back into the trenches—their original positions—for reasons that were never made clear. Ordering Foote to shell the Confederates from the river, Grant regrouped his men and counterattacked. By evening, he had regained all the ground that had been lost.

During the night, as the Confederates prepared to surrender, Generals Floyd and Pillow escaped with some 2,000 men by way of the river, leaving General Buckner in command. On the morning of February 16, Buckner sent a letter requesting Union terms. Grant's response was the ultimatum, "No terms except an unconditional and immediate surrender." Buckner felt his old classmate was "ungenerous and unchivalrous," but he had no choice: he accepted Grant's terms.

After one year of war, during which the Confederates had achieved several victories, Fort Donelson became the first important Union victory and a great morale booster for the North. More than 12,000 Confederate soldiers were captured or missing, and some 250 killed and 1,250 wounded. The Confederates had lost 48 cannon that would be very difficult to replace. More importantly, they had lost control of two major rivers that were the key to western Tennessee and all of Kentucky. Eventually, they would also lose Nashville. Union losses were 500 killed, with 2,108 wounded and 224 men missing or captured. The victory launched Grant's career as a general to be reckoned with, and led ultimately to his appointment as lieutenant general and commander of the Army of the Potomac in 1864.

Above: The Confederate Monument, erected in 1933, pays tribute to the Southern soldiers who fought and died at Fort Donelson.

Below: Fort Donelson, one mile west of Dover, Tennessee, was built to protect the Cumberland River batteries. With its capture, the North had opened a way to the Confederate heartland.

**FORT DONELSON
NATIONAL BATTLEFIELD**

MAILING ADDRESS
Superintendent, Fort Donelson National Battlefield, PO Box 434, Dover, TN 37058

TELEPHONE
Office, 615-232-5348; Visitor Center, 615-232-5706

DIRECTIONS
The fort is one mile west of Dover town square, on US 79.

VISITOR CENTER
Museum and a ten-minute slide program.

ACTIVITIES
Self-guided auto tour (rental tapes are available); interpretive talks and demonstrations are scheduled during the summer.

HOURS
The visitor center is open from 8 AM–4:30 PM, daily except December 25.

Pea Ridge

Following the battle at Wilson's Creek in August 1861, the opposing armies continued to skirmish across Missouri, each attempting to gain control of this important border state. In one of these efforts, Confederate General Sterling Price captured the northwestern town of Lexington, near Independence. His success was short-lived: Price's army was soon pushed back into southwestern Missouri by a force under Brigadier General Samuel R. Curtis, newly appointed commander of the Federal Southwest District of Missouri. By February 1862, Curtis and his army of nearly 11,000 Federal troops had forced Price and his Missouri State Guard as far south as the Boston Mountains, near Fayetteville, Arkansas. Once there, Price was joined by troops commanded by General Benjamin McCulloch.

In early March, Jefferson Davis appointed Major General Earl Van Dorn overall commander of Confederate forces west of the Mississippi. Van Dorn decided to move his new army, which included the troops of Price and McCulloch, north again to attack the Federals. When Curtis learned of the advance, he had his men form a defensive position on Pea Ridge, just over the Missouri border in Arkansas.

On March 6, the Confederates were joined by three regiments of Indians from the Cherokee Nation, commanded by General Stand Watie. These regiments included men who had been forcibly removed from their lands in North Carolina and Georgia by the Federal government during the 1830s. Van Dorn, with a force increased to 16,200, hoped to defeat

THE FIGHT FOR MISSOURI

On **March 7–8, 1862,** in the hill country of northern Arkansas, the battle of Pea Ridge ended in a decisive victory for the Union that secured control of the key state of Missouri. Union troops commanded by Brigadier General Samuel Ryan Curtis defeated a Confederate army led by Major General Earl Van Dorn. Pea Ridge is the only major battle in the Civil War in which Indians participated: the Confederates recruited about 1,000 members of the Cherokee Nation.

 USA Brigadier General Samuel R. Curtis; Brigadier General Franz Sigel

 CSA Major General Earl Van Dorn; Brigadier General Benjamin McCulloch (killed); Major General Sterling Price; General Stand Watie

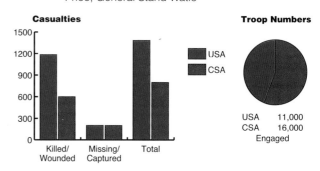

Casualties

Troop Numbers

USA 11,000
CSA 16,000
Engaged

Curtis quickly and follow up with a campaign to take St. Louis and stop Grant's advances on the Tennessee and Cumberland Rivers.

Finding his opponent thoroughly entrenched, Van Dorn discarded his original plan to attack the center of the Federal line. Instead, he planned a long night march around Curtis's defensive position. This would enable him to attack the Union army from the rear. During the march, McCulloch's troops fell behind, and Van Dorn decided to use this delay to his advantage and make a two-pronged attack. Van Dorn and Price's Missourians would march east toward Elkhorn Tavern. McCulloch and his army, which included the Cherokee, were ordered to the west end of Pea Ridge, near the small village of Leetown. However, Curtis's scouts (who included "Wild Bill" Hickock) had discovered the movements of the Confederate army; Van Dorn's delay had allowed Curtis to turn his entire force so that his front lines were ready to meet the Confederates. At Pea Ridge, both McCulloch and his second-in-command, General James McIntosh, were killed in the decisive Union victory.

At Elkhorn Tavern, Van Dorn attacked the Federal army. Both the first and second charges were unsuccessful, but a third swept the Union left back from Elkhorn Tavern and Telegraph Road, the main north-south artery. At nightfall, the Confederates held Elkhorn Tavern, but the Union defense was still intact and in the darkness, reserves moved up and stabilized the line.

Above: The rocky outcropping known as Pea Ridge backed up the Confederate entrenchments occupied by Van Dorn's Confederate troops, who enveloped Curtis's Union force near Elkhorn Tavern on March 7th.

Opposite: A Union army officer's sketch of the outbreak of hostilities at Pea Ridge, originally published in Leslie's Illustrated Newspaper.

Below: The reconstructed Elkhorn Tavern, focal point of the fighting.

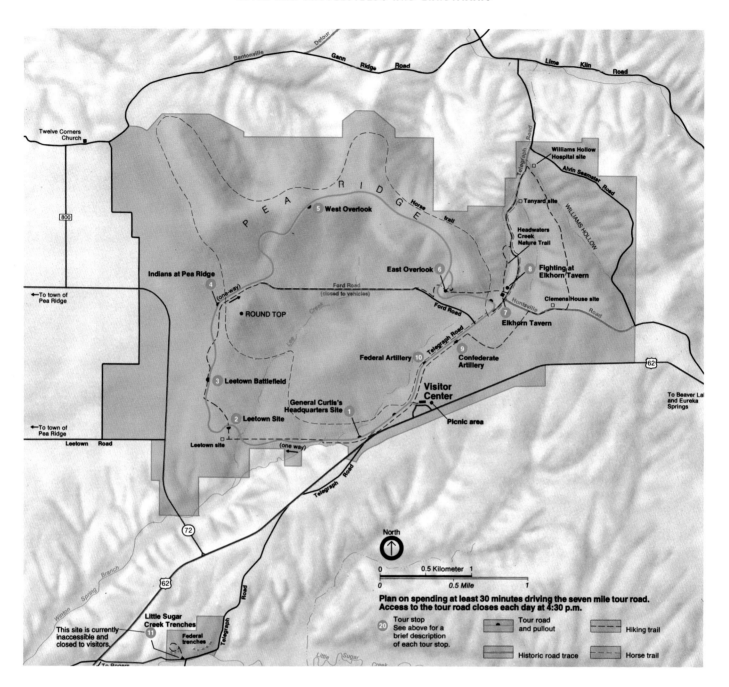

Plan on spending at least 30 minutes driving the seven mile tour road. Access to the tour road closes each day at 4:30 p.m.

1 General Curtis's Headquarters Site Shortly before the battle, the Union commander made his headquarters in this area.

2 Leetown The hamlet of Leetown once stood near this site. Nothing remains of the village as it was before the battle.

3 Leetown Battlefield Union soldiers successfully repelled a Confederate attack across Round Top to the right of this position.

4 Indians at Pea Ridge (see feature opposite)

5 West Overlook On the night of March 6, half the Confederate troops marched around this site to get into the rear of the Union position.

6 East Overlook The best view of the battlefield.

7 Elkhorn Tavern The tavern— the original building burned down shortly after the battle— was the focal point of the fighting at Pea Ridge.

8 Fighting at Elkhorn Tavern Fierce fighting raged around the tavern when the Confederates regrouped there.

9 Confederate Artillery On March 8, Tull's Missouri Battery was positioned here.

10 Federal Artillery Union artillery massed here and bombarded the Confederates from their positions around Elkhorn Tavern on March 8.

11 Little Sugar Creek Trenches On the bluff above the creek, remnants of the Union trenches and earthworks are visible.

PEA RIDGE NATIONAL MILITARY PARK

MAILING ADDRESS
Pea Ridge National Military Park, Highway 62 East, Pea Ridge, Arkansas 72751

TELEPHONE
501-451-8122

DIRECTIONS
The park is located twenty-eight miles north of Fayetteville, Arkansas. Take US 62 from Fayetteville to Rogers. The park is ten miles north of Rogers, on US 62.

VISITOR CENTER
Civil War museum exhibits and a twelve-minute slide program.

ACTIVITIES
A self-guided auto tour, a ten-mile hiking trail, and an eleven-mile horse trail; ranger talks on the battle are available depending on visitation and staffing.

HOURS
The visitor center is open daily from 8 AM–5 PM Elkhorn Tavern is open from 10 AM–4 PM, May through October. The park is closed Thanksgiving, December 25, and January 1.

On March 8, Federal artillery under General Franz Sigel fired on the Confederate position around Elkhorn Tavern. The Confederate artillery responded with equal ferocity. Following the bombardment, two divisions of Union infantry, followed by cavalry, attacked. With his whole line under assault and his troops running low on ammunition, General Van Dorn was forced to order a retreat. The Federal force pursued a company of Confederates moving along Telegraph Road, believing them to be the main body of the army. This mistake allowed Van Dorn and most of his force to escape.

During the 2-day battle, approximately 600 Confederates were killed or wounded and 200 captured or missing. Union casualties included 203 killed, 980 wounded, and 201 captured or missing. Pea Ridge was the first decisive Union victory in a battle west of the Mississippi.

Above: Telegraph Road, the Confederate line of retreat on March 8 after Union forces bombarded the Southern position at the tavern.

NATIVE AMERICANS IN THE CIVIL WAR

The Confederacy quickly forged alliances with a number of tribes early in the war, most notably with the "Five Civilized Tribes": the Cherokee, Chickasaw, Choctaw, Creek, and Seminole. All too familiar with the broken promises and harsh treatment of the Northern government, the Native Nations found themselves courted by an army with a common enemy. While some sought to remain neutral and others sided with the North, many influential tribal leaders like Cherokee John Ross were eventually won over and raised thousands of warriors for the Confederates.

Pea Ridge was the most significant battle of the war involving Native troops, with the First Cherokee Mounted Rifles and the First Choctaw-Chickasaw Regiment fighting for the Confederacy. The two companies of the Cherokee Mounted rifles led by Brigadier General Stand Watie (whose Cherokee name, Degataga, means "the immovable" or "stands together") fought in more battles than any other unit in the western theater. Watie executed a brilliant series of guerrilla actions throughout the war, and lived up to his name by being the final Confederate to surrender on June 23, 1865.

Shiloh

The Federal capture of Forts Henry and Donelson in Tennessee, and the battle at Pea Ridge, Arkansas, in the winter of 1862, forced the South and Confederate general Albert Sidney Johnston to abandon southern Kentucky and much of Tennessee. To stem the tide, General Johnston moved south to protect Corinth, Mississippi, the site of the South's Memphis and Charleston Railroad, the only direct rail link between Richmond and Memphis, and concentrated his troops—more than 40,000—at Corinth. Johnston's objective was to move north with this force and clear the Federals out of Tennessee.

Federal general Ulysses S. Grant, commanding the Army of the Tennessee, moved his troops to Pittsburg Landing on the Tennessee River, twenty miles north of Corinth. General Don Carlos Buell and his Army of the Ohio were ordered to join Grant there.

On April 2 Johnston ordered his troops to move out of Corinth with the intention of attacking Grant two days later. However, major delays the next day and heavy rains the following evening forced a change in the timetable. The two-day delay convinced Johnston he had lost the element of surprise. There had been skirmishing for several days, and General P. G. T. Beauregard, Johnston's second-in-command, wanted to call off the offensive, believing the delay had allowed Grant to be reinforced by Buell.

Contrary to the Confederate generals' reasonable assumptions, Grant was not, in fact, aware that the Southern troops

A BRUTAL LESSON UNDER FIRE

Shiloh, Tennessee, was the site of one of the bloodiest battles of the war. On **April 6, 1862,** Confederate generals Albert Sidney Johnston, Army of the Mississippi, and P.G.T. Beauregard (2nd in command), made a surprise attack on Major General Ulysses S. Grant's forces. The next day Grant, reinforced by Major General Don Carlos Buell's Army of the Ohio, counterattacked. The Confederates were forced to retreat beyond the Tennessee border to Corinth, Mississippi.

 USA Major General Ulysses S. Grant, Major General Don Carlos Buell, Brigadier General Benjamin M. Prentiss; Brigadier General William T. Sherman

 CSA General Albert Sidney Johnston, General P. G. T. Beauregard

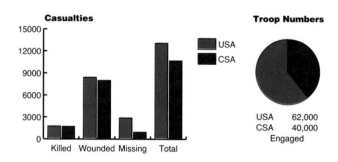

Casualties — USA / CSA

Troop Numbers
USA 62,000
CSA 40,000
Engaged

Opposite: This painting, entitled "The Battle of Shiloh," by Thure de Thulstrup, shows the ferocity of Union firepower in the "Hornet's Nest."

Left: The terrain was ill suited to defense of the Union position.

were so close. He and his senior division commander, General William T. Sherman, were planning their next offensive and did not expect an attack, so there was no sense of urgency in the movement of Buell's troops. The troops at Pittsburg Landing were not entrenched, there was no defensive arrangement, and the pickets set up were woefully inadequate. In addition, the Union position at Shiloh was poor: the river was behind them, and there was a creek on each flank. These creeks, which Sherman thought would guard his flanks, would prove to be dangerous obstacles in battle.

On the morning of April 6, while Grant was at his headquarters nine miles away in Savannah, the Confederates came out of the woods near Shiloh Church and attacked the unprepared Federals. Johnston's troop formation was awkward, with three corps positioned one behind the other across the whole battlefront—nearly three miles. Such a formation could not be commanded effectively, and it was impossible to know where reinforcements were needed.

Many of the troops on both sides had never been in battle before. With the first Confederate attack, some Union troops ran for the safety of the landing, but most fought stubbornly and fell back slowly. About three hours into the battle, the Confederate surge stalled along the Sunken Road, where the Federals, commanded by General Benjamin Prentiss, estab-

SAFETY OF THE UNION FIRST, EMANCIPATION SECONDARY

President Abraham Lincoln clarified his intentions during the early part of the war when he wrote the following letter in response to a New York Tribune *editorial by Horace Greeley, published on August 19, 1862:*

Executive Mansion,
Washington, August 22, 1862

Hon. Horace Greel[e]y:
Dear Sir

I have just read yours of the 19th, addressed to myself through the New York Tribune. If there be in it any statements, or assumptions of fact, which I may know to be erroneous, I do not, now and here, controvert them. If there be in it any inferences which I may believe to be falsely drawn, I do not, now and here, argue against them. If there be perceptible in it an impatient and dictatorial tone, I waive it in deference to an old friend, whose heart I have always supposed to be right.

As to the policy I "seem to be pursuing" as you say, I have not meant to leave any one in doubt.

I would save the Union. I would save it the shortest way under the Constitution. The sooner the national authority can be restored; the nearer the Union will be "the Union as it was." If there be those who would not save the Union, unless they could at the same time *save* slavery, I do not agree with them. My paramount object in this struggle *is* to save the Union, and is *not* either to save or to destroy slavery. If I could save the Union without freeing *any* slave I would do it, and if I could save it by freeing *all* the slaves I would do it; and if I could save it by freeing some and leaving others alone I would also do that. What I do about slavery, and the colored race, I do because I believe it helps to save the Union; and what I forbear, I forbear because I do *not* believe it would help to save the Union. I shall do *less* whenever I shall believe what I am doing hurts the cause, and I shall do *more* whenever I shall believe doing more will help the cause. I shall try to correct errors when shown to be errors; and I shall adopt new views so fast as they shall appear to be true views.

I have here stated my purpose according to my view of *official* duty; and I intend no modification of my oft-expressed *personal* wish that all men every where could be free.

Yours,
A. Lincoln

lished a defensive line. This site became known as the "Hornets' Nest" because of the stinging firepower the Confederates faced there. The Federals fought off 12 assaults, yielding only when 62 artillery pieces were brought to bear on their position. Although these troops were eventually overwhelmed and captured, their sacrifice probably saved the day by allowing Grant time to set up a defensive position near Pittsburg Landing on the river's edge.

The fighting became a confused melée, with regiments and divisions on both sides totally disorganized. General Johnston was mortally wounded while leading an assault on the Peach Orchard. Meanwhile, Grant's arrival on the field by midday, and the arrival of General Lewis "Lew" Wallace's division, bolstered Union resistance. By late afternoon, the Federals were secure in their final defensive line, able to repulse several Confederate attacks on the flanks. In the evening, Buell's troops arrived, reinforcing Grant's position.

Beauregard, unaware that Buell's entire army was in place, began an offensive on the morning of April 7th. It appeared promising, but the larger Union force counterattacked and regained the ground lost the day before. Beauregard ordered a retreat to Corinth, and the weary Federals did not pursue.

Shiloh (a Biblical word from the Hebrew for "place of peace") was the bloodiest battle fought in the United States to that point, although such carnage would become com-

EYEWITNESS

From the account of a Union officer at Shiloh, published in 1865 by P. F. Collier in The Civil War in Song and Story:

"On going to the field the second day, our regiment strode on in line over wounded, dying, and dead…The regiment halted amidst a gory, ghastly scene. I heard a voice calling, "Ho, friend! ho! for God's sake, come here!"

I went to a gory pile of dead human forms in every kind of stiff contortion: I saw one arm raised, beckoning me. I found there a rebel, covered with clotted blood, pillowing his head on the dead body of a comrade. Both were red from head to foot. The live one had lain across [the dead man] all that horrible long night in the storm. The first thing he said to me was, "Give me some water. Send me a surgeon—won't you! Oh God! What made you come down here to fight us? We never would have come up there."…

I filled his canteen nearly—reserving some for myself—knowing I might be in the same sad condition. I told him we had no surgeon in our regiment, and that we would have to suffer, if wounded, the same as he; that other regiments were coming, and to call on them for a surgeon; that they were humane."

Left: *A cannon near the "Bloody Pond," where wounded soldiers drank and bathed their wounds.*

Bottom: *A sketch of exhausted Union soldiers awaiting reinforcement by General Buell at Pittsburg Landing—General Grant had been overconfident.*

Opposite: *This photograph of a diorama at the Visitor Center shows the melée in the woods around Shiloh.*

Right: *campaign maps of the fighting at Shiloh. On the first day, General Grant's army of mainly untrained recruits were taken by surprise, suffered many losses, but held. Only the arrival of General Buell's reinforcements saved the Union Army from defeat on the second day.*

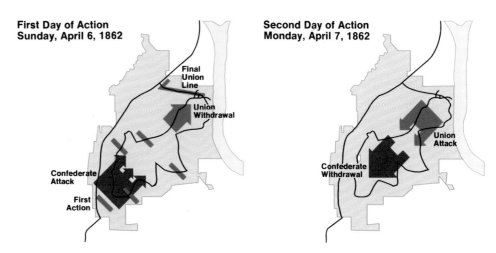

First Day of Action
Sunday, April 6, 1862

Final
Union
Line

Union
Withdrawal

Confederate
Attack

First
Action

Second Day of Action
Monday, April 7, 1862

Union
Attack

Confederate
Withdrawal

CIVIL WAR BATTLEFIELDS AND LANDMARKS

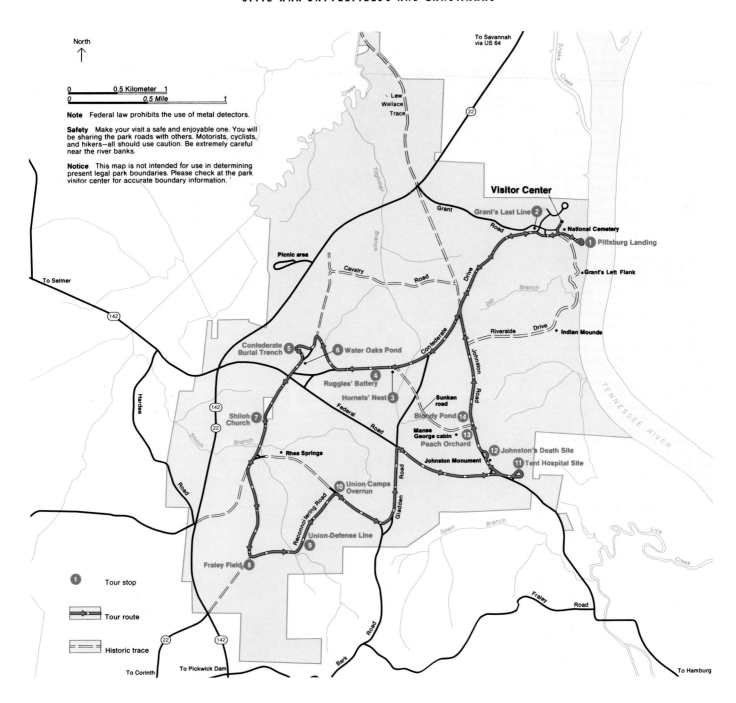

North

0   0.5 Kilometer   1
0   0.5 Mile   1

Note Federal law prohibits the use of metal detectors.

Safety Make your visit a safe and enjoyable one. You will be sharing the park roads with others. Motorists, cyclists, and hikers—all should use caution. Be extremely careful near the river banks.

Notice This map is not intended for use in determining present legal park boundaries. Please check at the park visitor center for accurate boundary information.

1 Tour stop

Tour route

Historic trace

1 Pittsburg Landing General Grant thought that the river at his back would afford protection, but instead it boxed in his artillery. Reinforcements crossed here the second day.

2 Grant's Last Line With reinforcements, victory ensued.

3 Hornet's Nest Union forces peppered Confederates through eleven engagements.

4 Ruggle's Battery Confederate artillery fire allowed the capture of 2,100 Union soldiers by General Daniel Ruggles.

5 Confederate Burial Trench 700 Confederate dead are buried in this mass grave.

6 Water Oaks Pond From here, General Beauregard withdrew.

7 Shiloh Church Site of the Confederate surprise attack.

8 Fraley Field First shots fired.

9 Union Defense Line First day, first line.

10 Union Camps Overrun From here, Union forces fell back to the Hornet's Nest.

11 Tent Hospital Union doctors created the first field hospital under tents.

12 Johnston's Death Site A monument shows where General A.S. Johnston was mortally wounded.

13 Peach Orchard The orchard was in bloom as Confederates tried to advance.

14 Bloody Pond Soldiers from both sides found welcome relief for their thirst and wounds at this pond.

monplace over the next three years. The battle claimed more than 13,000 Union casualties and more than 10,500 Confederate: in short, more than double the casualties at Manassas, Wilson's Creek, Fort Donelson, and Pea Ridge combined.

Although Grant was severely critized for having been taken by surprise, President Lincoln supported him, saying, "I can't spare this man—he fights!" For Grant and Sherman, Shiloh was an unforgettable lesson in the reality of total war. They no longer believed that the Confederates in the West would soon capitulate. It was said that Grant snatched victory from the jaws of defeat. At Shiloh, his overconfidence in his own position and underestimation of the enemy almost led to disaster, but his tenacity rallied Union forces and pushed back the Southern offensive.

Above: This painting by an unknown artist depicts the death of Confederate General Albert Sidney Johnston.

Below: An early twentieth century photograph of visitors paying their respects at the Shiloh Battlefield Cemetery, where many of the casualties from both sides lie.

SHILOH NATIONAL MILITARY PARK

MAILING ADDRESS
Superintendent, Shiloh National Military Park, Rt. 1, Box 9, Shiloh, TN 38376

TELEPHONE
901-689-5275

DIRECTIONS
The park is located ten miles south of Savannah, Tennessee and twenty-three miles north of Corinth, Mississippi. From Savannah take US 64 four miles west to where it intersects with TN 22. Drive south on TN 22 approximately six miles to the park. From Corinth, take US 45 five miles north to where it intersects with TN 22. Drive north and east on TN 22 approximately eighteen miles to the park.

VISITOR CENTER
Civil War exhibits, twenty-five-minute orientation film shown every half hour.

ACTIVITIES
Self-guided auto tours; nine-and-half-mile tour road for hiking or biking. Ranger interpretive programs are offered daily across the battlefield in summer and on weekends in summer and fall (weather permitting).

HOURS
The visitor center is open from 8 AM to 5 PM, with hours extended to 6 PM, in the summer. The battlefield is open from dawn to dusk year-round, except December 25.

Stones River

Early in the Civil War, the border states, divided in opinion over the issues of slavery and states' rights, tried to maintain neutrality. Kentucky, especially, found itself under pressure, surrounded as it was on three sides by Confederate states. A number of Southern sympathizers voted for the state's secession, and a star for Kentucky was actually added to the Confederate flag, although secession was never ratified. Later, the state was invaded by troops of both sides bent on forcing the issue: most engagements involved guerrilla bands. One of the few set battles was that at Perryville on October 7–8, 1862, between the Confederate Army of Tennessee, under General Braxton Bragg, and the Federal Army of the Ohio, commanded by Major General Don Carlos Buell. The Confederates were defeated, and Kentucky's allegiance to the Union was never really in question again.

After their defeat at Perryville, the Confederates moved into Tennessee. By the end of the year, when one division had been transferred to the defense of Vicksburg, the 38,000-man Army of Tennessee was concentrated near the town of Murfreesboro, about 30 miles south of the state capital at Nashville. Occupied by the Union Army since February, Nashville had become a major Federal depot. On December 26, 1862, some 43,000 Federal troops of the new Army of the

"HELL'S HALF ACRE"

At dawn on **December 31, 1862,** Confederate general Braxton Bragg's forces attacked Union troops led by General William S. Rosecrans near Stones River, Tennessee. By the time this fierce winter battle ended on **January 2, 1863,** both sides had sustained devastating losses. Although the Federals were too weak to pursue the retreating Confederates, the victory had given them access to central Tennessee, which they would soon control.

 USA Major General William S. Rosecrans

 CSA General Braxton Bragg; Major General John C. Breckinridge

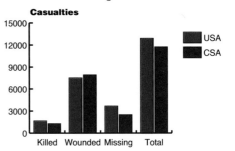

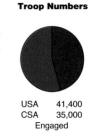

USA 41,400
CSA 35,000
Engaged

THE CRUCIAL RAILROADS

From the earliest battles, like Bull Run, railroads played a major role in the Civil War for troop transport and the movement of supplies and weaponry. This photograph shows an armored railroad car with cannon. In previous wars, horses, boats, and long marches were the only ways to move vast armies and heavy artillery. The advent of railroads was to transform military strategy through both increased troop mobility and the concentration of crucial supply lines. At the beginning of the war, the South had only 9,000 miles of track *versus* 21,000 for the North, a difference which—for the first time in the history of warfare—would prove pivotal. Throughout the war, this ratio never improved for the South.

Union generals targeted railroad hubs, like Richmond, and key stretches of track including Stones River, in Tennessee, where a Union victory meant control of the Nashville and Chattanooga rail system. Sherman's long march to Atlanta could not have been accomplished without first gaining control of key railroad supply lines and turning them into conduits for Union needs. Conversely, the sieges of Atlanta and Petersburg were effective when Union forces prevented railroads from bringing both food and military supplies to the entrapped soldiers and civilians.

Left: The oldest Civil War memorial here at Stones River National Cemetery, just west of Murfreesboro, marks where, in December–January 1862–63, thousands fell at "Hell's Half Acre." Both sides sustained losses of over 10,000, and the Confederate army was forced to retreat. The memorial was erected as a tribute to the Regular Brigade of the Army of the Cumberland.

Cumberland, (previously Buell's Army of the Ohio), commanded by Major General William S. Rosecrans, left Nashville in search of Bragg's army.

Union scouts soon found the Confederate troops and several skirmishes took place at the end of the year. Bragg ordered his cavalry commander, Brigadier General Joseph Wheeler, to move around the Federal army and destroy the Union supply wagons. Wheeler was successful and captured valuable weapons and mounts as well as hundreds of prisoners.

Bolstered by this success, Bragg decided to outflank his opponent, although he expected an immediate attack in response. However, Rosecrans did nothing. On the night of December 30, the two forces were camped northwest of Murfreesboro and only a few hundred yards apart. In fact, they were so close that every soldier could hear the bands in the enemy's camp, and at the end of the evening both sides, some 77,000 men, joined in the singing of "Home Sweet Home."

Rosecrans and Bragg had made similar plans—to attack the opponent on the right flank in the morning. The Federal assault was ordered for 7:00 AM, but the first Confederate troops, under General William Hardee, moved at dawn. In a wheeling movement from left to right, they surprised the Yankees at breakfast, as they had done at Shiloh, gaining an initiative that forced their opponents to withdraw. An attack by a Confederate corps under Major General Leonidas J. Polk

EYEWITNESS

Union soldier R. B. Stewart recounts the experience of battle and its aftermath:

"Down through the open fields we rushed, keeping in as good order as possible. Cannon thundered before us, to the right of us, and behind us. Shells shrieked over us, and, bursting, scattered their fragments through our ranks. But it was "close up," "guide right," and still forward until Stones River was reached, and we paused for a moment on its bank. A part of the line passed over, and the Southern ranks were broken. …

At night we rested where our work ended, but to most of us there was no rest. There was comfort in the thought that our defeat had turned to victory—that we who had fared so badly under the first stroke of the enemy were permitted to lay the last stroke on his back. All night long the rain poured down as though it would wash away every stain of blood. All night long we listened to the cries of the wounded where they lay upon the field. All night long the ambulances were busy gathering in the sheaves of this fearful harvest. All night long we waited and watched and wondered if the battle were really over."

YOUR OWN PROUD LAND'S HEROIC SOIL,
MUST BE YOUR FITTER GRAVE;
SHE CLAIMS FROM WAR HIS RICHEST SPOIL,
THE ASHES OF THE BRAVE.

soon followed; Major General Alexander McCook's men were pushed back toward the Nashville Turnpike, which was Rosecrans's supply line and best line of retreat. Only a strong stand by Union soldiers in the center right under Brigadier General Philip Sheridan prevented the Confederates from forcing the entire Union line over the Nashville Turnpike. The fighting was so fierce, and the sound of gunfire and artillery so loud, that many Confederates picked raw cotton from nearby fields to stuff into their ears.

At first, Rosecrans continued the planned offensive on the enemy's right despite this assault. However, he was soon persuaded that help was needed desperately to protect his supply lines on the right. Two divisions under Major General Thomas L. Crittenden were sent against the Confederate troops led by Major General John C. Breckinridge, former vice-president of the United States and Lincoln's opponent in the 1861 election.

Bragg now had a chance to fold up the two wings of the Union line, and he sent orders to Breckinridge to move his men across the Stones River and attack the apex of the two Union lines, which formed a right angle. Breckinridge was slow to respond, in part because he believed that his men still faced a threat from Rosecrans, who had, in fact, withdrawn. The Union troops at the apex of the angle, commanded by Brigadier General William B. Hazen, were strongly entrenched on a ridge called Round Forest. Against this point, the Confederates finally threw a wave of attacks that included four divisions of Breckinridge's men. Hundreds were lost in these assaults, due in part to lack of ammunition and to rifles that were still too wet to fire after the rain of the previous night. In spite of the constant pressure, the Union troops, with the

aid of strong artillery fire, held their position at what became known as "Hell's Half Acre." At the end of the day, the Confederate attacks ceased for lack of reinforcements, but Rosecrans did not withdraw, as Bragg had expected.

Over New Year's Day 1863, both sides maintained their positions while bringing up reinforcements. On the Federal side, batteries of artillery were emplaced and a division under Colonel Beatty took up a position on the far side of Stones River. The following day, Bragg ordered Breckinridge and his men to push this Federal force back to its own side of the river and retake a hill to the east. This was accomplished in an attack that began about 4:00 PM, but while pursuing the enemy the Confederates were drawn into range of 58 Federal guns: one witness recalled that they had "opened the door of Hell and the devil himself was there to greet them." Over 1,700 Confederates fell in the next 45 minutes, as the Union forces counterattacked with fresh troops. By the end of that day, Breckinridge's remaining men had been driven back to their original position.

Bragg's army, which had marched and fought over five days in intermittent rain and cold, was exhausted and isolated, and Bragg had just learned that Rosecrans's force would soon be reinforced. In the end, it was Bragg and his Confederates who withdrew the following night, with losses of 11,800 from a force of 35,000 men. The Union side had suffered 12,900 casualties, from a force of some 41,000 engaged. Both sides claimed victory, but soon afterward, Rosecrans's army was able to push the Confederates out of middle Tennessee, leaving those rich farmlands in Union hands. Rosecrans also established a strong supply base at Murfreesboro, which was used to launch the successful Union campaign against Chattanooga the following autumn.

The short, self-guided auto tour covers nine sites.

1 Visitor Center Start here, where the Chicago Board of Trade Battery pushed Confederate troops back to the cedar forest.

2 The Cedars General Rosecrans found the enemy hiding here.

3 Water's Alabama Battery Trees and rocks hindered the positioning of Confederate artillery.

4 Sheridan's Stand Union forces held long enough to allow reinforcements along the Nashville Pike.

5 Confederate Advance Fierce fighting at very close range in the cedar woods characterized the action here.

6 Rosecrans New Line Federal troops used the woods to their advantage.

7 Cemetery Only Union dead are buried here, some 6,100; Confederate dead were either removed to their hometowns or buried in mass unmarked graves.

8 Round Forest The oldest Civil War memorial stands here, marking the site of the determined Union army stand.

9 Breckinridge's Attack Federal artillery slaughtered General Breckinridge's advancing army.

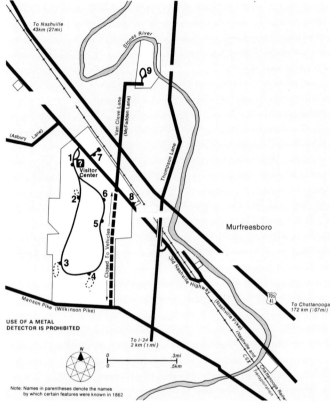

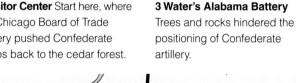

USE OF A METAL DETECTOR IS PROHIBITED

Note: Names in parentheses denote the names by which certain features were known in 1862

STONES RIVER NATIONAL BATTLEFIELD

MAILING ADDRESS
Superintendent, Stones River National Battlefield, 3501 Old Nashville Highway, Murfreesboro, TN 37129-3095

TELEPHONE
615-893-9501

DIRECTIONS
The Battlefield is located northwest of Murfreesboro, Tennessee. Take I-24 to exit 78 and drive east on US 231 to its intersection with US 70s/41. Drive northwest on US 70s/41 and follow signs to the park.

VISITOR CENTER
Museum, slide program, and publications for sale.

ACTIVITIES
Drive or bike the tour road. (A taped tour and brochure are available.) Interpretive talks by rangers, living history demonstrations, and cemetery lantern tours.

HOURS
The visitor center is open daily from 8 AM to 5 PM, except December 25.

Opposite: Row upon row of graves testify to the carnage at "Hell's Half Acre." During that fateful post-Christmas week, rain had soaked the men and guns malfunctioned. But at one point Federal artillery mowed down 1,700 Confederates in 45 minutes.

Left: A scene from the bitter fighting at Stones River.

Vicksburg

Two Mississippi River fortresses held the halves of the Confederacy together in 1863. Two Federal campaigns, one working south from Memphis, the other north from Baton Rouge, sought to capture the strongpoints, sever the Confederate nation and reopen the great river from the Midwestern heartland to the Gulf of Mexico.

The most important and powerful of the fortresses, Vicksburg, overlooked a long horseshoe bend of the Mississippi from a chain of hills rising from a drowned landscape of swamps, river bottoms, and bayous. All but unassailable from three sides, this Confederate "Gibraltar of the West" commanded the river for miles in both directions.

The Federals had failed in several earlier efforts to subdue Vicksburg. A Navy river flotilla tried to bombard the fortress into submission in the summer of 1862. A few months later, the Confederates repulsed a landward assault from the north. In early 1863, winter rains and rising water doomed a series of Federal operations known as the Bayou Expeditions including an effort to expand and use the old canal across the De-Soto Peninsula—"Grant's Canal."

In the spring, the Federal commander, General Ulysses S. Grant, conceived a daring plan to march his army down the west bank of the Mississippi, cross the river south of Vicksburg, advance inland onto high, dry ground, and attack the fortress from the east—the vulnerable fourth side, or so Grant hoped.

The campaign opened on the moonless night of April 16, 1863, when a flotilla of Union gunboats and transports ran past the water batteries at Vicksburg and joined up with Grant's land forces on the Louisiana bank between Vicksburg and Port Hudson. By month's end, the flotilla had ferried the army

UNION SPLITS THE CONFEDERACY

The fourteen-month Vicksburg Campaign was undertaken by Union general Ulysses S. Grant to gain total control of the Mississippi River and split the Confederacy. Late in 1862, Grant and General Sherman converged on Vicksburg but their attempt to storm it was repulsed. A grueling forty-seven day siege followed, and the city surrendered on **July 4, 1863,** marking what may have been the greatest Union military achievement of the Civil War.

 USA General Ulysses S. Grant; General William T. Sherman

 CSA General John C. Pemberton

Troop Numbers

USA	71,000
CSA	30,000
Engaged	

across the mile-wide river. On May 1 Grant, against the advice of General William T. Sherman and other senior subordinates, cut loose from his base and struck deep into enemy territory.

"All we want now are men, ammunition and hard bread," Grant explained to the skeptical Sherman. "We can subsist our horses on the country and obtain considerable supplies for our troops."

On firm ground at last, the Federals moved swiftly, taking Jackson, the Mississippi capital, in a headlong assault on May 14. Leaving Sherman's corps behind to wreck Jackson, Grant sent the other two corps toward Vicksburg forty miles to the

Left: Grant's entrenchments for the siege of Vicksburg, from a wartime sketch by F. B. Schell.

Left: Adm. David D. Porter's gunboat flotilla runs past the Vicksburg water batteries on the night of April 16, 1863. Confederate gunners sank only one of the 12 vessels; the others reached Grant's army at Hard Times on the west bank of the Mississippi below Vicksburg.

west. On the 16th, the Federals defeated a Confederate army under General John Pemberton at Champion's Hill. Next day, the Yankees routed Pemberton at the Big Black River and drove the Confederate remnants into the Vicksburg defenses. In only 19 days, Grant's army had crossed the Mississippi, marched 180 miles, fought and won 5 battles, and sealed up the enemy's mobile forces.

Grant ordered a frontal attack May 19 on the Stockade Redan, one of Vicksburg's strongpoints. He had thought the Confederates demoralized. If they had been, they recovered quickly, meeting the advancing Federals with a devastating fire. "The heads of the columns have been swept away as chaff thrown from the hand on a windy day," wrote Sherman after the repulse. Grant tried again three days later, with the same result. At a cost of 3,000 Federal killed, wounded, and missing in the May 22 attack, he learned that his army could not carry Vicksburg by assault.

"We'll have to dig our way in," he said.

Thus the Federals settled in for the five formal stages of a siege: investment, artillery bombardment, the construction of parallel and approach trenches, the initial breaching of the defenses, and the final assault.

With close to a year's notice, the Confederates had prepared a formidable defensive system on the high ground around Vicksburg—"frightful enough," one Yankee admitted, "to appall the stoutest heart." The lines extended in a seven-mile semicircle north to south along the steep, wooded bluffs, forming a mutually supporting complex of forts, redoubts, and deep-dug trenches.

The Federals built their own mirror-image works, some as close as 50 yards from Pemberton's lines. Grant had a three-to-one advantage in numbers, a reasonably secure supply line (apart from J. E. Johnston's troops in the rear), and supreme confidence in the eventual outcome. "The enemy are now undoubtedly in our grasp," he wrote Henry Halleck, the Union general-in-chief, in Washington. "The fall of Vicksburg and the capture of most of the garrison can only be a question of time."

For his part, Pemberton believed that his 30,000 Confed-

EYEWITNESS

From a letter written July 5, 1863, by Union soldier George W. Driggs, published in his history of the Eighth Wisconsin Volunteers:

"In strange contrast with the startling scenes of carnage, and the deafening roar of artillery around us, is the calm, sweet serenity of this beautiful Sabbath morning. So quiet that a feeling of loneliness creeps around the heart of one accustomed to hearing the constant booming of cannon and the sharp crack of musketry.…The tumultuous chaos of two great contending armies have ceased their struggles, and the Federal arms have gained another victory over the wily foe. Vicksburg, as you have long ere this been informed, has surrendered, after being besieged for forty-seven days. It was a gala day for our troops, I assure you, and the 4th of July was never before celebrated in Vicksburg with such a right hearty good feeling as on yesterday.

It was also surmised, from the appearance of a flag of truce which made its appearance early in the afternoon of Friday the 3d, that Grant and Pemberton were having an interview relative to the surrender of the city, and all waited in breathless suspense the cheering announcement that Vicksburg was ours. While in this suspense, the silence was broken by the appearance of Gen. Pemberton and staff, who approached our lines bearing in his hand a flag of truce, which was received by Gen. Grant with all the courtesy due from one high in rank. They met with a smile, each recognizing the other as old class-mates at West Point— shook hands and dismounted, and while Gen. Grant's staff entertained the gentlemanly officers of Pemberton's staff, the two distinguished generals proceeded arm in arm to the shade of an old oak tree near by—throwing themselves leisurely upon the grassy ground beneath the old shade tree, they reviewed the past in all kindness, and laughed as jocosely as if they had been daily associates and friends, instead of deadly foes."

erates could hold out until a relief column could reach Vicksburg. Northeast of Jackson, the Confederate general Joseph E. Johnston assembled a 30,000-strong field force to attempt a move on Grant's rear. Communicating via messages smuggled through the siege lines, Pemberton implored Johnston to move as swiftly as possible to his assistance.

"Am I to expect reinforcements?" he wrote Johnston. "From what direction, and how soon?"

By mid-June, Grant had some 70,000 men in 16 divisions in line, 9 divisions pressed up to Vicksburg, the remaining 7 facing east in anticipation of Johnston's appearance. Opposite the Confederate works, the digging went on—and the shooting, too—day after day in the rising heat and humidity of the Mississippi high summer. "The soldiers got so they bored like gophers and beavers, with a spade in one hand and a gun in the other," a Federal veteran recalled.

It was dull and dangerous work. The Confederate snipers were active, and accurate. Their marksmanship provided the Yankees with one of the few diversions of the siege. "A favorite amusement of the soldiers was to place a cap on the end of a ramrod and raise it just above the head-logs, betting on the number of bullets which would pass through it in a given time," recounted one of Grant's officers. With constant repetition, though, even gambling became stale. "The history of a single day was the history of all others," another Yankee observed.

Inside Vicksburg, the Confederates were short of food, supplies, and ammunition. In fact, they found themselves ill-equipped for the intimate exchanges that were such a feature of short-range static warfare. "Fighting by hand grenades was all that was possible at such close quarters," wrote one. "As the federals had the hand grenades and we had none, we obtained our supply by using such of theirs as failed to explode, or by catching them as they came over the parapet and hurling them back."

THE 1863 DRAFT RIOTS

Union victories at Vicksburg and Gettysburg in early July 1863 were turning points of the war. Still, Federal demands for manpower seemed insatiable. On July 12, 1863, New York City newspapers published the first names drawn for the draft. Mobs began to form that afternoon. In four days of rioting, gangs destroyed a church and orphanage, attacked the office of the abolitionist *New York Tribune,* and killed more than a dozen people. Front-line troops were called in to quell the uprising.

Below: The campaign for Vicksburg. Grant's western army crossed the Mississippi River on April 30, 1863, and executed a remarkable three-week campaign that forced the Confederates to fall back into the static defenses of the fortress of Vicksburg. Union troops occupied Jackson on May 14 and overwhelmed Gen. John Pemberton's Confederates at Champion Hill two days later. By May 18, Grant's forces had closed up on Vicksburg. The siege ended with the surrender of the fortress on July 4.

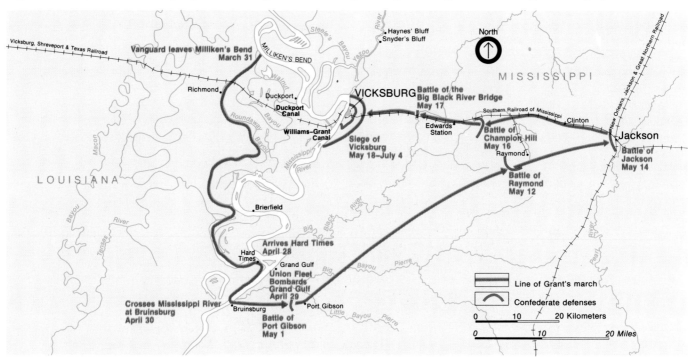

Grenades could be recycled; there was little the defenders could do about food. Pemberton put the garrison on half-rations, then quarter-rations. Vicksburg's bakers made their dough from a gritty compound of ground corn and dried peas. "The corn meal cooked in half the time the peas meal did, so the stuff was half raw," a siege survivor recalled. "It had the properties of india-rubber, and was worse than leather to digest." (The military song "Pea Bread" was a dubious tribute to this concoction.) Mule meat, on the other hand, proved palatable to all but the most squeamish, although it was expensive at a dollar a pound.

Vicksburg's prewar population approached 3,500, and Grant's sudden appearance trapped many civilians inside the fortress. They carved shelters out of the hillsides for protection against the Federal bombardments, a honeycomb of caves and dugouts the besiegers dubbed "prairie dog village." Although they were destructive of property, deafening, and nerve-racking, the cannonades caused surprisingly few civilian casualties, perhaps fewer than a dozen. It was the cumulative effect of hunger, fear, and unrelieved tension that inflicted most of the damage.

Wrote Vicksburg diarist Dora Miller Richards: "I have never understood the full force of these questions—what shall we eat? What shall we drink? And wherewithal shall we be clothed?"

Johnston, meantime, concluded he could do little for Vicksburg. On June 13 a two-week-old message from Johnston reached Pemberton. It sealed the garrison's fate. "I am too weak to save Vicksburg," Johnston wrote. "Can do no more than attempt to save you and your garrison. It will be impossible to extricate you unless you cooperate and we make mutually supporting movements. Communicate your plans and intentions if possible." A few days later, Pemberton replied that he could not hold out beyond the first few days of July. "My men have been thirty-four days and nights in the trenches, without relief, and the enemy within conversation distance," he informed Johnston. "We are living on very reduced rations, and, as you know, are extremely isolated. What aid am I to expect from you?"

Johnston suggested Pemberton try the impossible, given the half-starved condition of his troops—an escape across the Mississippi. He did, finally, put his field force in motion for Jackson, setting out on June 29, a day after Pemberton received what amounted to a threat of mutiny in the form of a petition from "many Soldiers" of the Vicksburg garrison.

"If you can't feed us," it read, "you had better surrender."

On July 3 Pemberton sent an emissary to Grant under a flag of truce. Pemberton wanted to discuss terms; Grant replied that he would accept nothing short of unconditional surrender. After thinking it over, and especially after calculating the number of river transports that would be required to ship 30,000 prisoners north, Grant relented. He offered to allow the Confederates to go home on parole—a promise not to take up arms again until they were exchanged for Federal captives.

That night, the troops observed an informal cease-fire. There were exchanges of news and gossip, and family reunions, too, through the short summer night. "Several brothers met," one Yankee remembered, "and any quantity of cousins." Pemberton surrendered at 10:00 AM on July 4, Independence Day, bringing the 48-day Siege of Vicksburg to a close.

On July 9 Federal forces led by General Nathaniel P. Banks captured Port Hudson, Louisiana, 240 miles to the south, the last remaining Confederate bastion on the Mississippi River. Here, too, a siege had followed unsuccessful efforts, by Union Admiral David Farragut to take seven vessels past the Confederate batteries overlooking the river (March 14, 1863). Banks's 45-five day siege resulted in the surrender of the garrison (6,000 men, 7,500 small arms, ammunition, and 2 river steamers) shortly after the arrival of word that Vicksburg had fallen. Victory at Vicksburg—perhaps the greatest Northern success of the Civil War—had cut the Confederacy in two and reopened the Mississippi from source to mouth. On July 16 a merchant steamboat glided up to the levee in New Orleans after an uneventful trip downriver from St. Louis.

"The father of waters," President Lincoln exulted, "again goes unvexed to the sea."

Right: In this F.B. Schell sketch, U.S. troops raise the Stars and Stripes over the Vicksburg courthouse on July 4, 1863. Grant's army took 27,000 officers and men prisoner and captured more than 200 field and siege guns as well as large quantities of ammunition and other supplies.

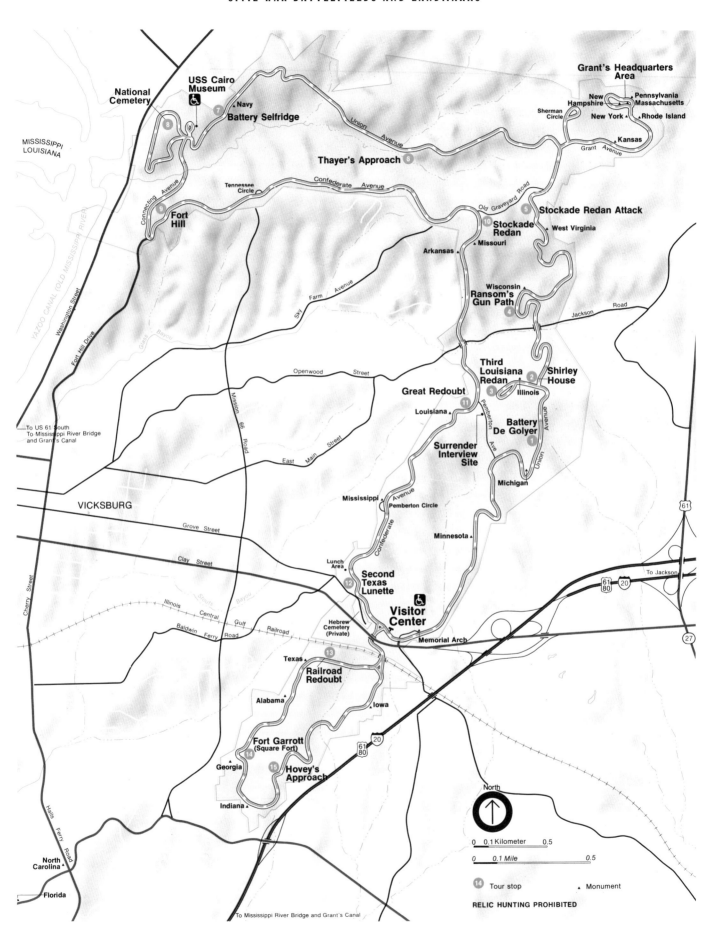

Grant's Headquarters Area

New Hampshire
Pennsylvania
Massachusetts
New York
Rhode Island
Sherman Circle
Kansas

USS Cairo Museum

National Cemetery

Navy

Battery Selfridge

Union Avenue

Grant Avenue

Thayer's Approach

MISSISSIPPI
LOUISIANA

Tennessee Circle

Confederate Avenue

Old Graveyard Road

Stockade Redan Attack

Stockade Redan

West Virginia

Fort Hill

Missouri

Arkansas

Connecting Avenue

Wisconsin

Ransom's Gun Path

Jackson Road

Sky Farm Avenue

Glass Bayou

Fort Hill Drive

YAZOO CANAL (OLD MISSISSIPPI RIVER)

Washington Street

Openwood Street

Third Louisiana Redan

Shirley House

Illinois

Great Redoubt

Louisiana

Battery De Golyer

Mission 66 Road

East Main Street

Surrender Interview Site

To US 61 South
To Mississippi River Bridge
and Grant's Canal

Michigan

VICKSBURG

Mississippi

Pemberton Circle

Grove Street

Minnesota

Clay Street

Cherry Street

Lunch Area

Second Texas Lunette

Illinois Central Gulf Railroad

Stouts Bayou

Baldwin Ferry Road

Hebrew Cemetery (Private)

Visitor Center

Memorial Arch

To Jackson

Texas

Railroad Redoubt

Alabama

Iowa

Fort Garrott (Square Fort)

Georgia

Hovey's Approach

Halls Ferry Road

Indiana

North Carolina

Florida

To Mississippi River Bridge and Grant's Canal

North

0   0.1 Kilometer   0.5
0   0.1 Mile   0.5

14 Tour stop   ▲ Monument

RELIC HUNTING PROHIBITED

The 16-mile battlefield tour begins at the Visitor Center off Clay Street.

1 Battery DeGolyer From here, guns of the 8th Michigan Artillery pounded the Confederate Great Redoubt just beyond. At one point during the siege, 22 great guns were mounted here.

2 Shirley House The "white house" to Union troops, it is the only surviving wartime building in the park. The 45th Illinois Infantry made its headquarters here.

3 Third Louisiana Redan This Confederate work commanded the Jackson Road approach to Vicksburg. Deciding it could not be taken by storm, Grant ordered his troops to tunnel under the fort and blow it up. Two mines were detonated but neither opened a breach in the line.

4 Ransom's Gun Path The 2nd Illinois Artillery, with help from Gen. Thomas Ransom's infantry, dismantled and dragged two 12-pound cannon over this trail to an earthen parapet 100 yards from the Confederate line.

5 Stockade Redan Attack Here and in this vicinity on May 19, 1863, Gen. William T. Sherman launched a series of attacks against Stockade Redan. Sherman's troops were driven off with heavy losses.

6 Thayer's Approach Brig. Gen. John M. Thayer led a Union attack up this hill on the afternoon of May 22nd. Thayer's troops used the tunnel under the road here to avoid the Confederate fire that swept the ridge.

7 Battery Selfridge U.S. Navy bluejackets manned the guns in this strongpoint, named after Lt. Cmdr. T.O. Selfridge, captain of the ironclad USS *Cairo*.

8 Vicksburg National Cemetery Established in 1866, this cemetery contains the remains of nearly 17,000 Union soldiers, including some 13,000 unknowns.

9 Fort Hill This bastion, so formidable that the Federals never hazarded an attack on it, anchored the Confederate left. Cannoneers here assisted the Vicksburg water batteries in the sinking of the gunboat *Cincinnati* on May 27, 1863.

10 Stockade Redan This Confederate fortification guarded the Old Graveyard Road approach to Vicksburg.

11 Great Redoubt Federal attacks here on May 22 were checked with heavy losses. Union great guns kept up a steady fire on this massive earthwork throughout the siege.

12 Second Texas Lunette The 2nd Texas Infantry manned this strongpoint, which commanded the Baldwin Ferry Road approach to Vicksburg. A furious battle boiled up here during the fighting of May 22.

13 Railroad Redoubt This stronghold protected the Southern Mississippi Railroad. Union forces overran it on May 22. The counterattacking Texas Legion regained the redoubt and, after a savage hand-to-hand encounter, drove the Federals out.

14 Fort Garrott Col. Isham Garrott's 20th Alabama held this bastion, where Garrott was killed on June 17th.

15 Hovey's Approach This is a restored section of two Union approach trenches. Col. Alvin P. Hovey's troops cut a zigzag trench to prevent enemy enfilade fire and keep Federal casualties to a minimum.

VICKSBURG NATIONAL MILITARY PARK

MAILING ADDRESS
Superintendent, Vicksburg National Military Park, 3201 Clay Street, Vicksburg, MS 39180

TELEPHONE
601-636-0583

DIRECTIONS
The park is located just inside Vicksburg on historic US 80, within one mile of I-20.

VISITOR CENTER
Interpretive audiovisual programs and exhibits, museum, and bookstore.

ACTIVITIES
Auto tours and guided and auto-tape tours. The U.S.S. Cairo Museum is adjacent to stop eight on the battlefield tour.

HOURS
The visitor center is open daily from 8:00 AM to 5 PM The tour road opens daily at 7 AM and closes at sunset. The U.S.S. Cairo Museum is open daily from 8:30 AM to 5 PM. Summer hours and programs are conducted from 9:30 AM until 6 PM, from June through mid-August. The park is closed on December 25.

Left: An equestrian statue of Ulysses S. Grant at Vicksburg. His capture of the great Confederate fortress proved to be one of the decisive episodes of the Civil War.

Chickamauga and Chattanooga

The contest for the Confederate heartland opened along the Duck River in middle Tennessee in late June 1863. It concluded an eventful five months later, just before the Northern Thanksgiving, on a high ridge commanding Chattanooga, the gateway to Georgia and the Deep South.

In one of the Civil War's decisive episodes, the opposing armies carried out a campaign of maneuver through the summer, clashed in the bloodiest battle of the war in the West at the time of the autumnal equinox, and endured numbing rain and cold in an early winter standoff in the Tennessee hills. In the end, one of the armies broke.

Chickamauga

In 1863 the Union Army of the Cumberland, led by General William S. Rosecrans, scored a series of bloodless successes late in the summer. Moving with speed and deception, Rosecrans forced Confederate General Braxton Bragg's Army of Tennessee to fall back through Chattanooga, across the Tennessee River, and into the Georgia hills. However, the Confederate retreat stopped in North Georgia. By mid-Sep-

THE TENNESSEE CAMPAIGN: CHICKAMAUGA

In the fall of 1863, Union forces led by General William S. Rosecrans advanced on Chattanooga. Confederate troops under General Braxton Bragg evacuated the city and attacked from nearby Chickamauga, Georgia, on **September 19–20, 1863,** driving the Union army back into the city. There they planned to cut supply lines on the Tennessee River and starve out the Northerners.

 USA General William S. Rosecrans; General George H. Thomas

 CSA General Braxton Bragg

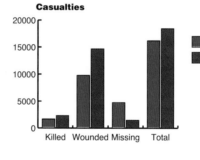

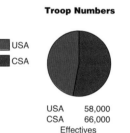

Troop Numbers

USA 58,000
CSA 66,000
Effectives

Left: This sketch from the evening of September 19, 1863, depicts one of the relentless series of Confederate charges during the Battle of Chickamauga. Union troops repulsed this attack, but were ultimately overwhelmed after a fatal gap opened their line.

tember, with substantial reinforcements in hand or on the way, including the 12,000-strong corps of General James Longstreet coming by rail from Virginia—a major logistical success—Bragg reversed direction and lashed out at the advancing Federals.

Only Confederate tactical mismanagement (not all of it Bragg's fault) spared the overconfident, overextended Rosecrans from disaster. Two attempts to pounce on elements of the divided Army of the Cumberland misfired. By the third week of September, Rosecrans had the army concentrated in the wooded, vine-choked valley of West Chickamauga Creek, a dozen miles south of Chattanooga.

The armies' outriders closed with each other on September 18th. The van of Longstreet's two divisions reached Bragg that day. At daybreak on the 19th, Saturday, the Federal XIV Corps under General George H. Thomas opened fire on probing Confederates near Jay's Mill, just west of Chickamauga Creek, touching off a general engagement.

The armies were roughly equal in size, each with some 65,000 men. The initiative lay with Bragg, whose first efforts were aimed at Thomas on the Union left. As the Federals fell back slowly to the LaFayette Road (now U.S. 27), Bragg's attack evolved into a series of savage individual encounters, defying overall control. Smoke from the discharge of thousands of muskets rose into the forest canopy and hung there, trapped. Only rarely could the opposing infantry see more than a few yards ahead through the dense undergrowth and stinging smoke.

Years later, an Indiana veteran recalled the day's fighting: "There was no generalship in it," wrote Colonel John T. Wilder. "It was a soldier's fight purely, wherein the only question involved was the question of endurance. The armies came together like two wild beasts, and each fought as long as it could stand up in a knock down and drag out encounter. If there had been any high order of generalship displayed, the disasters to both armies might have been less."

The fighting spread from north to south through the woods and ravines of the Chickamauga Valley. Thomas's corps held, though just barely, on the Union left. After noon, Bragg shifted his main effort southward, against Rosecrans's center and right. The Federals withstood the onslaught there, too, and with the last of the daylight, the battle sputtered out. As night fell, the sound of axes rang through the woods—Yankee troops furiously at work building log-and-brush breastworks against an expected renewal of the battle Sunday morning.

In a late-night council of war, Rosecrans and his corps commanders decided to remain in place and await events. On the other side of the line, Bragg reorganized his army into two wings, the right under General Leonidas Polk, the left under Longstreet, who had only just reached the battlefield. Bragg directed Polk to open the proceedings at dawn. The attack would continue in echelon from north to south, passing from Polk to Longstreet.

Polk's assault jumped off late—not until 9:30 AM, in fact, some four hours behind schedule. On the extreme left, the Federals stopped the initial Confederate charge. The eche-

EYEWITNESS

From a letter by Benjamin Abbott, aide to Confederate general Henry Benning of Georgia, on the victory at Chickamauga dated September 26, 1863:

Shouts began to go up from the right, and we knew it was our boys. It soon spread along the whole line. The enemy was firing away all along the line. On the left, musketry was heavy but retiring, the cannon seeming to play a small part in it. The yell of victory became louder and fiercer as the sun declined. There seemed to be no enemy in our front. General Benning ordered me to go forward a short distance to see what was in front. We had become afraid of firing into our own men and being fired into by them. I went as ordered and came to the Chattanooga road. I was sure I saw the enemy sending men across attempting to reinforce their left. I rode back and told what I had seen. General Benning suggested artillery and sent a courier to the division commander for it. In a few minutes a number of pieces were sending shell down that road like lightning. I watched from behind one of the guns and saw with intense excitement the shot as it would rise, curve over and explode at the very spot aimed among the demoralized Federals....

Around us the enemy's dead and wounded lay very thick. I walked among them, while we waited for orders. I came upon a young officer and found he was mortally wounded and suffering very much. I saw at once he would die and asked if I could do anything for him. He replied, "I am dying. Wash me clean and bury me decently." I promised him all I could under the circumstances and asked his name. His answer was, "Lieutenant Colonel D.J. Hall of Chicago." I had him moved in the hut and in less than an hour he died. As far as I could I complied with his request and marked his grave with board on which I carved his name with my knife....In my own heart before the battle I felt very bitter against these men who had invaded our soil, as I believe against every principle of right, and yet in the hour of victory we soldiers were touched with pity for these wounded and dying enemies. It was not the place to discuss right and wrong: it was simply a question of humanity.

lon attack rippled on down the line. Thomas's corps stood its ground through the morning, aided by a steady stream of fresh troops drawn from Rosecrans's right.

Toward noon, Longstreet's turn came. By then the frequent comings and goings of troops had created some confusion in the Federal command. Someone reported, mistakenly as it happened, that one such shift had opened a gap in the center of the line. Acting on the report, Rosecrans put a front-line division in motion to fill the place—in fact, creating a gap where none had existed before. Longstreet's 16,000-strong storming column broke out of the woods, swept across the LaFayette Road, and drove straight for the opening.

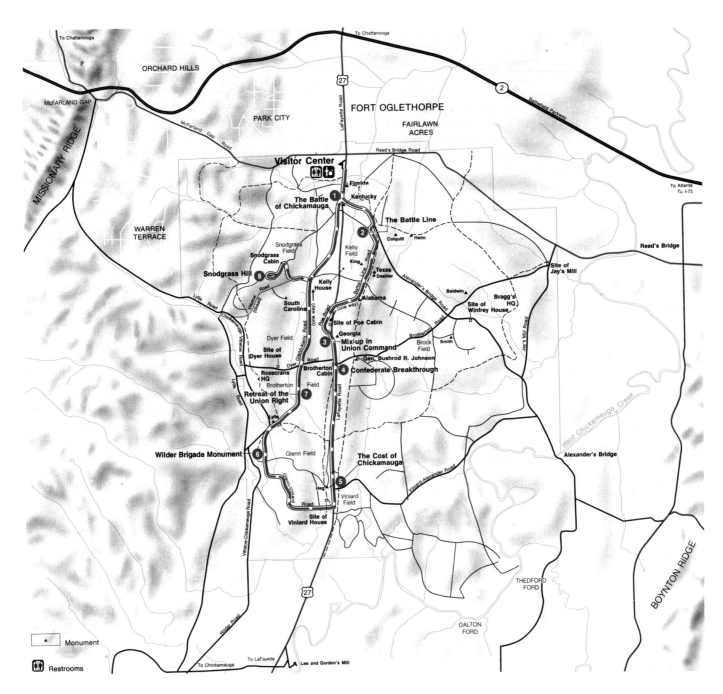

1 Battle of Chickamauga

Union and Confederate forces clashed in the dense woods of the valley of Chickamauga Creek in northwest Georgia. Monuments and markers along the tour road establish the locations of units that took part in the two-day encounter.

2 The Battle Line The

second day's battle opened near here on Sunday, September 20.

3 Mix-up in the Union Command Around 11:00 AM, Rose-

crans received an erroneous report that one of the center divisions had drifted out of position, leaving a gap in the line. In moving another division to fill the non-existent opening, Rosecrans in fact created one.

4 Confederate Breakthrough

Confederate Gen. James Longstreet launched his attack toward the just-opened gap.

5 The Cost of Chickamauga

One of the war's bloodiest battles, Chickamauga cost the Confederates more than 18,000 casualties. The monuments across the road mark troop positions on September 19.

6 Wilder Tower This 85-foot

monument honors Col. John Wilder and his brigade of mounted infantry. It stands on the site of Rosecrans' tactical headquarters.

7 Retreat of the Union Right

Longstreet's attack shattered the Federal line and sent thousands of fugitives streaming back toward Chattanooga. Rosecrans and two of his corps commanders joined the flight.

8 Snodgrass Hill Here George

Thomas earned the sobriquet "the Rock of Chickamauga."

It was one of the war's great strokes of fortune. Encountering slight resistance, Longstreet's infantry advanced a full mile into the Federal rear. On either side of the Confederate wedge, Federal units broke and ran, racing in panic for McFarland's Gap and the safety of the far slope of Missionary Ridge.

The swelling roar of Longstreet's attack interrupted the catnap of the War Department observer Charles Dana. When he looked up, he saw Rosecrans making the sign of the cross. "Hello," Dana said to himself. "If the general is crossing himself, we are in a desperate situation." As the larger scene swam into focus, Dana saw that the entire Federal right wing had been blown away "like leaves before the wind." Yipping the Rebel yell, the Confederate infantry came surging through in an unstoppable wave. As the disaster unfolded, Rosecrans turned to his staff and said calmly: "If you care to live any longer, get away from here."

Thousands of Yankees already had figured that out for themselves. They choked the roads back to Chattanooga and safety. From time to time, one conscientious officer or another would stop to deliver a harangue to the retreating infantry. "We'll talk to you, my son, when we get to the Ohio River," one veteran called out to a young staff colonel who tried to stem the flow.

On the left, meantime, Thomas—who had held fast against Confederate pressure all day—pulled back to a shorter, stronger line on the rise of Snodgrass Hill, deployed such scattered units from the right as had not set off in full flight for Chattanooga, and fought on through the afternoon.

Later, Longstreet estimated that the Confederates launched twenty-five separate charges at Thomas, whose refusal to yield earned him the sobriquet of "the Rock of Chickamauga." Thomas's stand saved what remained of the Army of the Cumberland. At about 5:00 PM, an hour or so before sundown, he issued orders for a withdrawal. The first troops began pulling out of the line half an hour later. By nightfall Thomas had disengaged the entire corps and set it on the road for McFarland's Gap.

"Like magic," wrote Longstreet, "the Union army had melted away in our presence."

For the record, the Confederates had won a smashing victory, breaking up a Yankee army and taking 8,000 prisoners, 51 guns, and thousands of small arms. Longstreet and others pressed Bragg to organize a rapid pursuit toward Chattanooga. The commanding general refused. Confederate casualties had been crippling—20,000 men killed, wounded, or missing over two days, roughly 30 percent of the army's strength. There would be time enough, Bragg thought, to occupy the high ground around Chattanooga and starve the enemy into surrender.

The failure to follow up the tactical victory of Chickamauga disgusted Bragg's chief subordinates, then and later. One of the most aggressive and outspoken of them, the cavalry commander Nathan Bedford Forrest, could barely contain his anger when he learned that Bragg intended to let the beaten and demoralized Army of the Cumberland escape.

"What does he fight battles for?" Forrest snarled.

Chattanooga

Two days after the battle, Bragg's forces occupied the heights of Missionary Ridge, planted artillery on Lookout Mountain, and posted infantry at the Tennessee River crossings, essentially sealing off Chattanooga. Confederate command of the rail and wagon routes into the town left the defenders with only one tenuous supply line, a rough mountain road over the Cumberlands from the north.

In Washington, President Lincoln and his secretary of war, Edwin Stanton, acted swiftly to contain the disaster. Two corps of the Army of the Potomac, the 11th and 12th under General Joseph Hooker, were detached and sent west by railroad. These troops would more than make up for Rosecrans's Chickamauga losses of about 15,000 killed, wounded, and missing. In addition, General William T. Sherman and the Army of the Tennessee were en route to Chattanooga.

Stanton also made changes at the top. He relieved two of Rosecrans's corps commanders and considered removing Rosecrans as well. Defeat had paralyzed the commanding general. "Our fate is in the hands of God," he wired Lincoln resignedly. Rosecrans seemed, the president thought, "confused and stunned, like a duck hit on the head." In mid-October, Lincoln assigned General Ulysses S. Grant to command the newly created Department of the Mississippi, with headquarters in the field—Chattanooga. Grant at once replaced Rosecrans with George Thomas.

Grant's advent meant immediate relief for the troops. He put in train a series of operations that broke the siege and

THE TENNESSEE CAMPAIGN: CHATTANOOGA

Grant, now commander of all Western forces, replaced Rosecrans with General George H. Thomas, who had distinguished himself at Chickamauga. Grant led part of his Army of the Tennessee to Chattanooga, where the Union won a decisive victory on **November 23-25, 1863**. The eastern half of the Confederacy was split in two when Chattanooga became the base for Union incursions into Georgia and Alabama.

 USA: General Grant, General Philip Sheridan, General Joseph Hooker, General William T. Sherman

 CSA: General Braxton Bragg, Major General William J. Hardee, Lt. General Patrick Cleburne

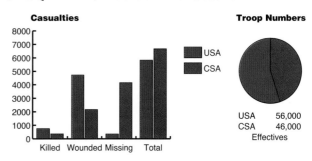

Casualties

Troop Numbers

USA 56,000
CSA 46,000
Effectives

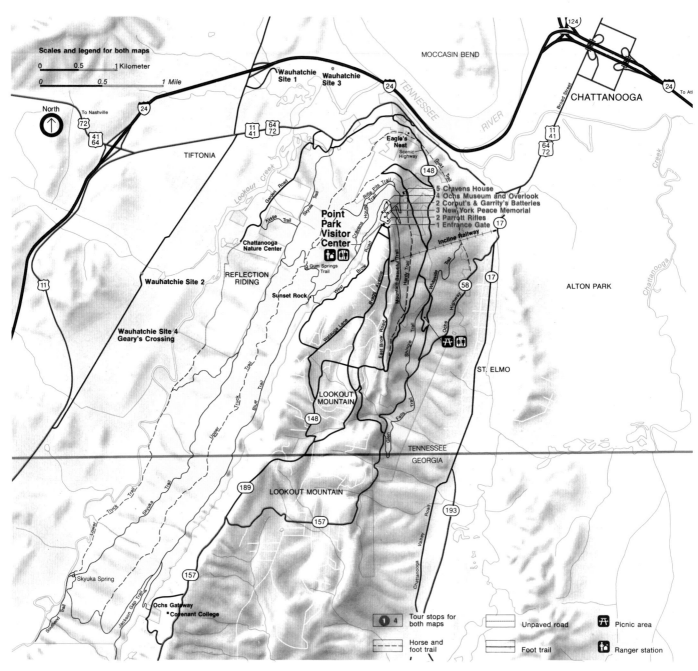

Scales and legend for both maps
0   0.5   1 Kilometer
0   0.5   1 Mile

North
72
41
64
24
To Nashville

TIFTONIA

Wauhatchie Site 1
Wauhatchie Site 3

24
TENNESSEE RIVER

MOCCASIN BEND

CHATTANOOGA
Broad Street
24   To Atl
11
41
64
72

11
41
64
72

11
41

Eagle's
Nest
Scenic
Highway
148

5 Cravens House
4 Ochs Museum and Overlook
2 Corput's & Garrity's Batteries
3 New York Peace Memorial
2 Parrott Rifles
1 Entrance Gate
17

Rifle Pits Trail
Cravens House Trail

Point
Park
Visitor
Center

Chattanooga
Nature Center

Garden Road
Skyuka Trail
Kiddie Trail

REFLECTION
RIDING

Gum Springs Trail
Weir Trail

Bragg Avenue
East Brow Road

Mountain Beautiful Trail
Hardy Trail

Whiteside Trail

Ochs Highway

58
17

Incline Railway

ALTON PARK

Chattanooga Creek

Wauhatchie Site 2

Sunset Rock

Wauhatchie Site 4
Geary's Crossing

Truck Trail
Bluff Trail

Upper Trail

Wehutty Lane

LOOKOUT
MOUNTAIN
148

ST. ELMO

Shingle Trail

Glen Falls Trail

Ochs

TENNESSEE
GEORGIA

Lower Trail
Truck Trail
Skyuka Trail

189

LOOKOUT MOUNTAIN

157

193

Chattanooga Valley Road

Skyuka Spring

157

Jackson Gap Trail

Ochs Gateway
Covenant College

1   4   Tour stops for
both maps

Horse and
foot trail

Unpaved road

Foot trail

Picnic area

Ranger station

opened the "Cracker Line"—so named for the army's hard-bread staple food—into Chattanooga. Soon goods of all kinds were pouring in. Sherman turned up in mid-November. With some 60,000 men and a now reliable supply line, Grant prepared to take the offensive against Bragg on Missionary Ridge.

The besiegers, it turned out, had been as hungry, cold, and demoralized as the besieged. "Nothing to eat but we are well supplied with lice," a Florida soldier remarked wryly. Bragg's army had been weakened as well by the detachment of Longstreet's corps, sent northeast to recapture Knoxville for the Confederacy. Dissension wracked the senior leadership of the Army of Tennessee. Most of Bragg's lieutenants detested him.

Grant's battle plan gave the leading role to Sherman on the left, with supporting help from Hooker's two corps on the right, opposite Lookout Mountain. Grant assigned a minor part to

the Army of the Cumberland in the center. Thomas's troops, still under the cloud of Chickamauga, were merely to demonstrate against the Confederate center on Missionary Ridge.

The battle opened well. Sherman saw his four divisions across the Tennessee River without incident on November 24th. On the right, Hooker's troops captured Lookout Mountain against light resistance, moving upslope in a heavy mist that gave the encounter the name "Battle Above the Clouds." The main event on November 25 went less smoothly, at least at first. A Confederate division under Patrick Cleburne fought Sherman to a standstill through the morning. Suspecting (wrongly) that Bragg had been borrowing from the center to strengthen Cleburne, Grant directed Thomas to take the Confederate advance line at the base of Missionary Ridge, an operation conceived to ease the pressure on Sherman.

Point Park/Lookout Mountain is a walking tour that involves some fairly steep steps.

1 The Entrance Gate The U.S. Army Corps of Engineers built this monument in 1905.

2 The Batteries The three gun batteries in the park are a small surviving part of the Chattanooga siege lines. The first consists of two Parrott rifles. The second, Garrity's Battery of Napoleon 12-pounder cannon, overlooks the valley. The third, Corput's Battery, is near the western overlook from which Sunset Rock may be seen. Longstreet observed the Wauhatchie Valley night attack from the rock.

3 New York Peace Memorial On the top of the shaft of the 95-foot-high monument, Union and Confederate soldiers shake hands under one flag.

4 The Ochs Museum and Overlook High above the Tennessee River, the museum exhibits and pictures tell the story of the struggle for Chattanooga and the city's strategic importance as a communications center and a gateway to Atlanta and the Deep South.

5 Cravens House Some of the hardest fighting on Lookout Mountain took place here. Union artillery fire badly damaged the house, which the Confederates used as a headquarters.

6 The Bluff Trail This main hiking trail is reached by way of metal steps to the left of the Ochs Museum. Here Kentucky troops climbed to Lookout Point to plant the American flag. A number of well-marked trails branch off from the main trail.

Right: The scene of battle at Lookout Mountain.

Thomas's attack decided the battle. At 3:30 PM, 23,000 troops of the Army of the Cumberland advanced on a 2-mile front and swept over Bragg's first-line rifle pits. The Confederates fell back to a second line midway up the ridge, where they began to pour effective fire into the Yankees below. "We can't live here," concluded a Federal regimental commander. At about the same time, the assault troops reached an unspoken consensus. Faced with the choice of continuing uphill or dropping back, they opted to resume the advance. From his command post on Orchard Knob, Grant watched anxiously.

"Thomas, who ordered those men up the ridge?" he asked. "I don't know," Thomas answered. "I did not."

The Federal wave broke over the second line. Groups of infantry scrambled on uphill, finding cover among the rocks and in slight dips of ground. The defenders fell back in disorder. Forty-five minutes after the bugles sounded the advance, the Federals reached the crest of Missionary Ridge.

There the Confederate front wavered, then collapsed. Bluecoats shouting "Chickamauga!" swarmed over the top of the ridge and sent the dazed enemy stumbling down the reverse slope. "My God, come see them run!" an Indiana infantryman called out.

The outcome of this improvised assault seemed a miracle— "as awful," in Charles Dana's words, "as a visible interposition of God." Bragg's army kept on going south, covering some thirty miles down the road to Atlanta before slowing to an exhausted halt around Dalton, Georgia. Bragg hardly knew what to make of the rout. "No satisfactory excuse can possibly be given for the shameful conduct of our troops," he wrote the Confederate president, Jefferson Davis. In Bragg's view, a line of skirmishers ought to have been able to hold Missionary Ridge.

Grant felt the same way. No more than Bragg could he account for the miracle. Told years later that the Confederate high command had believed the Missionary Ridge line to be impregnable, Grant thought for a moment, then replied: "Well, it *was* impregnable.

CHICKAMAUGA AND CHATTANOOGA NATIONAL MILITARY PARK

MAILING ADDRESS
Superintendent, Chickamauga and Chattanooga National Military Park, PO Box 2128, Fort Oglethorpe, GA 30742

TELEPHONE
706-866-9241

DIRECTIONS
The Chickamauga Unit is located near Fort Oglethorpe on US 27 off I-75 south of Chattanooga. The Point Park and Lookout Mountain Units are just west of downtown Chattanooga off US 64/72. The Orchard Knob Unit is located in downtown Chattanooga off Orchard Knob Avenue. The Missionary Ridge Units are located just east of downtown Chattanooga on Crest Road.

VISITOR CENTERS
Museum, bookstore, research facilities, interpretive exhibits, a twenty-six-minute multimedia presentation on the Battle of Chickamauga., and the Fuller Collection of American Military Arms.

ACTIVITIES
Living history demonstrations, hiking, self-guided auto tour (rental tapes are available), and horseback riding.

HOURS
The park is open 24 hours except for the Lookout Mountain Unit, which is open during the Visitor Center hours, from 8 AM to 4:45 PM, with hours extended to 5:45 PM in the summer. The park is closed December 25.

Brices Cross Roads

One of General William T. Sherman's greatest concerns during his invasion of Georgia was the ever-increasing length of his supply lines, especially the single line of track from Nashville to Chattanooga. It was vulnerable to guerrilla bands and raiders commissioned by the Confederacy, and the lack of food and equipment in the South made the Union supply trains essential. At one point, Sherman wrote that "the Atlanta Campaign was an impossibility" without a secure supply line.

One of the fiercest Confederate raiders was General Nathan Bedford Forrest, whose exploits at Shiloh had made him well known to both sides. Early in 1864, Forrest had obtained an independent command from President Davis; in May his cavalrymen were harrying Federal forces in northeast Mississippi. Then Lieutenant General Stephen D. Lee sent orders to move against Sherman's supply line in Middle Tennessee in the hope of slowing—perhaps stopping—the Federal advance toward Atlanta.

Sherman planned a preemptive attack on Forrest and sent an expedition of 8,000 men to Mississippi from Union-held Memphis to find and destroy the raider's command. Brigadier General Samuel D. Sturgis—who had taken command of the Union forces at Wilson's Creek after the death of General Lyon—was commander of cavalry in the military dis-

BRILLIANT GENERALSHIP AT BRICES CROSS ROADS

In a battle that demonstrated the tactical skill of Confederate major general Nathan Bedford Forrest, his outnumbered cavalrymen routed a Union force in densely forested Brices Cross Roads, Mississippi, on **June 10, 1864.** Union general Samuel D. Sturgis retreated to Memphis, pursued by Forrest's troops for more than twenty miles. The Confederates captured much-needed supplies, but the Union defeat was only temporary.

 USA Brigadier General Samuel D. Sturgis

 CSA Major General Nathan Bedford Forrest

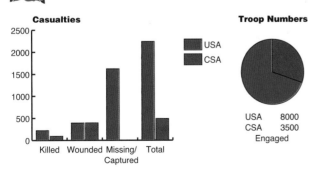

trict of West Tennessee and led the expedition. On June 1, Sturgis and his troops left Memphis and made their way into northern Mississippi, heading toward the Confederate position at Tupelo.

On June 3, Forrest was recalled from Russellville, Alabama, where he was poised to attack Sherman's supply line, and ordered to combat the Federal force advancing through Mississippi. Forrest and his raiders hurried back, took up positions north of Tupelo, and waited for Sturgis. Outnumbered more than two to one, Forrest selected familar territory—a densely wooded area known as Brice's Cross Roads—from which to attack. His strategy was twofold: to conceal the fact that his force was a small one and to attack and dispense with the Union cavalry before the infantry arrived. He assumed that the infantry would hasten its pace once the battle began and that the troops marching double time in the June heat would arrive exhausted. His assessment proved remarkably accurate.

Forrest reached Tupelo on June 9, divided his 3,500 men into four brigades, and sent them out on patrol. The first contact between the two forces took place at 9:45 AM, when Union cavalrymen commanded by General Grierson came up against one of Forrest's patrols. They chased the Confederates down the Baldwyn Road until they were confronted by a brigade of dismounted cavalry. The Confederates drew the enemy into a fight and defended themselves until relieved by more troops commanded by Forrest himself.

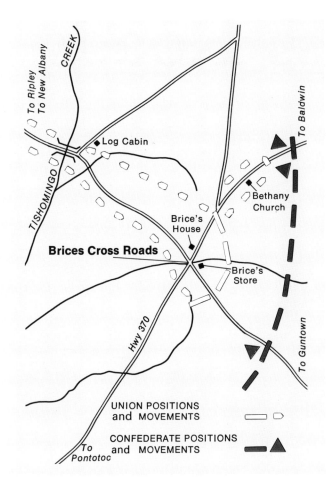

To Ripley
To New Albany

CREEK

Log Cabin

TISHOMINGO

Brice's House

Bethany Church

To Baldwin

Brices Cross Roads

Brice's Store

Hwy 370

To Guntown

To Pontotoc

UNION POSITIONS and MOVEMENTS

CONFEDERATE POSITIONS and MOVEMENTS

The small site provides a view of the area of action.

1 Confederate Positions One mile behind Bethany Church and Brice's Store, General Nathan Bedford Forrest's troops waited in the woods, poised to attack. They pushed the Union forces back toward the river.

2 Union Positions Heading toward Tupelo, General Samuel D. Sturgis marched his men over the river toward Brice's House and the cross roads where disaster awaited.

3 Tishomingo Bridge Exhausted Federal troops were routed, and their retreat was impeded by a toppled supply wagon on the bridge and by the rain-swollen river.

Opposite: A memorial to those fallen at Brices Cross Roads, the site of a major Confederate victory.

BRICE'S CROSS ROADS NATIONAL BATTLEFIELD SITE

MAILING ADDRESS
Superintendent, Natchez Trace Parkway, RR 1, NT-143, Tupelo, MS 38801

TELEPHONE
601-680-4025

DIRECTIONS
The site is located six miles west of Baldwyn, Mississippi, on MS 370.

VISITOR CENTER
There are no visitor facilities or park personnel at the site; information can be obtained at Tupelo Visitor Center.

ACTIVITIES
Folders are available at the site. Signs and markers provide interpretation. Ten granite markers with bronze tablets on the highway leading to the site, describe the action that took place at specific locations and list the units involved.

HOURS
Open 24 hours, closed December 25.

As he had planned, Forrest was able to defeat the Union cavalry before the infantry arrived. In fact, Sturgis, hearing the sounds of battle in the distance, ordered his men to move even faster in the punishing heat. They arrived on the field exhausted, just as Forrest had predicted. Forrest attacked the raggedly formed Union line, and after two hours of a ferocious frontal assault combined with charges on both flanks, the Federal troops began to give way. They withdrew in an orderly fashion until they reached Tishimingo Creek. During the retreat, a wagon had overturned on the only bridge crossing the stream and blocked it. The Union soldiers were forced to seek fords up- and downstream through water swollen by the recent rains. This increased their sense of panic, and the retreat became a rout. The Confederates pursued until nightfall and resumed the chase in the early hours of the morning, capturing hundreds of men. Not until the morning of June 13 did Sturgis and his remaining soldiers limp back into Memphis.

Forrest's victory over a force more than twice the size of his own gave a great psychological boost to the Confederate cause. His plan for Brice's Cross Roads became a model for the twofold use of cavalry, both mounted and dismounted to serve as infantry. Brice's Cross Roads also earned the Confederates a dozen cannon and 170 wagons loaded with ammunition, food, and 5,000 stands of badly needed small arms. However, in deflecting Forrest from Sherman's supply lines, it benefited the Union cause.

EYEWITNESS

From a letter to Secretary of War Edwin M. Stanton by General William T. Sherman after Union forces in Mississippi were defeated by Confederate general Nathan Bedford Forrest.

"I will have the matter of Sturgis critically examined, and if he should be at fault he shall have no mercy at my hands. I cannot but believe he had troops enough. I know I would have been willing to attempt the same task with that force; but Forrest is the devil, and I think he has got some of our troops under cover. I have two officers at Memphis who will fight all the time…I will order them to make up a force and go out and follow Forrest to the death, if it cost ten thousand lives and breaks the Treasury. There will never be peace in Tennessee until Forrest is dead!"

Tupelo

Almost before the smoke of Brice's Cross Roads had cleared, Sherman had taken new steps to ensure that Forrest would be stopped. After the battle, he wrote to Edwin M. Stanton, the secretary of war, "I have two officers at Memphis that will fight all the time. I will order them to go out and make up a force and follow Forrest to the death, even if it cost ten thousand lives and breaks the Treasury. There will never be peace in Tennessee until Forrest is dead."

In early July, Major General Andrew Jackson Smith and Brigadier General James Mower led a force of 14,000, including a brigade of black troops and 24 cannon, out of Memphis toward northern Mississippi. Following Sherman's orders, Smith's soldiers practiced the same destruction on Confederate civilian property that would mark the March to the Sea. Both Forrest and Lieutenant General Lee realized that the Union troops had been ordered to prevent Confederate attacks on Sherman's supply lines. Through their scouts and pickets, they learned that Smith's force was approaching Tupelo, a station on the Mobile and Ohio Railroad—an important Confederate supply line.

Union troops reached Tupelo on July 13 and began a systematic and rapid destruction of the railroad. Then they moved west to the small town of Harrisburg, which had been deserted by its inhabitants. Here they built a defensive network out of cotton bales, pieces of fencing, and anything else that came to hand against the expected Confederate assault.

This came at 7:00 AM on July 14, when the Confederates, who now numbered approximately 9,500, launched themselves against the Union defenses. They had been ordered to attack simultaneously, but in the confusion a number of brigades went forward on their own and unsuccessfully, "all gallantry and useless sacrifice," in a series of frontal assaults. Smith's force pushed each one back with cannon and concentrated mus-

SHERMAN'S SUPPLY LINE SECURED

After the Battle of Brice's Cross Roads, General Nathan Bedford Forrest's Confederate cavalry battled another Union force, in Tupelo, Mississippi, on **July 13–14, 1864**. Technically, the battle ended in a draw, but the Federals frustrated Forrest's attempt to disrupt General Sherman's supply line, thus ensuring the successful invasion of Georgia.

 USA Major General Andrew Jackson Smith

 CSA Major General Nathan Bedford Forrest

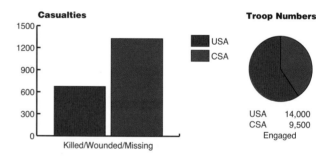

Casualties

Troop Numbers

	USA	CSA

USA	14,000
CSA	9,500
	Engaged

Killed/Wounded/Missing

ket fire, and by 1:00 PM, the fighting had let up. Forrest made another attack during the night, using the Union campfires to aim his artillery. This, however was equally unsuccessful, as was a subsequent attack against the Union left flank.

The following day, in a somewhat surprising move for a victorious army, the Union force, now low on ammunition and rations, began to move back toward La Grange, one of the stops on their march from Memphis, while the Confederates continued to attack the column and the rear guard. During one assault, at Old Town Creek, Forrest was wounded, and many soldiers on both sides fell to heat exhaustion. Smith continued to withdraw and by July 23 was back in Memphis.

The Battle of Tupelo, a Union victory for its impact on Forrest, had cost Forrest 1,326 men, against 674 Union casualties. It also succeeded in keeping him away from the Federal supply lines, even if he had not been followed "to the death." Sherman and his men were now on the outskirts of Atlanta.

The following month, when Smith commanded another expedition to keep the Confederates away from Sherman's supply lines, Forrest and his men raided Memphis. In the fall, Forrest made another incursion into western Tennessee. He also commanded the cavalry during the disastrous Tennessee campaign of late 1864. Promoted to lieutenant general in February 1865, Forrest soon suffered one of his few failures when he was unable to stop a Union raid on Selma, Alabama. He and his men did not surrender to a Union force until May 4, 1865, almost a month after Lee met Grant at Appomattox.

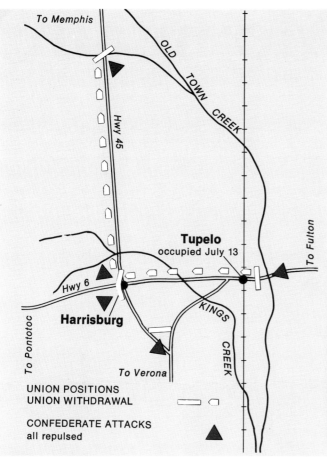

To Memphis

OLD TOWN CREEK

Hwy 45

To Fulton

Tupelo
occupied July 13

Hwy 6

KINGS CREEK

Harrisburg

To Pontotoc

To Verona

UNION POSITIONS
UNION WITHDRAWAL

CONFEDERATE ATTACKS
all repulsed

1 Visitor Center The center is near the location of Confederate lines where General Nathan Bedford Forrest's attack plan was bungled, resulting in an uncoordinated assault that was "all gallantry and useless sacrifice."

2 Union Positions The Federal army retreated toward Memphis, despite its success in repulsing Confederate attacks in Tupelo and Harrisburg. Forrest was wounded in the pursuit.

3 Mobile and Ohio Railroad This rail line was a vital Confederate supply line, which Union forces destroyed before they were attacked.

TUPELO NATIONAL BATTLEFIELD

MAILING ADDRESS
Superintendent, Natchez Trace Parkway, RR 1, NT-143, Tupelo, MS 38801

TELEPHONE
601-680-4025

DIRECTIONS
The one-acre site is within the city limits of Tupelo, Mississippi, on MS 6 about one-and-one-third miles west of its intersection with US 45. It is one mile east of the Natchez Trace Parkway.

VISITOR CENTER
Park interpreters can provide information on the Tupelo and Brice's Cross Roads battlefields.

ACTIVITIES
Folders are available on site. Signs and markers provide interpretation.

HOURS
The Visitor Center is open from 8 AM to 5 PM.

Opposite: The Tupelo Battlefield Memorial near the Visitor Center honors both Union and Confederate soldiers.

Left: A sultry sunrise presages the heat that sapped the strength of both armies.

Kennesaw Mountain

I n March 1864, Ulysses S. Grant was promoted to the rank of lieutenant general and, soon after, appointed commander of all the Union armies, as general-in-chief. He quickly developed a strategy for Federal forces on all fronts of the conflict that included a policy of total war. This would bring the conflict to the civilian population, whom he saw as opponents to be conquered, exactly like enemy troops. One campaign was to cut through the center of Georgia, one of the few granaries left to the Confederacy, with troops commanded by Grant's old friend William Tecumseh Sherman. His orders from Grant were "to move against [Joseph E.] Johnston's army, to break it up, and to get into the interior of the enemy's country as far as you can, inflicting all the damage you can against their War resources." Sherman wrote about the campaign. "Atlanta was too important a place in the hands of the enemy to be left undisturbed, with its magazines, stores, arsenals, workshops, foundries, and more especially its railroads, which converged there from the four great cardinal points."

On May 6, 1864, Sherman set off from Chattanooga, Tennessee, with a force totaling almost 110,000 men, divided into three columns, and 254 pieces of artillery. The 60,000-man Army of the Cumberland, commanded by General George Thomas, marched in the center. The Army of the Tennessee, (General James B. McPherson, with 30,000 troops) was on the right, and the Army of the Ohio, 17,000 troops, under General John M. Schofield, on the left.

General Joseph E. Johnston, commanding the Confederate Army of Tennessee (together with corps from the Army of the Mississippi under the command of Lieutenant General Leonidas Polk, who was also the Episcopal Bishop of Louisiana) knew that an offensive campaign against Sherman with his smaller force would be suicidal. Instead, he planned a defensive strategy, constantly blocking Sherman's advance toward Atlanta and using his knowledge of the countryside to place his 65,000 men and 187 artillery pieces in the best-defended and -protected positions. Johnston also had to safeguard the Western & Atlantic Railroad, which ran up from Atlanta to Chattanooga and served as his supply route. At the same time, he was forced to destroy a number of railroad bridges to the north and pull up track to delay Sherman's movements, since Union forces were also using the Western & Atlantic line, as a link to their supply base at Nashville and a route into enemy territory. They replaced the destroyed track and bridges quickly with supplies brought in from the North.

Because he had surveyed much of the Georgia countryside as a young lieutenant fresh out of West Point, Sherman was also familiar with the terrain and could make calculated guesses on how Johnston would deploy his men. To avoid a head-on

ON THE ROAD TO ATLANTA

The battle of Kennesaw Mountain, on **June 27, 1864,** was the climax of the hard-fought Atlanta Campaign. General William T. Sherman and his armies made a frontal assault on strong Confederate positions commanded by General Joseph E. Johnston, who had impeded the Federal advance against Atlanta since May. Here, too, Union forces were set back, but a week later, Sherman outflanked his adversary and resumed his drive on Atlanta.

 USA General William T. Sherman

 CSA General Joseph E. Johnston; General Benjamin F. Cheatham

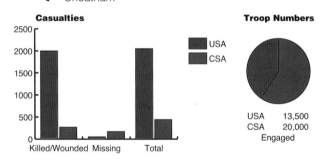

assault, Sherman favored a series of flanking attacks to maneuver around his opponent. Slowly but surely, he did, in fact, press Johnston's Confederates back, sending the Army of the Tennessee on a secret march to attack the railroad near Resaca. The Confederates were too strongly entrenched at Dalton for McPherson's men to move them, but several days later they were forced to withdraw to Resaca and then further south, when Sherman's men crossed the Oostanaula River and threatened the railroad again.

By the end of May, Sherman's armies had fought with the Confederates at New Hope Church, Pickett's Mill, and Dallas, while trying to outflank Johnston's men in the Allatoona Mountains at Cassville. The engagements were undecided, although Sherman's casualties—4,500—surpassed the Confederates', who lost only 3,000 men. Johnston retreated again, this time into a strong defensive position in a ten-mile-long line running from Brush Mountain to Pine and Lost Mountains. Sherman described the scene as follows: "On each of these peaks, the enemy and his signal station, the summits were crowned with batteries and the spurs alive with men busy in felling trees, digging pits and preparing for the grand struggle impending." The Federals placed their guns as well as they could and on June 14, during a barrage aimed at a group of Confederate officers, including Johnston and his subordinates, they killed General Polk.

After further skirmishing, Sherman moved to the left, and on June 19 Johnston withdrew to a new line at Kennesaw Mountain, west of Marietta and only twenty miles from Atlanta. Here, on a site described by one Union soldier as "about 700 feet high and entirely separated from all mountain ranges and swelling up like a great bulb from the plain," the Confederates established artillery positions, trenches, and rifle pits among the natural ravines and steep rock escarpments. To prevent discreet maneuvering by the Federals, they cut down a number of trees, opening up the hillsides to reveal the obvious approach routes.

Sherman and his men besieged Kennesaw Mountain, setting up artillery batteries to shell the Confederates out of their positions. On June 21, the Federals tried a flanking maneuver, extending their lines to the south at Kolb's Farm, below the left flank of the Confederate line. However, this was soon observed and repulsed by a Confederate force under General John B. Hood.

On June 27, Sherman decided to attack. Perhaps he believed that the Confederate line was extremely thin, since it had been stretched so far. He decided to send his main force up the mountain in a frontal assault against the Confederate center, with diversionary attacks against both flanks. If he could break through Confederate lines, the way would be open to Marietta and the Western & Atlantic Railroad. The battle began with the usual shelling by Federal artillery, some 200 guns, and at 8:00 AM 5,500 men charged along Burnt Hickory Road toward Pigeon Hill, a spur of Kennesaw Mountain. Their difficulties were increased by 100-degree heat, and by the rains of previous days, which made the ground soft and muddy. Confederate defenders pinned them down with heavy crossfire before they reached their objective. Another 8,000 men, attacking to the south near the Dallas Road, were just as easily thwarted by the heavy underbrush and strongly positioned Confederate artillery. Beyond them, on a hill now known as Cheatham for its Confederate defender, General Benjamin F. Cheatham, the two sides met in fierce hand-to-hand fighting at a place soon called Dead Angle. Again, the Confederates were able to beat back the enemy from a strong defensive position. A number of Federal soldiers, unable to return to their lines under heavy fire, were forced to dig them-

selves in barely thirty yards from the Confederate lines, and there they remained for almost six days. After three days, an armistice was declared to allow both sides to bury their dead and treat their wounded. Altogether, the Union force lost more than 2,000 men, while Confederate casualties were one-fifth that number.

A week later, recognizing that he would not be able to take Kennesaw Mountain in a frontal assault, Sherman resorted again to flanking maneuvers. Men from the Army of the Ohio crossed Olley's Creek, toward the south, and established themselves on the Confederate left. Subsequently, Sherman moved the entire Army of the Tennessee from its position on his left to join the Army of the Ohio on the extreme right. With his line of retreat threatened, Johnston was forced to withdraw, first to Smyrna, and eventually to the city of Atlanta itself.

Despite his valiant delaying tactics, Johnston was removed from command of the Army of Tennessee by President Davis. His replacement was General John Bell Hood, a veteran of Gettysburg. Hood struck aggressively at Federal forces traversing Peachtree Creek on July 20, but was repulsed by Union batteries at a cost of 4,800 casualties. Two days later, the day-long Battle of Atlanta ended in another Confederate defeat: Union artillery including 17,000 rifles and several batteries brought down some 8,000 of Hood's men—more than twice the Union casualties. The Siege of Atlanta ensued, and Hood was forced to withdraw on September 1st. Atlanta fell to Sherman, who had systematically worked his way around the city, cutting the rail connections. His victory was a terrible blow to the Confederacy, as the armaments factories that made the city so valuable were burned and destroyed. The fall of Atlanta was a great triumph for the Union, coming as it did after a long period of stalemate, and, in fact, it may have ensured Lincoln's reelection of November 8th. The next week, Sherman began his March to the Sea.

PRISON CAMPS

Andersonville, in Georgia, is considered the worst prison camp of the Civil War: some 13,000 Union enlisted men died here, at times as many as 97 a day. (A National Cemetery is nearby.) As many as 30,000 prisoners were confined without shelter or sanitary facilities.

After the war ended, the commandant, Capt. Henry Wirz, was the only person convicted of war crimes. The charges included "murder, in violation of the laws and customs of war." He was hanged November 10, 1865, in Washington's Old Capitol Prison at the foot of Capitol Hill. While conditions at Andersonville were deplorable, Wirz's trial was tainted, as no one was allowed to testify in his favor. He refused the offer of a pardon for testimony against Jefferson Davis.

During the course of the war, 30,218 Union prisoners died in various Confederate prison camps, as compared with 25,976 deaths in Union prison camps. These figures represent about 12 percent of the war's fatalities.

Previous page: The battle at Kennesaw Mountain took place in 100-degree heat. The illustration shows General William Tecumseh Sherman's forces below and General Joseph E. Johnston's forces defending the ridge.

Left: The capture of Atlanta in September 1864 was a dispiriting defeat for the Confederacy and a grand victory for Sherman's men, depicted here. Shortly thereafter, Sherman announced his "March to the Sea."

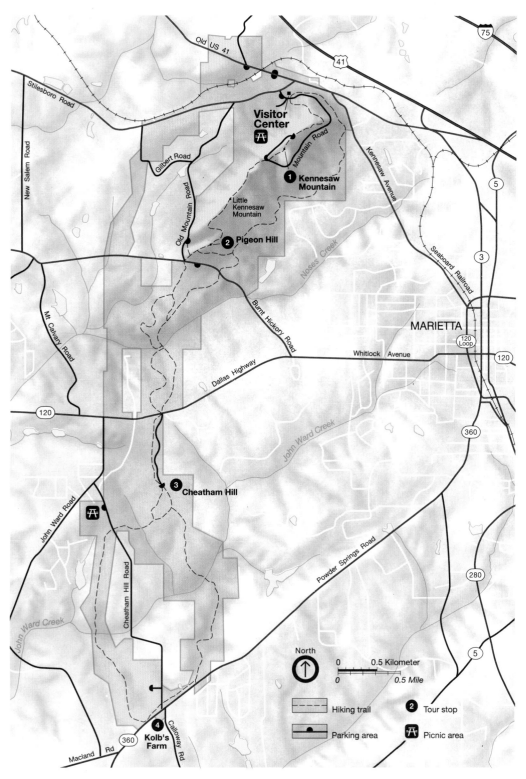

Visitor Center

1 Kennesaw Mountain

Little Kennesaw Mountain

2 Pigeon Hill

3 Cheatham Hill

4 Kolb's Farm

MARIETTA

North

0   0.5 Kilometer

0   0.5 Mile

- - - - Hiking trail
●―――― Parking area

2 Tour stop
Picnic area

KENNESAW MOUNTAIN NATIONAL BATTLEFIELD PARK

MAILING ADDRESS
Superintendent, Kennesaw Mountain National Battlefield Park, 900 Kennesaw Mountain Drive, Kennesaw, GA 30144-4854

TELEPHONE
404-427-4686

DIRECTIONS
The park is located three miles north of Marietta, Georgia. Take exit 116 off of I-75 and drive approximately one mile northwest on US 41 to its intersection with Old US 41. Drive approximately two miles northwest on Old US 41 to its intersection with Stilesboro Road. Turn left onto Stilesboro Road and drive one quarter mile west to the park entrance.

VISITOR CENTER
Exhibits, audiovisual programs, and brochures (including some foreign language versions) are available.

ACTIVITIES
Interpretive programs on weekends in the summer, self-guided auto tours, and hiking.

HOURS
The park is open daily from 8:30 AM to 5 PM, with extended hours to 6 PM on weekdays in the summer. December 25 the park is closed. The grounds are open until 8 PM during the summer.

1 Kennesaw Mountain This eminence west of Marietta, Georgia, is steep and rocky—a feature that helped the Confederates defend its twin peaks from trenches and rifle pits.

2 Pigeon Hill The scene of an abortive 5,500-man Union charge on June 27th.

3 Cheatham Hill Site of a staunch Confederate defense led by General Benjamin F. Cheatham.

4 Kolb's Farm This was the southernmost extent of the Union lines, reached on June 21 in an unsuccessful flanking maneuver that was observed and repulsed by General John B. Hood's Confederates.

Map of the Eastern Theater

OTHER SITES OF INTEREST IN VIRGINIA

Kernstown: Site of two battles: the first, on March 23, 1862, set the stage for the Shenandoah Valley Campaign in which Federal forces eventually gained control of the valley but at a heavy price. The second battle, on July 24, 1864, marks the period when Washington was threatened again by Confederate advances. Following Union losses, General Grant replaced the previous generals with Major General Philip Sheridan.

Cedar Creek (near Middletown): The last major battle of the 1864 Shenandoah Valley Campaign took place here on October 19, 1864.

Fisher's Hill (near Strasburg): This battle on September 22, 1864, marked the beginning of the "Red October" destruction of the Shenandoah Valley.

New Market: The first battle of the Shenandoah Valley Campaign was fought here on May 15, 1864, and was so critical to the Confederacy that General Lee ordered use of 247 cadets from the nearby Virginia Military Institute. Important railroad lines and passage over Massanutten Mountain were at stake.

Cross Keys and Port Republic: General Stonewall Jackson's victories at Cross Keys (June 8) and Port Republic (June 9, 1862) mark the climax of the Confederacy's Shenandoah Valley Campaign, a military masterpiece in which Jackson had defeated portions of four Union armies.

Piedmont: The Union victory in this battle on June 5, 1864, shattered the Confederate's military force in the Shenandoah Valley, opening the upper valley for the first time in the war.

Brandy Station (near Culpeper): The Union cavalry charge in this battle on June 9, 1863, was called the most "brilliant and glorious" of the war. General Robert E. Lee, who had observed the battle—his son Rooney Lee led a brigade—praised the gallantry of both sides.

Cedar Mountain (near Culpeper): This battle on August 9, 1862, was the only occasion on which General "Stonewall" Jackson, who led the victorious Confederate charge, drew his sword.

North Anna River (near Richmond): Site of a huge battle, involving 130,000 men (May 23–26, 1864), in which General Grant got around General Robert E. Lee's trenches and began his drive to the Capital of the Confederacy.

Map of the Western Theater

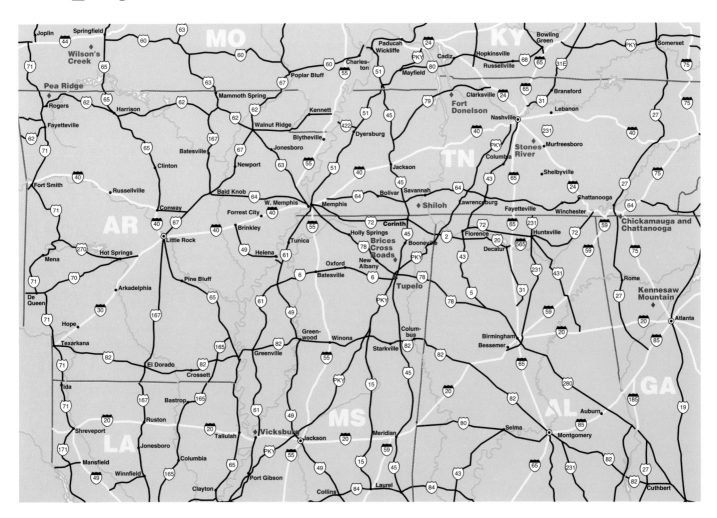

Civil War Soldiers

Union or Confederate, most Civil War soldiers were American-born, from farm or small-town backgrounds. Most were young, in their twenties. A substantial majority of Northerners could read and write; literacy rates were lower in the Southern forces. And most were volunteers, serving in the infantry.

That said, the armies, North and South, were astonishingly diverse in composition. Hundreds of thousands of foreign-born men enrolled; in one Union regiment, the officers called out orders in seven languages. Boys marched with old men. The famous Yankee drummer boy Johnny Clem enlisted at the age of nine; an Iowa infantry regiment carried an eighty-year-old on its muster roll.

More than 180,000 Americans of African descent, two-thirds of them newly freed slaves, joined the Union armies. Both sides raised regiments of Native American troops. Sarah Seelye, age twenty, enlisted in the 2nd Michigan infantry in May 1861 under the name Franklin Thompson and served for nearly two years before she acknowledged her gender and left the ranks to become a nurse. Some women served their cause as intelligence agents. Thousands of women tended the sick and wounded. Thousands more followed the camps as laundresses and vivandieres. The 1st Wisconsin Heavy Artillery regiment elected a woman chaplain.

The Volunteers

North and South, volunteers fought the Civil War. With the firing upon Fort Sumter in April 1861, President Lincoln sent out a call for 75,000 troops to reinforce the small, widely scattered U.S. regular army of around 13,000 officers and men. Existing militia regiments responded first, among them the gaudily outfitted Zouaves, their name and their uniform of bloomers, short jackets and fezzes copied from the French Colonial light infantry.

The Union debacle at Bull Run in July 1861 foretold a long, difficult war. In consequence, both armies stepped up their recruitment efforts. Hundreds of thousands of men rallied to the colors in 1861 and 1862. In most cases, enrollment officers and regimental surgeons rewarded patriotism and enthusiasm, accepting on good faith such material as came to hand.

"You have pretty good health, don't you?" a medical officer asked Massachusetts recruit Charles Barker in November 1861.

Barker said he felt perfectly fit.

"You look as though you did," the surgeon agreed, and passed Barker for enlistment.

Observant eyes discerned subtle physical differences between ordinary Northern and Southern soldiers. The Northern small-town and country people generally seemed fitter and more prosperous. Edward Porter Alexander, a U.S. Army officer who resigned to fight for the Confederacy, traveled through New York, Ohio, and Indiana on a roundabout journey to Richmond in the spring of 1861.

"They were all fine healthy looking men," he remarked of the Northerners, "with flesh on their bones & color in their cheeks, thoroughly well uniformed, equipped and armed." As his train wound its way through the hills of Tennessee and Georgia, he could not help marking the contrast. "Our men were less healthy looking," Alexander thought, "they were sallower in complection & longer & lankier in build, & there seemed too to be less discipline & drill among them."

Later in the war, when manpower needs had become acute, especially in the Confederacy, judgments could be uncharitable. Watching a detachment of Texas cavalry pass, a Louisianan remarked: "They look more like Baboons mounted on goats than anything else."

New Yorker or Georgian, country- or city-bred, artisan or laborer, college graduate or illiterate, most recruits landed in the infantry. The Union army contained the equivalent of 1,696 infantry regiments, compared with 272 cavalry regiments and 78 regiments of artillery. The proportions in the Confederate service were roughly the same.

Volunteers were organized in regiments of 10 companies each, designated by number and state: the 1st Minnesota, the 32nd Massachusetts, and so on. Three or more regiments made up a brigade; three or more brigades, a division; two or more divisions, a corps; two or more corps, an army. Union brigades and divisions were numbered; corresponding Confederate units were called by the names of their commanders: Toombs' brigade, Kershaw's division. Northern armies were generally named after rivers, Confederate armies after states or regions.

Union regiments carried an authorized strength of around 1,000 men. In practice, most units went into battle with fewer than half that number. The Union average at Gettysburg, for example, fell short of 400 men. Toward the close of the fighting, many Confederate infantry regiments had been bled down to company size, fewer than a hundred men.

The North-South sectional conflict brought on the Civil War, and sectional and state rivalries sometimes flared with nearly equal intensity within the Union and Confederate armies. Eastern troops, especially those in the Army of the Potomac, regarded Westerners as loutish, ill-mannered, and undisciplined. Soldiers of Grant's (later Sherman's) Army of the Tennessee and Rosecrans's (later Thomas's) Army of the Cumberland derided Easterners as "paper-collar soldiers" or bandbox troops.

"General feeling is that the Potomac Army is only good to draw greenbacks and occupy winter quarters," remarked an Illinois soldier in a Western army after the battle of Antietam, reflecting the common view.

Potomac veterans gave as good as they got. They compared Robert E. Lee's army to those of the West and found it a far tougher and more skilled opponent. "The Western rebels are nothing but an armed mob," one Easterner said, "and not anything so hard to whip as Lee's well-disciplined soldiers." Eastern and Western Confederates had similar views. Veterans of

James Longstreet's Army of Northern Virginia, sent west to Chattanooga in 1863, made no attempt to disguise their contempt for Braxton Bragg's troops.

Confederate troops, although nearly always ferocious in battle, were, as Alexander suggested, generally less disciplined and soldierly on parade than the Yankees. A Georgia infantryman wrote home to complain that the men of his regiment had been ordered to doff their caps when approaching the colonel or a general. "You know that is one thing I won't do," he insisted. "I would rather see him in hell before I would pull off my hat to any man and they just as well shoot me at the start." Caste loomed larger in the South, too. Cavalier types sometimes balked at taking orders from rough-mannered hill country yeomen. A privileged Mississippi planter's son could hardly stand the thought of serving under the plebeian general Nathan Bedford Forrest: "I must express my distaste to being commanded by a man having no pretension to gentil-

ity — a negro trader, gambler, an ambitious man, careless of the lives of his men so long as preferment is *en prospectu*," he wrote in his diary. "Forrest may be & no doubt is the best Cav officer in the West, but I object to a tyrannical, hotheaded vulgarian's commanding me."

Foreign-born Volunteers

Some 200,000 German-born Americans fought for the Union from 1861 to 1865, making them the most numerous of the foreign-born contingents. New York State alone raised ten largely German-speaking regiments; natives of the German states served in nearly every unit in the Northern armies.

Ireland supplied 150,000 men for the Union cause, and the Irish were the largest single foreign contingent to serve the Confederacy. In one Alabama company, 104 of 109 enrollees listed themselves as Irish born. New York raised five all-Irish regiments, which went into battle carrying emerald green flags with harp and sunburst emblems alongside the national colors. Massachusetts, Pennsylvania, Ohio, and Indiana each raised two Irish regiments. The Irish Brigade of the 1st Division, II Corps, Army of the Potomac, distinguished itself at Antietam and at Marye's Heights, Fredericksburg. North or South, the Irish were usually held in high regard as attacking troops: "They fight like tigers," one Yankee veteran wrote of the Irish 9th Massachusetts after Antietam, "& no regt. of Rebs can stand a charge from them. They have a name which our Regt. will never get."

Some 50,000 Canadians, 45,000 Englishmen, and thousands of Scots and Welsh volunteers fought for the Union. Norwegians were the norm in the 15th Wisconsin, with a few Swedes and Danes intermixed. One company of the 15th contained five men named Ole Olsen. Louisiana, with cosmopolitan New Orleans, supplied more foreign-born soldiers to the Confederate armies than any other state.

Union or Confederate, native-born men occasionally rebelled at taking orders from some heavily accented immigrant officer. A German who sought to reprimand a disorderly New York cavalryman provoked this xenophobic reply: "Hold your barking and speak English, you damned Dutch son of a bitch."

Black Troops

Louisiana, partly Union-occupied after the spring of 1862, supplied the greatest number of black recruits, some 24,000 men, to the Union armies. From Pennsylvania, New York, and Massachusetts came a total of 16,000 black enlistees. Several Union divisions were predominately black, as was the XXV Corps, units of which were among the first to enter Richmond, the Confederate capital, in April 1865.

Advocates of black recruitment encountered heavy initial resistance in the North, and even supporters expected that black troops would be used only for garrison and labor service. "Give them a chance," the abolitionist leader Frederick Douglass, himself a former slave, argued. "I don't say they will fight better than other men. All I say is, give them a chance!" Sixteen months into the war, in August 1862, the War Department finally announced that it would recruit former slaves.

Black enlistees ran up against stubborn racial prejudice. Union white troops were often hostile. "Jack what do you think about them dam niger Regiments," a Pennsylvania soldier wrote. "They better not send them out hear for if they do our own Soldiers hate a niger more than they do a Reb." Few black officers were commissioned; blacks nearly always served under white officers. At the outset, black enlistees were paid only ten dollars per month, three dollars less than whites. There were inequities in clothing and equipment as well.

In late 1862, men of the Port Royal, South Carolina, region formed the first regiment of freed slaves to be mustered into U.S. service: the 1st South Carolina Volunteers. It was a high-stakes venture, as the regimental commander, the Massachusetts abolitionist Thomas Wentworth Higginson, fully recognized: "A single mutiny, such as happened in the infancy of a hundred regiments, a single miniature Bull Run, a stampede of desertions, and it would have been all over with us," Higginson wrote. "The party of distrust would have got the upper hand, and there might not have been, during the whole contest, another effort to arm the negro."

The 1st South Carolina went on to make a successful war record. Two Louisiana regiments, the 1st and 3rd Louisiana Guards, composed mainly of New Orleans free black recruits, were the first black units to take part in a general engagement—at Port Hudson on the Mississippi River in May 1863. Sent in with the first assault wave, the Louisianans lost 20 percent of their strength in killed, wounded, and missing.

All too often, Confederate troops reacted with ungovernable fury in encounters with black formations. At Milliken's Bend, Fort Pillow, the Crater at Petersburg, and elsewhere, Rebels dealt with captured black troops summarily on the battlefield: "Several [were] taken prisoner and afterwards either bayoneted or burnt," a North Carolina infantryman wrote after one skirmish. "The men were perfectly exasperated at the idea of negroes opposed to them & rushed at them like so many devils."

As the war ground on and casualties mounted, many Yankee whites were grateful for the contributions of African-American soldiers. "We called upon them in the hour of our trial, when volunteering had ceased, when the draft was a partial failure, and the bounty system a senseless extravagance," recalled Colonel Norwood Hallowell, a white officer in the black 55th Massachusetts. Without question, black enlistees contributed largely to the final margin of victory for the Union armies.

As for the Confederates, in early 1865, they turned in desperation to the possibility of black enlistments. A year before, the Irish-born general Patrick Cleburne had called for the enrollment of blacks in the Confederate army in return for a promise of emancipation. Not until March 1865, however, did President Davis authorize black recruitment. In the few weeks that remained to the Confederacy, only a few companies were organized.

After Appomattox

The armies melted away seemingly overnight in the spring of 1865. The beaten Confederates, clutching their parole slips, struck out for home, some by rail or steamer, some on horseback, others on foot, traveling in ragged, hungry groups. Grant's two great armies, Meade's from Virginia and Sherman's from the Carolinas, marched on Washington for the Grand Review on May 23–24, 1865. Some 150,000 men marched past the president, other senior politicians, and the leading generals.

Then, one after another, the Union volunteer regiments were mustered out. Close to a million Northerners turned toward home, soon to begin the often painful process of reabsorption into civilian life. For all its hardships, soldiering had introduced drama and high purpose into the lives of tens of thousands of ordinary men. "I do feel so idle and lost to business that I wonder what will become of me," a home-bound Iowan wrote in his diary. "Can I ever be contented again?" In late June 1865, General Meade issued the order that formally disbanded the Army of the Potomac.

The Generals: USA

NATHANIEL P. BANKS (1816–1894)

A career politician, a veteran member of Congress, and an antebellum governor of Massachusetts, he used his political contacts to obtain a major general's commission in May 1861. In the event, Banks proved far more successful at winning elections than at winning battles.

He became Stonewall Jackson's foil in Jackson's brilliant Shenandoah Valley campaign of 1862. Transferred west to command the Department of the Gulf, his messy Red River Campaign of 1863 yielded the fall of Port Hudson on the Mississippi, but only after the capture of Vicksburg had made the downriver fortress untenable.

Banks's failed Red River Campaign of 1864 led to his removal from field command. He returned to political life after the war, serving several more terms in Congress.

AMBROSE E. BURNSIDE (1824–1881)

His magnificent muttonchop whiskers gave a new word to the language: sideburns. Born and raised in Liberty, Indiana, Burnside graduated from West Point in 1847, noteworthy more for his impressive appearance than for his abilities as a soldier or a scholar.

Burnside rose rapidly in the Union Army after the outbreak of war. He commanded the land forces in the capture of Roanoke Island, North Carolina, and led a corps at Antietam. His fumbling performance at the Stone Bridge there helped rob the Union of a decisive victory.

Placed in command of the Army of the Potomac, he presided over the disaster at Fredericksburg. Removed early in 1863, he later commanded a corps at Petersburg, where his mismanagement of the battle of the Crater led to his final removal from authority.

SAMUEL R. CURTIS (1805–66)

An 1831 West Point graduate, he left the army after a year and eventually entered the law and politics. In 1861 Curtis resigned his Iowa congressional seat to become colonel of the 2nd Iowa Volunteer Infantry.

Rising rapidly to command of the Army of the Southwest, he defeated a Confederate army at the battle of Pea Ridge, Arkansas, in March 1862, then captured Helena, Arkansas, after a difficult 1,000-mile march in July and August.

Troops under Curtis's command checked Sterling Price's Missouri Raid of 1864. Although Price claimed success, it came at the cost of thousands of small arms, all his cannon, and most of his men.

ULYSSES S. GRANT (1822–1885)

The Ohio-born son of a tanner, Grant graduated from West Point in 1843 and served ably in the Mexican War. But he failed to adapt in peacetime army. Bored, lonely, and increasingly addicted to drink, he resigned under pressure in 1854.

He hardly fared better in civil life, moving from job to job, even selling firewood in the streets for a time. The coming of war altered his fortunes overnight. By September 1861, Grant had risen from clerk in a dry goods store to brigadier general commanding the military district of Cairo, Illinois.

Grant won his military reputation in the West, proving himself a bold strategist and a master of logistics. His list of successes mounted: capture of Forts Henry and Donelson in February 1862; recovery from near-disaster and eventual victory at Shiloh in April; the brilliant overland campaign in the spring of 1863 that yielded one of the Civil War's decisive victories, the surrender of the Confederate fortress of Vicksburg.

His victory at Missionary Ridge near Chattanooga in November 1863 opened the invasion route to Atlanta and the Deep South. It led, too, to Grant's ascension to commander-in-chief of all Union land forces. Headquartered in the field with the Army of the Potomac, he launched a relentless campaign against the Confederates in the spring of 1864. In a continuous shifting battle, from the Wilderness to Spotsylvania to Cold Harbor, he ground down Robert E. Lee's army mercilessly. By late June, after a surprise crossing of the James River, he had forced Lee into the Petersburg lines, robbing him of all freedom of movement.

The 1864 battles had been fought at an unprecedented cost—66,000 casualties in the Army of the Potomac between May 4 and June 19, half the army's strength at the outset of the campaign. But Grant would not be deflected from his goal. As Lincoln had said after Shiloh, in response to calls for Grant's removal: "I can't spare this man; he fights." With great directness of purpose, Grant pursued his strategy to the end: destruction of the Confederate armies, one by one.

Lee's army collapsed first, at Appomattox Court House, Virginia, on April 9, 1865. The others soon followed. As the chief architect of victory, Grant found the greatest American prize within his grasp: the presidency. Elected in 1868, returned to office in 1872, his two terms were marred by scandal and corruption on a grand scale. Grant had one final triumph—the completion, just before his death on July 23, 1885, of his *Personal Memoirs*, widely regarded as a classic of Civil War literature.

JOSEPH HOOKER (1814–1879)

Vain, self-applauding "Fighting Joe" Hooker, grandson of a Revolutionary War officer, graduated from West Point in 1837 and fought in Mexico before quitting the army to take up farming in California.

He accepted a Union commission at the start of the war and led a division on the Peninsula and a corps at Antietam. After Fredericksburg, he succeeded Burnside, against whom he had schemed, in command of the Army of the Potomac. In May 1863, he launched a campaign that he boasted would destroy the Army of Northern Virginia. Instead, Hooker became the victim of the most brilliant of Lee's victories, Chancellorsville.

Removed from command on the eve of Gettysburg and transferred west, he led two corps under Grant at Chattanooga. Passed over for command of one of Sherman's armies in 1864, he asked to be relieved of duty and never returned to the field.

GEORGE B. McCLELLAN (1826–1885)

He seemed a favorite of fortune, born into a prominent Philadelphia family, second in his West Point class of 1846, a veteran of the Mexican War, president of a railroad at the age of thirty-one.

McClellan succeeded to the command of the Union Army of the Potomac after the disaster at Bull Run (Manassas) in July 1861. A brilliant organizer, he inspired devotion in the troops and transformed the army. In the field, though, he lacked dash and aggressiveness.

His caution was legendary. "If McClellan does not want to use the army," President Lincoln once said, "I would like to borrow it." He advanced so slowly toward Richmond in the spring of 1862 that his critics dubbed him the "Virginia Creeper." At Antietam, he missed several opportunities to crush the Confederate army, although he claimed a strategic victory.

Lincoln relieved McClellan after Antietam and he never saw field service again. Running as a Democrat, he challenged Lincoln for the presidency in 1864, but carried only three states.

GEORGE G. MEADE (1815–1872)

The Union victor at Gettysburg, Meade rates as a solid if unspectacular commander, cautious and careful in the field despite his notoriously ungovernable temper.

A Pennsylvanian and an 1835 West Point graduate, he performed capably as a division and corps commander at Antietam, Fredericksburg, and Chancellorsville. Praised for his efficient handling of troops at Gettysburg, he has been faulted for failing to pursue the wounded and vulnerable Army of Northern Virginia after the battle.

Meade remained in nominal command of the Army of the Potomac after Grant came east in 1864. However, he played a secondary role to that of Grant's protégé Sheridan in the pursuit to Appomattox in April 1865, the campaign that brought the long war to an end.

JOHN POPE (1822–1892)

An 1842 West Pointer and an Old Army veteran, the Kentucky-born Pope rose swiftly to senior command in the West. By the late winter of 1862, his success in clearing New Madrid and Island No. 10 of Confederates had opened the Mississippi River almost as far as Memphis.

Lincoln chose him in the summer of 1862 to replace the popular McClellan in command of the Army of the Potomac. A bombastic opening address alienated the troops at the outset, and things quickly got worse for Pope. Robert E. Lee humbled him at the second battle of Bull Run on August 29–30, 1862, and he was relieved of command the next day.

Sent to frontier Minnesota for his sins, Pope never again held a field command during the Civil War.

Opposite: Ulysses S. Grant Above: George B. McClellan

WILLIAM S. ROSECRANS (1819–1898)

The Ohio-born Rosecrans, an 1842 West Pointer, interrupted a successful career as an engineer and miner to return to the army at the start of the Civil War.

In spite of a notoriously unruly temper, he rose quickly to command the Union Army of the Cumberland, which he led to a disputed victory (the Confederates claimed a draw) at Stone's River near Murfreesboro, Tennessee, in late 1862.

Rosecrans's embarrassing defeat at Chickamauga in September 1863 ended in his removal from command; he saw no further service in the field. Rosecrans enjoyed postwar success in business and in public service. He represented California in Congress from 1881 to 1885.

PHILIP H. SHERIDAN (1831–1888)

The son of immigrants from the County Cavan, Ireland, the explosive, hard-mannered Sheridan survived a year's suspension for fighting and other deficiencies of deportment to graduate a few places from the bottom of his West Point class of 1853.

He seemed born for the swirl of battle. Sheridan's aggressive handling of a Michigan cavalry regiment in 1861–62 won him promotion and an eventual infantry command. He led the impulsive infantry charge that carried Missionary Ridge in November 1863.

Sheridan came east with Grant in 1864 to take charge of the Army of the Potomac's cavalry corps. In August, Grant sent him into the Shendandoah Valley to lay waste to that Confederate granary. In one report to Grant, he claimed to have burned 2,000 barns and 700 mills.

Grant gave his protégé the starring role in the last campaign. His rout of the Confederates at Five Forks on April 1, 1865, flanked Lee out of the Petersburg defenses and sent him into a precipitous westward retreat. Sheridan, with cavalry and infantry, pursued without letup, trapping the remnants of the Army of Northern Virginia at Appomattox Court House.

Like Sherman, Sheridan stayed on in the postwar army. He organized a series of punitive expeditions against the Plains Indians in the 1870s and, in 1884, became second in succession to Grant as army commander-in-chief.

WILLIAM T. SHERMAN (1820–1891)

Some authorities rank Sherman as the outstanding Federal commander of the Civil War. His masterly campaigns of 1864–65 carried Union forces a thousand miles, from Chattanooga through Georgia and the Carolinas to the southern marches of Lee's Virginia.

Born in Ohio, orphaned at age nine, Sherman graduated from West Point in 1840 and endured the dull, dispiriting routines of old army life until 1853, when he resigned to become a banker. Like so many soldiers of his era, Sherman found the civilian world a hostile place. He returned to the cloistered life in 1859 as superintendent of the Louisiana Military Academy.

Sherman re-entered the army on the outbreak of war. He commanded a division under Grant at Shiloh in 1862, the

beginning of the most successful military partnership of the war. In March 1864, he succeeded Grant as the senior Union commander in the west. Two months later, he launched the grand offensive that, in combination with Grant's relentless pursuit of Lee in Virginia, closed out the war in less than a year.

Sherman's campaigns were noteworthy for their promiscuous destruction of property and their comparatively low casualty rates. He preferred maneuver to frontal assault and held that the war would end only when its realities were brought home starkly to the civilian population. "War is cruelty," he told Atlantans not long before their city went up in flames, "and you cannot refine it."

Sherman succeeded Grant as commander-in-chief of the army in 1869, waged merciless war on the Plains Indian tribes, and resisted all blandishments to enter politics, for which he had a profound and anti-democratic contempt.

GEORGE H. THOMAS (1816–70)

A Virginian, he graduated from West Point in 1840, saw action in Mexico, and participated in punitive campaigns against Indian tribes in Florida and on the Plains.

Although Southern-born, Thomas remained loyal to the Union. His stout defense at Chickamauga in September 1863 made him a national hero and earned him the sobriquet of the "Rock of Chickamauga" and promotion to command of the Army of the Cumberland. Thomas's troops launched the assault on Missionary Ridge that ended in a decisive Confederate defeat. He checked the advancing Army of Tennessee at Franklin, Tennessee, in November 1864 and two weeks later routed and nearly destroyed the Confederates at the battle of Nashville.

The Generals: CSA

PIERRE G.T. BEAUREGARD (1818–1893)

Born into a prosperous Creole family, he graduated from West Point in 1838, served in various engineering billets in the Old Army, and resigned to accept a senior Confederate command in 1861.

Beauregard directed Confederate forces in the bombardment of Fort Sumter in April 1861, the incident that touched off the Civil War. He received much credit for the Confederacy's first significant battlefield victory, at Bull Run (Manassas) in July.

Never a favorite of President Davis, Beauregard bounced from one command to another, serving at Shiloh, Charleston again (during the Union siege of 1863), and Petersburg, where his skillful initial conduct of the defense saved the city for the Confederacy in 1864. Toward war's end, he served as second-in-command to Joseph E. Johnston in the Carolinas and surrendered with Johnston's army in April 1865.

BRAXTON BRAGG (1817–1876)

The North Carolina-born Bragg, an 1837 West Pointer, inspired indifference in the troops he commanded and widespread contempt, even hatred, in many of his senior lieutenants.

Bragg's 1862 invasion of Kentucky ended in failure and retreat after the drawn battles of Perryville in October and Stone's River at year's end. His Army of Tennessee defeated Union forces at Chickamauga in September 1863, but he failed to follow up his success. In November, Grant routed Bragg's demoralized army at Missionary Ridge.

He served as President Davis's military advisor in 1864. Returning to the field near the war's end, he fought his last battle, against Sherman in North Carolina, in March 1865.

NATHAN BEDFORD FORREST (1821–1877)

An indifferently educated blacksmith's son, Forrest built a fortune as a cotton planter and slave trader in his native Tennessee. When war broke out in 1861, he enlisted in a cavalry regiment he had raised and equipped at his own expense.

Within a few weeks, Forrest had risen to command the regiment and embarked on the career that would make him the best-known and most-feared Confederate cavalry commander of the Civil War. He led a series of destructive raids behind the Union lines and checked Union cavalry penetrations of Confederate territory. His operations were so successful that Sherman vowed to stop him "if it costs ten thousand lives and bankrupts the federal treasury."

In April 1864, Forrest's command carried out the infamous massacre of surrendering black troops at Fort Pillow, Tennessee. After the war, he had a brief involvement with the Ku Klux Klan in his native state and may have served as its Grand Wizard for a time.

Opposite: William T. Sherman Above: "Stonewall" Jackson

A. P. HILL (1825–1865)

Ambrose Powell Hill needed five years to finish at West Point, although he finally graduated in 1847 in time to see front-line service in Mexico later in the year.

Hill resigned from the U.S Army during the secession crisis and first achieved prominence on the Virginia Peninsula in 1862, where he earned a reputation as one of the hardest-hitting of Lee's division commanders. Following Jackson's death, Hill succeeded to corps command and fought at Gettysburg and in a number of heavy engagements during the Petersburg siege of 1864–65.

Hill once said that he had no wish to survive the collapse of the Confederacy. On April 2, 1865, advancing Union troops shot him dead as he rode toward the front to rally his broken command.

THOMAS J. JACKSON (1824–1863)

Jackson survived a pinched, poverty-blighted orphan childhood in western Virginia to become the best known and most brilliant of Lee's lieutenants. Educated at West Point, a combat veteran of the Mexican War, he struggled in peacetime army life and resigned in 1852 to teach mathematics.

Like Grant, Jackson showed in civilian life little of the dash that would mark his brief, incandescent wartime career. His students at the Virginia Military Academy dubbed him Tom

Fool Jackson. He earned his permanent *nom de guerre* at Bull Run (Manassas) in July 1861, repulsing a Federal assault so that the world knew him thereafter as "Stonewall."

Austere, obsessively religious, deeply eccentric, Jackson fought with an intelligent slashing audacity that seemed to paralyze his opponents. "Always mystify, mislead and surprise the enemy," he said. His Shenandoah Valley operation of 1862, which put those principles into almost perfect practice, has been judged one of the great campaigns in military history.

Jackson distinguished himself at the Second Battle of Bull Run (Manassas), Antietam, and, most notably, Chancellorsville, where his flank march and assault on the Federal right wing set up Lee's masterpiece victory.

Jackson died on May 10, 1863, as a result of wounds inflicted by his own troops in the confused aftermath of the Battle of Chancellorsville. "I do not know how to replace him," Lee said in eulogy.

ALBERT SIDNEY JOHNSTON (1803–1862)
A Kentucky-born Texan and an 1826 West Point graduate, Johnston led U.S. troops in the Utah Expedition against the Mormons in 1858. When Texas seceded, he resigned to accept command of all Confederate forces in the west.

Although President Davis judged him the most capable soldier of his time, Johnston built a record of unbroken defeat in Kentucky and Tennessee in 1862, retreating from Fort Donelson through Nashville to northern Mississippi.

In April 1862, he attacked Grant's Union army near the country church of Shiloh in southwestern Tennessee. He died of wounds received on the first day of battle.

JOSEPH E. JOHNSTON (1807–1891)
Virginia-born, an 1829 West Point classmate of Robert E. Lee, Johnston ranks as one of the most skillful Southern commanders. With Beauregard, he led Confederate forces to a resounding victory at First Bull Run (Manassas). In sole command on the Virginia Peninsula, Johnston dropped back steadily before McClellan's forces. Wounded near Richmond, he yielded command to Lee and never returned to the eastern army.

In command of the Army of Tennessee in 1864, Johnston retreated toward Atlanta before Sherman's superior force. President Davis relieved him on July 17, charging that he had failed to bring Sherman to battle. He returned to the field in North Carolina in February 1865 and surrendered to Sherman on April 26th.

Johnston's partisans claimed, rightly, that he never lost a decisive battle. On the other hand, this cautious commander never actually won one on his own, either.

ROBERT E. LEE (1807–1870)
One of history's great generals, Lee (above) led the Army of Northern Virginia from July 1, 1862, to the Confederacy's end at Appomattox Court House on April 9, 1865. For nearly three years, the brilliant, daring, and resourceful Virginian fought the always larger, more powerful Union Army of the Potomac to a stalemate.

Born in Alexandria, Virginia, the son of an improvident Revolutionary War hero, Lee graduated from West Point in 1829, served in frontier garrisons, fought in Mexico, and commanded the detachment that captured the insurrectionary John Brown at Harpers Ferry. Secession forced him to choose between his officer's oath and his loyalty to Virginia. In April 1861, he refused President Lincoln's offer to command the Federal army in the field. Within a few weeks, he had accepted a brigadier's commission in the Confederate Army.

In mid-1862, with Union forces in sight of Richmond, Lee succeeded to command of the Confederacy's main army. In the counteroffensive known as the battles of the Seven Days, he drove the Federals away from the capital. Lee followed the Seven Days with a smashing success at Second Bull Run (Second Manassas). A few weeks later, his first invasion of the North, a bold move with political and diplomatic as well as military aims, came to grief in the drawn battle of Antietam. Victory at Fredericksburg in December 1862 restored Lee's aura of invincibility. In May 1863, he conducted the brilliant battle of maneuver that yielded his greatest triumph, Chancellorsville.

Lee's second great gamble, the Pennsylvania campaign of June–July 1863, resulted in a decisive defeat at Gettysburg. From then on, the Confederates fought on the defensive. By mid-1864, the Federal commander, Ulysses S. Grant, had forced the once-nimble Army of Northern Virginia into static lines covering Richmond and Petersburg. After a confused, desperate retreat in early April 1865, Lee surrendered to Grant at Appomattox Court House.

Even in his own day, Lee attained mythic stature. Handsome, courtly, unfailingly kind in manner, he inspired in his troops a near-absolute confidence and devotion. "We looked forward to victory under him as confidently as to successive sunrises," one of his officers wrote. As a tactical commander, Lee had no peer. Critics have faulted him, however, for a strategic short-sightedness that placed the defense of his beloved Virginia above all else.

The U.S. authorities did not trouble Lee after the war. In the autumn of 1865, he accepted the presidency of Washington College (now Washington and Lee) in Lexington, Virginia. He died there on October 12, 1870.

JAMES LONGSTREET (1821-1904)

He was Lee's "Old War Horse," prosaic, reliable, brave as a lion. Born in South Carolina, raised in Georgia and Alabama, Longstreet graduated from West Point in 1842 near the bottom of his class and had an unremarkable career in the old army.

He resigned in 1861 to accept a Confederate commission. A veteran of First Bull Run (Manassas) and the Seven Days' battles, Longstreet found his true vocation as a corps commander under Lee—a methodical, precise, and hard-hitting complement to the elusive, fast-moving Jackson.

His corps launched the powerful counterattack that broke Pope's army at the Second Battle of Bull Run (Manassas) and bore the greater share of the fighting at Fredericksburg. Stubborn and self-assured, Longstreet did not hesitate to challenge Lee, especially after Jackson's death. He vigorously opposed the Pennsylvania campaign of 1863 and tried to argue Lee out of attacking at Gettysburg on July 2nd and 3rd. Events, especially the debacle of Pickett's charge, proved him right.

Badly wounded in the Wilderness in the spring of 1864, Longstreet returned to duty in the autumn and served with the Army of Northern Virginia to the end. He became a deeply controversial postwar figure, not least because he embraced the Republican party. Moreover, "Lost Cause" diehards unfairly stigmatized him for the defeat at Gettysburg and its ultimate consequence, the collapse of the Confederacy.

JOHN C. PEMBERTON (1814–1881)

The Pennsylvania-born Pemberton, an 1837 West Pointer, had a long and adventurous career in the Old Army, serving in Mexico, on the frontier, and with the Utah Expedition. Married into a Virginia family, he elected to fight for the Confederacy in 1861.

Promoted beyond his abilities, he took command at Vicksburg in late 1862 and soon proved himself no match for U.S. Grant. After a short campaign of maneuver and a six-week siege, Pemberton surrendered the strategic Mississippi River fortress on July 4, 1863.

Southerners unfairly suspected the Northern-born Pemberton of treachery at Vicksburg. Taken captive and later exchanged, he served out the war in a backwater ordnance inspectorate in Virginia.

JAMES EWELL BROWN STUART (1833–1864)

Born in Patrick County, Virginia, the son of a prosperous planter, "Jeb" Stuart (above) graduated from West Point in 1854, served in Kansas during the border troubles there, and joined the Confederate army at the outbreak of war in 1861.

Stuart rose to prominence as the chief of Robert E. Lee's cavalry—the "eyes and ears" of the Army of Northern Virginia. Only his failure to keep Lee informed of Union movements during the Gettysburg campaign marred an otherwise distinguished war record.

Stuart's plumed hats, red-trimmed capes, and long flowing beard were legendary in the Confederacy. He was mortally wounded in a clash with Sheridan's cavalry at Yellow Tavern near Richmond on May 11, 1864. "He never brought me a false piece of information," Lee said of him.

EARL VAN DORN (1820–1863)

Unlucky in war, the Mississippian Van Dorn had less luck still in love.

Trained at West Point, from which he graduated in 1842, Van Dorn fought in Mexico and on the frontier. Assigned to senior command in the Confederate army, he suffered a defeat at Pea Ridge in March 1862. In October, forces under Van Dorn's command were routed at Corinth, Mississippi. Transferred to the cavalry after these two setbacks as an independent commander, he was shot in a lover's quarrel in May 1863. The assailant claimed Van Dorn had been carrying on an affair with his wife.

Strategy, Tactics, Weapons, and Innovations

The national forces had to conquer to win—to subdue and occupy the rebellious states in order to restore the Union. A less complicated task faced the Confederacy. The South could win simply by not losing.

The U.S. Army's aging commander-in-chief, Winfield Scott, developed the initial Union grand strategy: an advance down the Mississippi River to divide the Confederacy and a naval blockade of Southern ports to strangle it. Northerners derided the "Anaconda" plan, as Scott dubbed the strategy, as plodding and slow. It proved effective, though, and the Union leadership pursued its chief features, the Mississippi line of operation and the blockade, to a successful conclusion.

In the early months, the Union blockade seemed to exist only on paper. In 1861 a Confederate blockade runner risked only a one-in-ten chance of seizure. But Northern shipyards soon were turning out dozens of vessels to reinforce the blockading fleets. By 1864, with some 600 Federal warships on patrol, the main Confederate ports had been so effectively sealed off that the odds of running the blockade had fallen to one in three.

It was tedious work for the Northern bluejackets. "Day after day, day after day, we lay inactive, roll, roll," wrote the Union naval officer Alfred T. Mahan. On average, an individual warship participated in only a dozen sightings and one or two captures a year. And for all the risk, blockade runners still managed to bring in an estimated $200 million in goods, including 600,000 small arms essential to the Confederate war effort.

With some exceptions, notably Lee's invasions of the North in September 1862 and June–July 1863, the Confederacy stood on the strategic defensive. Tactically, though, Southern commanders were usually quick to go over to the attack—often bolder, at least in the earlier phases of the war, than their Union counterparts. Here Lee himself set the standard, during the Seven Days' battles, at Second Bull Run, and at Chancellorsville and Gettysburg.

According to Clausewitz, "Tactics is the art of using troops in battle; strategy is the art of using battles to win the war." By this standard, Lee ranks as the master tactician of the Civil War. As strategists, Grant and Sherman had no peer. Their two most brilliant operations, Grant's Vicksburg campaign of 1863 and Sherman's march through Georgia and the Carolinas in 1864–65, were decisive in bringing about the Union's final victory.

Small Arms

The two Civil War armies used similar tools for the job—weapons, in most cases, whose basic designs dated from the 1840s and 1850s. Prewar refinements improved the range, accuracy, and lethality of the small arms of 1861–65. Percussion caps had made flintlocks obsolete; the widespread use of rifling greatly increased the capabilities of the standard smoothbore musket.

In both armies, the primary small arms were cap-and-ball percussion-fired pistols, rarely employed to much effect except for close-in self-defense, and muzzleloader rifled muskets firing to an effective range of a thousand yards or so. Later in the war, innovative breechloading small arms were widely available, although they were used mainly to equip Union cavalry.

Many types of revolver pistols made an appearance during the war. The Colt and Remington models were by far the best-known and most numerous. U.S. forces bought nearly 150,000 of Connecticut gunsmith Samuel Colt's .44-caliber "Army" and .36-caliber "Navy" models. These reliable weapons used a percussion cap to discharge a prepackaged cartridge of black powder, wad and lead ball wrapped in paper or oiled silk and inserted in the front end of the revolver chambers. Colt's rival Remington supplied some 125,000 Army and Navy models to Union forces.

War conditions allowed Confederate manufacturers to ignore patent restrictions without risk of penalty, and they copied Colt and Remington designs for small-scale production. Southern industrial limitations, however, meant that larger proportions of foreign-made pistols, particularly British-made ones, were in use in the Confederate armies.

Most Civil War muskets had started life as .69-caliber smoothbores firing a round ball. With the appearance of the conically shaped Minie bullet in the 1850s, most smoothbores were rebored and rifled for greater range and accuracy. Throughout the war, the principal weapon of both armies was the .58-caliber Springfield firing the Minie—officially, the United States Rifle Musket Model 1861.

Northern manufacturing capacity seemed boundless. The Springfield (Massachusetts) Arsenal produced 1,200 rifles per year at the outset of the war. By mid-1864, capacity had risen to 300,000 annually. Between January 1861 and December 1865, Springfield alone turned out nearly 800,000 Model 1861 and 1863 rifled muskets for the Union armies. Altogether, some four million small arms were issued to Union troops during the war. The Confederates could not hope to keep up. From 1864, when the blockade took full effect, Southern forces were chronically short of small arms.

Confederate blockade runners smuggled in some 100,000 English-made Enfield rifles. The Yankees, too, were unwittingly a major supplier of Southern small arms. After Jackson's capture of Harpers Ferry on September 15, 1862, for instance, Confederate ordnance officers forwarded captured muskets and cannon to Lee in time for their use against their former owners at Antietam only two days later.

War spurred the development of more efficient breechloading weapons, although many senior officers, conservative and

Left: Railroads were a decisive strategic asset for the Union. The North's extensive railroad net essentially negated the South's main strategic advantage— shorter interior communications. In one of the most impressive logistical operations of the Civil War, the Union army transferred two corps from the Virginia theater to Chattanooga in the autumn of 1863, moving 20,000 men with their artillery, horses, and equipment 1,233 miles in only 11 days.

content with the tried and true, resisted their introduction. One of the best breechloaders was the Sharps rifle, patented in 1848 by Christian Sharps of Philadelphia. The U.S. Ordnance Department purchased some 80,000 Sharps rifles during the war, mostly for cavalry use.

Connecticut gunmaker Christopher M. Spencer patented the first effective breechloading repeater carbine (1860). It fired a quickly replaceable 9-cartridge magazine. Said one impressed Confederate of the Spencer: "That tarnation Yankee gun they loads on Sunday and shoots the rest of the week." The Union army bought some 77,000 Spencers and 60 million cartridges during the war. Union troops used them to great effect on the first day at Gettysburg, at Darbytown Road, Virginia, in October 1864 and Franklin, Tennessee, in November 1864.

Cannon

To begin, some brief definitions: according to Mark Boatner's *Civil War Dictionary*, a standard reference, cannon is the most accurate generic term for anything larger than small arms. Mounted, a cannon is designated artillery. A gun fires a flat trajectory; a howitzer projectile follows an arching path; a mortar has a high-angle trajectory. Civil War guns fired a solid ball; howitzers fired an explosive shell.

The 12-pounder Napoleon smoothbore muzzle-loader proved to be the basic field artillery weapon of the Civil War, with rifled cannon, according to Boatner, in a lesser role despite their greater range and accuracy. The most effective and versatile 12-pounder Napoleon could fire both shot and shell, and so carried the designation of gun-howitzer.

North and South, the standard field artillery pieces, along with the 12-pounder gun-howitzer, were 6- and 12-pounder

guns; 12-, 24- and 32-pounder howitzers; 12-pounder mountain howitzers; 10- and 20-pounder Parrott rifles; and the 3-inch Ordnance rifled gun. Maximum effective ranges were around 1,500 yards for smoothbores, 2,500 yards for rifles. Civil War artillerists could maintain a rate of fire of two to three rounds per minute.

Union resources were more than adequate to supply the armies with sufficient numbers of cannon—more than 7,800 pieces were issued to Northern gunners from 1861 until 1866. Southern capacities, however, were extremely limited. The Tredegar Iron Works in Richmond supplied most of the cannon manufactured in the South. Once again, the Yankees were an important provider: "Gradually we captured Federal guns to supply most of our needs," wrote the Confederate artillerist Edward Porter Alexander.

As for ammunition, solid shot and explosive shell were used for long-range work. Case shot (also called shrapnel after its inventor, Henry Shrapnel), a hollow cast-iron projectile filled with lead bullets, scattered death and ruin over a wide area when it burst. Canister, a shorter-range version of case shot, broke apart on firing and sent musket balls toward an enemy with the effect of a large-scale shotgun blast. Grape shot, usually a cloth bundle filled with lead shot, worked well only at close ranges.

Both armies experienced difficulties with unreliable fuses and defective ammunition, but such problems were far more severe in the Confederate artillery service. Badly fused shells bursting prematurely caused so many casualties among Confederate frontline troops at Fredericksburg, Alexander reported, that the gunners were ordered to use solid shot only when friendly infantry were nearby. At Knoxville, in November 1863, a Confederate battery of 10-pounder Parrott rifles fired off 120 long-range rounds. According to Alexander, all but two of the shells either tumbled or burst prematurely. "We were handicapped by our own ammunition until the close of the war," he said.

Innovations

From time immemorial, a soldier's instinctive reaction to danger has been to burrow. Civil War armies advanced the art of field fortifications immeasurably. Intricate systems of trenches and bombproofs, designed to give the defender overlapping fields of fire, ringed important strategic objectives such as Vicksburg and Petersburg. Southerners, so often on the defensive after 1863, became especially adept throwing up protective works quickly and with minimal tools—at times, little more than bayonets and tin cups.

Both sides, but particularly the Union armies, made widespread use of technological innovations in communications. Alexander, who served as an aerial observer during the Peninsular Campaign in 1862, communicated with the ground via black cambric balls suspended from the basket of his hot air balloon (top right). The Federals took aeronautical communications a step further, rigging a telegraph to provide an air-to-ground signals link.

The Civil War saw the first extended use of the electrical telegraph and the first use of the field telegraph. George W. Beardslee developed a portable field telegraph, with a range of around ten miles, on which messages were composed via an alphabet dial and pointer. Burnside used it to effect at Fredericksburg in December 1862, when fog and battlesmoke made visual communications across the Rappahannock impossible.

Ponderous and vulnerable, the field telegraph saw little use later in the war. Instead, the armies relied on faster, more powerful commercial telegraphy. The Union's Military Telegraph System employed some 12,000 operators and strung 15,000 miles of wire. It remained under civilian control throughout the war, under the direction of Anton Stager, a prewar Western Union general superintendent. In a 12-month period in 1862–63, the system averaged 3,300 military messages a day.

As all wars do, the Civil War stimulated invention as weapons-smakers worked overtime to develop more efficient killing machines. "Battery guns" were primitive rapid-fire weapons in which multiple rifle barrels were mounted on a wheeled carriage. One of the best known, the Ager Battery Gun, claimed a rate of fire of 100 rounds per minute. But U.S. ordnance officers were skeptical, and only about 50 were manufactured.

A Confederate officer designed the first machine gun to see action in war, the Williams gun. Northerner Richard J. Gatling developed the best-known and most effective machine gun, and named it after himself. A side crank turned the weapon's six barrels to provide a high rate of small-arms fire.

Gatling, too, had difficulty penetrating the military bureaucracy, and his weapon saw only limited service during the war. Union General Benjamin Butler spent $12,000 of his own money to buy a dozen Gatlings for use around Peters-

burg in 1864, and a few other Federal commanders ordered a small number for the infantry and for gunboat service. The U.S. Army did not, however, adopt the Gatling for general use until 1866.

Advances Afloat

Important military uses were found for new combinations of steam, iron, and explosives. In 1861–62, the Indiana manufacturer James B. Eads built seven flat-bottomed, broad-beamed, armor-sheathed gunboats for river warfare. Grant and the commander of the river flotilla, Flag Officer Andrew Foote, employed the steam-driven vessels to great advantage during the Cumberland-Tennessee River Campaign in early 1862.

The war's best-known ironclad, the *U.S.S. Monitor*, armed with great guns in a unique revolving turret, provided the answer to the Confederacy's armored marauder, the *C.S.S. Virginia*. Converted from the raised hull of the scuttled steam frigate *Merrimac*, with her superstructure sheathed with heavy iron plating, the *Virginia* looked, thought a Union soldier watching from shore, "like a house submerged to the eaves, borne onward by the flood." In the world's first clash of ironclad ships, *Monitor* and *Merrimac* fought to a draw in Hampton Roads, Virginia, on March 9, 1862.

The Confederate Navy experimented seriously with submersible vessels as a potential means of piercing the Union blockade. The *David*, a steam-driven semi-submersible, approached the *USS New Ironsides* on station off Charleston, South Carolina, the night of October 15, 1863, and rammed her 14-foot-long spar torpedo into the Union warship's side. The blast nearly swamped the *David*, but did not cause sufficient damage to sink the target.

A fully submersible vessel, the *H.L. Hunley*, named after her builder, had greater success, but at a high cost. The submarine, driven by eight crewmen operating a crank that turned the propeller, attacked and sank the *USS Housatonic* off Charleston the night of February 17, 1864. But the explosion sent the submarine to the bottom, too. Many years later, divers found the wrecked hull of the *Hunley*, with the skeletons of the crew of nine inside.

Conflict Statistics

Estimates vary, sometimes widely, on the numbers of troops involved and casualty figures for Civil War conflicts. The editors of this book have used *Civil War Day by Day: An Almanac*, by E.B. Long and Barbara Long, as the primary source for the statistics quoted. The figures used to create the graphs for the featured battles are listed below.

Battle	Effectives	Engaged	Killed	Wounded	Missing/Captured	Total Casualties
First Manassas						
USA		37,000	460	1,124	1,312	2,896
CSA		35,000	387	1,582	13	1,982
Second Manassas						
USA		75,000	1,724	8,372	5,958	16,054
CSA		48,500	1,481	7,627	89	9,197
Harpers Ferry						
USA		12,800	44	173	12,520	12,737
CSA		23,000	39	247		286
Antietam						
USA	75,000		2,010	9,416	1,043	12,469
CSA		40,000	2,700	9,024	2,000	13,724
Richmond/Seven Days						
USA	115,000	83,000	1,734	8,062	6,053	15,849
CSA	88,000	86,500	3,286	15,909	946	20,141
Fredericksburg						
USA		114,000	1,284	9,600	1,769	12,653
CSA		72,500	595	4,061	653	5,309
Chancellorsville						
USA	133,868		1,606	9,762	5,919	17,287
CSA	60,000		1,665	9,081	2,018	12,764
Stones River						
USA	41,400		1,677	7,543	3,686	12,906
CSA	35,000		1,294	7,945	2,500	11,739
Gettysburg						
USA		85,000	3,155	14,529	5,365	23,049
CSA		65,000	2,592	12,709	5,150	20,451
Wilson's Creek						
USA	5,400		258	873	186	1,317
CSA	11,000		279	951	0	1,230
Fort Donelson						
USA	27,000		500	2,108	224	2,832
CSA	21,000			1,500	12,000	13,500
Pea Ridge						
USA		11,000	203	980	201	1,384
CSA		14,000		600	200	800
Shiloh						
USA	62,000		1,754	8,408	2,885	13,047
CSA	44,000		1,723	8,012	959	10,694
Chickamauga						
USA	58,000		1,657	9,756	4,757	16,170
CSA	66,000		2,312	14,674	1,468	18,454
Chattanooga						
USA		56,000	753	4,722	349	5,824
CSA		46,000	361	2,160	4,146	6,667
Brices Cross Roads						
USA		8,000	223	394	1,623	2,240
CSA		3,500	96	396	0	492
Tupelo						
USA		14,000	77	559	38	674
CSA		9,500				1,347
Kennesaw Mountain						
USA	13,500			1,999	52	2,051
CSA	20,000			270	172	442

Chronology

1859

October 16 – 18   John Brown's raid on Harpers Ferry.

1860

November 6   Abraham Lincoln is elected president of the United States.

December 3   Outgoing president James Buchanan informs Congress that "the election of any one of our fellow-citizens to the office of President does not of itself afford just cause for dissolving the Union."

December 20   The first Southern state, South Carolina, secedes.

1861

January 9   Mississippi becomes the second state to secede.

January 10   Florida secedes.

January 11   Alabama secedes.

January 19   Georgia secedes.

January 26   Louisiana secedes.

February 1   Texas becomes the seventh state to secede. All are from the Deep South.

February 4   Representatives of the seceding states meet in Montgomery, Alabama, and create a provisional Confederate government.

February 9   The Montgomery convention names Jefferson Davis, of Mississippi, president and Alexander Stephens, of Georgia vice-president of the Confederate States of America.

February 18   Jefferson Davis inaugurated president of the Confederacy.

March 4   Inauguration of Abraham Lincoln as sixteenth president of the United States.

March 11   The Constitution of the Confederacy is adopted. Similar in content to the United States Constitution, except in its formal recognition and protection of the institution of slavery.

April 11   General P. G. T. Beauregard, commander of Confederate forces in Charleston, demands that the Federals surrender Fort Sumter in Charleston Harbor.

April 12   At 4:30 AM, the bombardment of Fort Sumter begins.

April 13   Fort Sumter surrenders and is evacuated the following day.

April 15   Lincoln calls for 75,000 volunteers to put down the rebellion that he now declares exists in the Southern states.

April 17   Virginia becomes the eighth state to secede, although her western counties object.

April 18   Federal troops abandon and burn the U.S. Armory at Harpers Ferry.

April 19   Lincoln declares a blockade of the Confederate coast. A mob in sympathy with secession attacks troops in transit through Baltimore, Maryland

April 20   Colonel Robert E. Lee resigns his commission in the U.S. Army. Federal troops evacuate the navy yard at Norfolk, Virginia.

May 6   The Confederate Congress recognizes a state of war between the Confederacy and the United States. Arkansas secedes, the ninth state to join the Confederacy. Tennessee legislature passes secession ordinance to be voted upon by the people in June. However, the ordinance itself is tantamount to seccession.

May 20   North Carolina secedes. Kentucky's governor issues a proclamation of neutrality.

May 21   Richmond, Virginia, is chosen as the Confederate capital.

June 8   Tennessee secedes, the eleventh and last state to join the Confederacy.

June 10   A minor battle at Big Bethel, Virginia, is a Confederate victory.

June 11   Engagement at Rich Mountain in western Virginia, a Union victory, helps create reputation of General George B. McClellan.

July 21   The first Battle of Manassas (Bull Run), the first serious engagement of the war, is a major Confederate victory.

July 27   Irvin McDowell, defeated Union commander of the Army of the Potomac, is replaced by General George B. McClellan.

August 10   The battle of Wilson's Creek, Missouri, the first major engagement in the Western theater, is a Confederate victory.

August 28   Union troops take Fort Hatteras, North Carolina.

September 6   Union forces commanded by General Ulysses S. Grant occupy the strategic city of Paducah, Kentucky.

October 21   Confederates repulse Union troops at the Battle of Ball's Bluff, Virginia.

November 1   General McClellan is appointed general-in-chief of Union armies.

November 7   Union troops capture Port Royal, South Carolina. Confederates win a minor victory at Belmont, Missouri.

November 8   The British ship *Trent*, carrying the Confederate commissioners to Great Britain James M. Mason and John Slidell, is stopped by threat of force by the U.S.S. *San Jacinto* on the high seas. Mason and Slidell are arrested. The incident threatens war between Britain and the United States.

December 26   Mason and Slidell are released by the United States to end the international crisis.

1862

January 13   Edwin M. Stanton is appointed secretary of war by Lincoln.

February 6   Fort Henry, Tennessee, is captured by a Union flotilla commanded by Flag Officer Andrew Foote.

February 8   A Union force captures Roanoke Island, North Carolina.

February 13–16   Fort Donelson, Tennessee, falls to General Grant after a four-day siege.

February 25   The fall of Fort Donelson enables a Union force under General Don Carlos Buell to capture Nashville, the first major Confederate city to fall, without bloodshed.

March 6–8   Battle of Pea Ridge in Arkansas ends in a Union victory.

March 8   The ironclad C. S. S. *Virginia* (better known as the *Merrimac*) defeats the frigates U. S. S. *Cumberland* and *Congress.*

March 9   The C. S. S. *Virginia* engages the ironclad U. S. S. *Monitor* at Hampton Roads. This first battle of ironclads ends in a draw.

March 11   McClellan is relieved of command as general-in-chief of Union armies, but retains command of the Army of the Potomac. In the West, military departments are consolidated to report to the secretary of war.

March 14   New Madrid, Missouri, falls to a Union army under Pope.

March 17   McClellan begins to move the Army of the Potomac toward Richmond in what becomes known as the Peninsula Campaign.

March 23	Lincoln orders General McDowell and his troops to stay in Washington in case it is threatened by General Thomas "Stonewall" Jackson.	*August 11*	Confederate guerrillas capture Independence, Missouri.
		August 16	The Army of the Potomac completes its evacuation of Harrison's Landing.
March 28	The battle of La Glorieta Pass in New Mexico Territory, the most westerly engagement of the war, is a Union victory.	*August 27–28*	A Confederate force under General Braxton Bragg begins its campaign into Tennessee and Kentucky.
April 6–7	Union forces commanded by Grant are surprised by a Confederate attack at Shiloh (Pittsburg Landing) in Tennessee. The Federals regain the ground initially lost. Confederate commander General Albert Sidney Johnston is killed.	*August 29–30*	The Second Battle of Manassas (Bull Run) is a Confederate victory after armies under James Longstreet and Jackson force a Federal retreat back to Centreville.
		September 1	Battle of Chantilly, Virginia, is a victory for Lee.
		September 4	Lee begins the Confederates' first invasion of the North.
April 8	Island Number 10 in the Mississippi falls to a Union force under Pope.	*September 14*	The Battle of South Mountain, Virginia, is a Union victory.
April 11	After a thirty-hour artillery assault, Fort Pulaski, Georgia, surrenders to a Union force. Such masonry forts are made obsolete by rifled cannon.	*September 15*	Confederates commanded by Jackson capture Harpers Ferry, Virginia.
April 24	A Union flotilla under Admiral David Farragut defeats Confederates in a naval engagement below New Orleans.	*September 17*	The Battle of Antietam (Sharpsburg), the bloodiest single day of the war, is a Union victory in that Lee's invasion is stopped.
April 25	The Federal fleet captures New Orleans.	*September 19*	A Union force under General William S. Rosecrans defeats Confederate armies led by Sterling Price and Earl Van Dorn at Iuka, Mississippi.
May 3	Confederates evacuate Yorktown and retreat toward Richmond.		
May 5	Federal forces under McClellan and the Confederate rear guard battle at Williamsburg, Virginia.	*September 22*	Lincoln issues a preliminary version of the Emancipation Proclamation.
May 8	At the beginning of the Shenandoah campaign Jackson triumphs at McDowell, Virginia.	*October 3–4*	The battle of Corinth, Mississippi, is a Union victory.
May 9	Confederates evacuate the naval base at Norfolk, Virginia. Two days later they destroy the ironclad C. S. S. *Virginia* to prevent its capture.	*October 8*	The Union victory at Perryville, Kentucky, forces the Confederates to retreat to Tennessee, ending the invasion of Kentucky.
May 15	Union flotilla moving up the James River toward Richmond is turned back by Confederate artillery at Drewry's Bluff.	*October 9–12*	Jeb Stuart's raid in the north takes him as far as Chambersburg, Pennsylvania.
		October 25	Grant takes command of the thirteenth Army Corps and the Department of Tennessee.
May 23	Confederates under Jackson are victorious at Front Royal.	*November 7*	McClellan is replaced by General Ambrose E. Burnside.
May 25	Jackson achieves another victory at Winchester, Virginia.	*November 13*	A Federal force occupies the rail center of Holly Springs, Mississippi.
May 31	McClellan defeats General Joseph E. Johnston at Seven Pines (Fair Oaks), east of Richmond.	*December 11–12*	Union forces under Burnside move across the Rappahannock in order to attack Fredericksburg, Virginia.
June 1	General Lee is given command of the Army of Northern Virginia.	*December 13*	During the Battle of Fredericksburg, well-entrenched Confederate forces on Marye's Heights repulsed the attacking Union soldiers, creating heavy casualties.
June 6	Union troops capture Memphis, Tennessee.		
June 9	The Shenandoah Valley Campaign ends with Jackson's victory at Port Republic	*December 14*	Burnside retreats from Fredericksburg.
June 12–15	Confederate cavalry under Brigadier General James Ewell Brown "Jeb" Stuart rides around McClellan's entire army, encamped outside Richmond.	*December 30*	U.S.S. *Monitor* sinks in the Atlantic off the coast of North Carolina, near Cape Hatteras.
		December 31	The battle of Stones River, Tennessee, (Murfreesboro) begins.
June 25	The Seven Days' campaign before Richmond begins with the battle of Oak Grove, Virginia.	**1863**	
June 26	An attack by Confederate troops commanded by A. P. Hill at Mechanicsville pushes Federal troops into a strong defensive position.	*January 1*	The Emancipation Proclamation, stating "all persons held as slaves within said designated States, and parts of States, are, and henceforward shall be free," is signed.
June 27	A concerted attack by Confederates under Generals John Bell Hood and George E. Pickett temporarily breaks the Union line during the Battle of Gaines' Mill.	*January 2*	The conflict of Stones River resumes, but the Confederate advantage is lost, and the battle ends inconclusively.
June 29	During the battle of Savage's Station the Confederates continue to assault McClellan's army as it withdraws.	*February 10*	General Fitz-John Porter is court-martialed and cashiered, for failure to follow orders at Second Manassas.
June 30	The Confederate attacks continue at White Oak Swamp, but the Federal army still holds together.	*February 19*	Federal troops under Burnside attempt to cross the Rappahannock and resume campaign against Fredericksburg.
July 1	Lee attempts unsuccessfully to destroy McClellan at Malvern Hill, and the superior Federal force withdraws.	*February 22*	The "Mud March," the Federals campaign to cross the Rappahannock fails, Burnside accepts the inevitable and attempts to return to the nearest camp, over roads that the January weather has rendered nearly impassable. Grant resumes digging a canal through marsh south of Vicksburg.
July 2	Seven Days' Campaign ends as McClellan retreats to Harrison's Landing.		
July 11	General Henry Halleck is named general-in-chief of all Union land forces by Lincoln.	*February 26*	General Joseph Hooker assumes command of the Army of the Potomac, replacing Burnside.
July 13	A Confederate force under General Nathan Bedford Forrest takes Murfreesboro, Tennessee.	*March 3*	The Union Conscription Act, which calls for the enlistment of all able-bodied male citizens between the ages of twenty and forty-five, is passed.
July 17	Grant is given command of the Union armies in the West.		
August 9	The Battle of Cedar Mountain in the Shenandoah Valley is another Confederate victory for Jackson.	*March 8*	In a daring raid at Fairfax County Court House, Con-

federate Captain John S. Mosby captures Union General E. H. Stoughton while he is asleep.

April 2 — Richmond is wracked by the bread riot.

April 16 — Acting Rear Admiral David D. Porter's fleet manages to run below the bluffs at Vicksburg despite the Confederate batteries.

May 1–4 — The Battle of Chancellorsville, Virginia is a brilliant southern victory, but during it, Stonewall Jackson is mortally wounded by his own men.

May 10 — Jackson dies at Guiney's Station, south of Fredericksburg.

May 14 — Grant captures Jackson, Mississippi.

May 16 — After the Battle of Champion Hill, Mississippi, the most severe of the Vicksburg campaign, the Confederates retreat toward the city of Vicksburg.

May 19–22 — After a series of attacks on the city fail, the Union siege of Vicksburg begins.

June 3 — Lee begins his second invasion of the North.

June 9 — Brandy Station, the largest and most severe cavalry battle of the war, is a Confederate victory.

June 20 — West Virginia officially becomes a Union state, the thirty-fifth, by presidential proclamation.

June 27 — A Confederate force under Jubal Early captures undefended York, Pennsylvania, and acquires supplies. General George Gordon Meade is given command of the Army of the Potomac.

July 1–3 — The Battle of Gettysburg, marks the "high tide of the Confederacy." Lee's attempt to surround Meade's army fails, as the Union troops hold the high ground. Despite a gallant charge on the third day by Pickett's division, the battle is a great Union victory.

July 4 — After a six-week siege, at the end of months of campaigning, Vicksburg falls to the Union. Lee retreats from Gettysburg.

July 8 — With the surrender of Port Hudson, Louisiana, the last Confederate garrison on the Mississippi River, the river is open to Federal ships and the Confederacy is cut in half.

July 11 — The first names of the new Federal draft are drawn. They are published two days later.

July 13–16 — Draft riots take place in New York and other northern cities. Figures are unclear, but there are estimates that nearly a thousand people were killed or wounded.

August 8 — Lee offers to resign the command of the Army of Northern Virginia, pleading ill health. President Davis refuses.

August 16 — Federal troops move toward the Tennessee River in the opening of the Chickamauga Campaign.

August 17 — Union forces begin a bombardment of Fort Sumter.

August 21 — Lawrence, Kansas, is sacked and burned by William Clarke Quantrill's guerrillas. Only women and small children are spared.

September 2 — General Burnside's troops occupy Knoxville, Tennessee, cutting the railroad link between Chattanooga and Virginia.

September 5 — Charles Francis Adams, American Minister to the Court of St. James threatens war against Britain if the building of the two almost-completed ironclads for the Confederacy is not halted. The British comply.

September 9 — Bragg moves out of Chattanooga, Tennessee, but is reinforced by Longstreet's forces from Virginia.

September 19–20 — At the Battle of Chickamauga, Tennessee, Bragg is victorious, but doesn't follow up his advantage, and Rosecrans is able to retreat to Chattanooga.

September 23 — Confederates begin siege of Chattanooga, Tennessee.

October 14 — Meade and Lee fight an indecisive engagement at Bristoe Station, Virginia.

October 16 — Grant is named to command the new military Division of the Mississippi, which combined the Departments of the Ohio, the Cumberland, and the Tennessee.

October 23 — Grant arrives in Chattanooga and takes command.

November 19 — Lincoln delivers the Gettysburg Address at the ceremonies dedicating the military cemetery.

November 23–25 — Grant captures Missionary Ridge and defeats Bragg in the Battle of Lookout Mountain (Chattanooga).

December 2 — Bragg is relieved of command of the Army of Tennessee, and is replaced by Lieutenant General William Hardee.

December 16 — General Joseph E. Johnston takes over command of the Army of Tennessee.

1864

January 19 — The Arkansas pro-Union Constitutional Convention adopts an antislavery constitution.

February 3 — Sherman's campaign against Meriden, Mississippi, begins.

February 14 — Federals capture Meriden, Mississippi.

February 17 — Confederate submarine C.S.S. *Hunley* sinks the U.S.S. *Housatonic* off Charleston, South Carolina.

March 9 — Grant is promoted to the newly revived rank of lieutenant general.

March 10 — Grant is put in command of the Armies of the United States.

March 12 — Henry Halleck is named chief of staff. Red River Campaign begins.

April 4 — Major General Philip Sheridan takes command of the cavalry of the Army of the Potomac.

April 12 — Confederate General Nathan Bedford Forrest captures Fort Pillow, Tennessee, above Memphis. High Union casualties lead to persistent rumors of the massacre of both white and blacks in the Federal Army after surrender.

May 4 — Grant leads his army across the Rapidan River, beginning the Wilderness Campaign.

May 5–6 — Grant and Lee fight the inconclusive Battle of the Wilderness. Instead of retreating, Grant moves towards Spotsylvania Court House.

May 7 — Sherman moves towards Atlanta.

May 8–21 — Grant repeatedly attacks Lee's forces which are firmly entrenched at Spotsylvania, saying "I propose to fight it out on this line if it takes all summer."

May 11 — Jeb Stuart is mortally wounded at Yellow Tavern, Virginia.

May 13–29 — Sherman drives south toward Atlanta. His opponent Joseph E. Johnston fights a delaying action.

May 14–15 — Battle for Resaca, Georgia.

May 16 — Beauregard stops Butler south of Richmond at the Battle of Drewry's Bluff, Virginia.

May 25 — Beginning of Campaign of New Hope Church, Georgia, in which Sherman's advance is stalled by Johnston.

June 1–3 — The Battle of Cold Harbor. On June 3, the Union charge resulted in around 7,000 casualties in under an hour.

June 8 — Lincoln is nominated for a second term.

June 10 — Forrest defeats Sturgis at Battle of Brices Cross Roads, Mississippi.

June 12 — Grant begins flanking movement across James River to Petersburg, Virginia.

June 16–18 — Grant launches a surprise attack at Petersburg, but command delays deny him victory, and the siege of Petersburg begins.

June 19 — U.S.S. *Kearsarge* sinks the Confederate raider C.S.S. *Alabama* off Cherbourg, France.

June 27 — Sherman is defeated at the battle of Kennesaw Mountain, but continues the drive toward Atlanta.

July 2 — Marietta, Georgia, is evacuated by Confederates.

July 6 — General Jubal Early crosses the Potomac, enters Maryland, and captures Hagerstown.

July 8 — Union general John Schofield crosses the Chattahoochee River, forcing Johnston into the last defenses before Atlanta.

July 9	Lew Wallace musters volunteers to defend Washington D.C. from Early, loses the Battle of Monocacy to Early, but delays his advance until the capital is reinforced.
July 11–12	Confederates under Early reach suburbs of Washington, but seeing Federal troops fortify the capital, decides to withdraw.
July 14	Forrest wins a battle near Tupelo, Mississippi.
July 17	Davis relieves Johnston, gives command to General John Bell Hood.
July 20	Hood attacks Sherman at the Battle of Peachtree Creek, Georgia, but falls back.
July 27–29	The siege of Atlanta. Diversionary cavalry raids toward Richmond are launched by Sheridan, north of the James River.
July 30	Petersburg Mine explodes and the subsequent Union assault is a failure.
August 5	Farragut, with a fleet of fourteen wooden ships and four ironclads, wins the Battle of Mobile Bay, reportedly shouting, "Damn the torpedoes, full speed ahead!"
August 7	Sheridan is given command of Union troops in the Shenandoah Valley.
August 18–22	Sherman conducts a wheeling movement to strike at Jonesboro, southeast of Atlanta.
August 31	Democrats nominate General McClellan for President. Hood attacks Sherman at Jonesborough, but falls back once more.
September 1	Hood evacuates Atlanta.
September 19	Sheridan defeats Early at the Third Battle of Winchester, Virginia.
September 29–30	Grant pushes his lines west of Petersburg with the Battle of Peebles' Farm.
October 19	Confederates attack Sheridan's cavalry at Cedar Creek, Virginia, while he is away; in his famous "twenty-mile ride," Sheridan returns to save the day. It is the last major battle in the Shenandoah Valley. Confederates raid St. Albans, Vermont, from Canada.
October 22	Hood begins the Tennessee campaign.
November 8	Lincoln is reelected, with Andrew Johnson as his Vice President.
November 16	Sherman leaves Atlanta for the "March to the Sea."
November 22	Milledgeville, Georgia, is occupied by Federal troops.
November 25	Confederate attempt to burn New York City fails.
November 30	At the Battle of Franklin, Tennessee, six Confederate generals die, including Cleburne, as Hood's frontal attack on Thomas fails.
December 13	Sherman captures Fort McAllister, near Savannah, Georgia.
December 15–16	At the Battle of Nashville, the last major battle in the West, Thomas routs Hood and captures the city. Hood's Army of Tennessee is decimated.
December 20	Hardee takes his troops out of Savannah, Georgia.
December 22	Sherman wires Lincoln, "I beg to present to you as a Christmas gift, the city of Savannah."

1865

January 13	Hood resigns and turns command of his Army of Tennessee to Lieutenant General Richard Taylor under the supervision of Beauregard.
January 15	Fort Fisher, at Wilmington, North Carolina, falls to Union landing force.
January 31	The Confederate Congress names Lee General-in-Chief of all the Southern armies. U. S. House passes, 119 to 56, the Thirteenth Amendment abolishing slavery.
February 1	Sherman begins march through the Carolinas.
February 3	Lincoln and Secretary of State William Seward confer with Confederate Vice President Stephens at Hampton Roads.

February 17	Columbia, South Carolina, is ravaged by fire after falling to Sherman. Confederates evacuate Charleston.
February 18	Charleston is occupied without a fight.
February 22	Schofield takes Wilmington, North Carolina.
March 4	Lincoln is inaugurated for a second term.
March 11	Sherman takes Fayetteville, North Carolina.
March 13	The Confederate Congress authorizes the recruitment of black soldiers.
March 18	The Confederate Congress adjourns for the last time.
March 19–21	Confederates defeated at the Battle of Bentonville, North Carolina.
March 25	Gordon makes unsuccessful assault on Fort Stedman, in Union lines before Petersburg.
March 29	The Appomattox Campaign begins with flanking movements by the Federal army.
April 1	Sheridan overwhelms Pickett at Five Forks, Virginia.
April 2	The assault on Petersburg begins. A. P. Hill is killed. The Confederates evacuate Richmond. Night finds the city in flames.
April 3	Lee pulls his army out of the defense of Petersburg and moves west. Richmond occupied by Federal troops.
April 4–5	Lincoln visits Richmond.
April 6	Confederates defeated at Sayler's Creek, Virginia.
April 9	Lee surrenders to Grant at Appomattox Court House. The stage is set for the general surrender of Southern forces.
April 12	The Confederate government meets at Greensborough, North Carolina. Mobile, Alabama, surrenders.
April 14	Lincoln is shot by John Wilkes Booth at Ford's Theatre in Washington, D.C.
April 15	Lincoln dies and Andrew Johnson becomes President.
April 17	Johnston asks Sherman for terms of surrender. The Stars and Stripes are raised over Fort Sumter.
April 26	The Confederate government meets at Charlotte. Johnston surrenders to Sherman near Durham Station, North Carolina. Booth is shot dead in a blazing barn near Bowling Green, Virginia.
May 4	Lincoln is buried at Springfield, Illinois. General Taylor surrenders all remaining troops east of the Mississippi at Citronelle, north of Mobile.
May 10	Davis is captured by Federal troops near Irwinville, Georgia, and is taken to Fort Monroe, Virginia to await trial. President Johnson proclaims the end of armed resistance.
May 12	The last land fight of the war takes place in the Battle of Palmito Hill near Brownsville, Texas.
May 23–24	Grand Review of Federal armies in Washington, D.C.
May 26	General S. B. Buckner acting for General Kirby Smith surrenders the Trans-Mississippi.
May 29	Johnson proclaims amnesty for all citizens of the South who pledge allegiance to the United States, Confederate officers and a few others excepted.
June 23	President Johnson declares Federal blockade of Southern states at an end.
June 30	Lincoln conspirators convicted.
July 7	Lincoln conspirators executed.
November 6	Confederate cruiser C.S.S. *Shenandoah* surrenders to British officials at Liverpool.
December 18	Thirteenth Amendment to the Constitution abolishing slavery declared "in effect."

Bibliography

Anders, Curt. *Hearts in Conflict.* New York: Birch Lane Press, 1994.

Andrews, J. Cutler. *The North Reports the Civil War.* Pittsburgh: University of Pittsburgh, 1985.

———. *The South Reports the Civil War.* Princeton, NJ: Princeton University Press, 1970.

Boatner, Mark M. III. *The Civil War Dictionary,* rev. ed. New York: David McKay Company, 1988.

Botkin, B. A. *Civil War Treasury of Tales, Legends and Folklore.* New York: Random House, 1960.

Bowman, John S., ed. *The Civil War Almanac,* New York: Gallery Books, 1983.

———. *Who Was Who in the Civil War.* New York: Crescent Books, 1994.

Catton, Bruce. *Mr Lincoln's Army.* New York: Doubleday, 1951.

———. *Glory Road.* New York: Doubleday, 1952.

———. *A Stillness at Appomattox.* New York: Doubleday, 1953.

———. *The Centennial History of the Civil War,* 3 volumes. New York: Doubleday, 1961–1965.

Clark, Champ, and the editors of Time-Life Books. The Civil War Series. *Gettysburg: The Confederate High Tide.* Alexandria, VA: Time-Life Books, 1985.

Cromie, Alice. *A Tour Guide to the Civil War* (4th ed.) Nashville, TN: Rutledge Hill Press, 1992.

Davis, William C., and the editors of Time-Life Books. The Civil War Series. *First Blood: Fort Sumter to Bull Run.* Alexandria, VA: Time-Life Books, 1983.

———. *Death in the Trenches: Grant at Petersburg.* The Civil War Series. Alexandria, VA: Time-Life Books, 1986.

Davis, William C. *Jefferson Davis: The Man and His Hour.* New York: Freedom Press, 1977.

Denney, Robert E. *The Civil War Years: A Day-by-Day Chronicle of the Life of a Nation.* New York: Sterling Publishing Co., 1994.

Elson, Henry W. *The Civil War Through the Camera.* Springfield, MA: Patriot Publishing Co., 1912.

Foote, Shelby. *The Civil War, A Narrative,* 3 volumes. New York: Random House, 1958–1974.

Freeman, Douglas S. *R. E. Lee: A Biography,* 4 volumes. New York: Scribner, 1934–1935.

Golay, Michael. *To Gettysburg and Beyond: The Parallel Lives of Joshua Lawrence Chamberlain and Edward Porter Alexander.* New York: Crown Publishers, 1994.

Grant, Ulysses S., ed. w/notes by E. B. Long. *Personal Memoirs of U. S. Grant* (De Capo unabridged paperback ed.), 1952.

Greene, A. Wilson, and Gary W. Gallagher. *National Geographic Guide to the Civil War National Battlefield Parks.* Washington, DC: National Geographic Society, 1992.

Harwell, Richard Barksdale, ed. *The Union Reader.* New York: Longmans, Green & Co., 1958.

———. *The War They Fought.* New York: Longman's, Green & Co., 1960.

Katcher, Philip. *The Civil War Source Book.* Facts on File, New York, 1992.

Kennedy, Frances H., ed. *The Civil War Battlefield Guide.* Boston: Houghton Mifflin Company, 1990.

Lane, Mills, ed. *"Dear Mother: Don't Grieve About Me If I Get Killed, I'll Only Be Dead." Letters from Georgia Soldiers in the Civil War.* Savannah, GA: Beehive Press, 1977.

Lawliss, Chuck. *The Civil War Sourcebook: A Traveler's Guide.* New York: Harmony Books, 1991.

Long, E. B., and Barbara Long. *Civil War Day by Day: An Almanac.* New York: Doubleday, 1971.

Luraghi, Raimondo. *Storia della Guerra Civile Americana.* Turin: G. Einaudi, 1966.

MacNeice, Jill. *A Guide to National Monuments and Historic Sites.* Englewood, NJ: Prentice Hall, 1990.

McFeely, William S. *Grant: A Biography.* New York: Norton, 1981.

McPherson, James M. *Battle Cry of Freedom: The Civil War Era.* New York: Oxford University Press, 1988.

———. *What They Fought For—1861–1865.* Baton Rouge, LA: Louisiana State University Press, 1994.

———. *Ordeal by Fire: The Civil War and Reconstruction.* New York: Knopf, 1982.

McWhiney, Grady, and Perry D. Jamieson. *Attack and Die: Civil War Military Tactics and the Southern Heritage.* University, AL: University of Alabama Press, 1982.

Nolan, Alan. *The Iron Brigade.* Bloomington, IN: Indiana University Press, 1994.

Paludan, Phillip S. *The Presidency of Abraham Lincoln.* Lawrence, KS: University Press of Kansas, 1994.

Randall, James G., and David Herbert Donald. *The Civil War and Recontruction,* 2nd ed. Lexington, MA: D. C. Heath, 1969.

Rhodes, Robert Hunt, ed. *All for the Union: The Civil War Diary and Letters of Elisha Hunt Rhodes.* New York: Orion Book/Crown, 1991.

Robertson, James L. *Civil War Virginia: Battlefield for a Nation.* Charlottesville, VA: University Press of Virginia, 1991.

Roland, Charles P. *An American Iliad: The Story of the Civil War.* Lexington, KY: University Press of Kentucky, 1991.

Sears, Stephen W., ed. *The Civil War: A Treasury of Art and Literature.* New York: Hugh Lauter Levin Associates, 1992.

———. *The Civil War: The Best of American Heritage.* Boston: Houghton Mifflin Company, 1991.

Sifakis, Stewart. *Who Was Who in the Civil War.* New York: Facts on File, 1988.

Straubing, Harold Elk. *Civil War Eyewitness Reports.* Hamden, CT: Archon Books, 1985.

Stevens, Joseph, E. *America's National Battlefield Parks.* Norman, OK: University of Oklahoma, 1990.

Struggle for Tennessee, The: Tupelo to Stones River. The Civil War Series. Alexandria, VA: Time-Life Books, 1985.

Symonds, Craig L. *A Battlefield Atlas of the Civil War.* 1983.

Thomas, Benjamin. *Abraham Lincoln.* New York: Knopf, 1952.

Vandiver, Frank E. *Blood Brothers: A Short History of the Civil War.* College Station, TX.: Texas A&M University Press, 1992.

———. *Their Tattered Flags: The Epic of the Confederacy.* New York: Harper's Magazine Press, 1970.

Walker, Steven L., and Matti P. Marjorin. *Civil War Parks: The Battlefields of Freedom.* Scottsdale, AZ: Elan Publishing, 1991.

Ward, Geoffrey C., and Ric and Ken Burns. *The Civil War.* New York: Alfred A. Knopf Inc., 1990.

Wheeler, Richard. *Voices of the Civil War.* New York: Thomas Y. Crowell, 1976.

Wiley, Bell Irvin. *The Life of Billy Yank: The Common Soldier of the Union.* Baton Rouge, LA: Louisiana State University Press, 1971.

Woodward, C. Vann, ed. *Mary Chesnut's Civil War.* New Haven: Yale University Press, 1981.

Index

Acknowledgements

The publisher would like to thank the following people for their expertise, advice, and assistance, in the preparation of this book: the Superintendents of the National Parks featured in this book and the staff of the National Park Service, Harpers Ferry Publications Division, especially Tom Patterson for his help with the National Park maps and for the art on pages 90–91, and Tom Durant for help with picture research; Claire Gordon for preparing the index. Grateful acknowledgement is also made to the individuals and institutions who supplied pictures; all are courtesy of the Prints and Photographs Division, Library of Congress, or the National Archives, except those listed below with their page numbers:

Anne S. K. Brown Military Collection, Brown University Library: 108. **The Bettmann Archive**: 14 (above), 15, 20, 20–21 (bottom), 26 (bottom), 28 (top), 34, 37 (bottom), 41 (both), 48, 51, 53 (both), 56 (both), 57, 59 (top), 62, 74 (both), 76, 83, 101, 114, 119, 129, 136. **Museum of the Confederacy, Richmond, VA**: 105 (top, photo by Katherine Wetzel). © 1995 **Michael A. Smith**: 2–3; 19, 22, 26 (top), 27, 30–31, 35, 36–7, 37 (top), 39, 40, 42, 43 (bottom), 52, 54 (both), 55 (top), 58, 59 (bottom l & r), 61, 63, 70, 71, 73, 75 (top), 78 (both), 79 (bottom), 99 (bottom). **UPI/Bettmann**: 82. Courtesy, **U.S. Department of the Interior, National Park Service Division**: all maps except on pages 138–139; 12, 13 (all), 16 (top), 66, 68 (top), 69 (bottom), 84, 103, 105 (bottom), 110, 111, 113, 115, 116, 117, 130, 132, 133; photo Fred R. Bell,: 51 (top); photos Jack E. Boucher: 29 (bottom), 100, 123; photo Carl G. Degan: 103; photos Richard Frear: 47 (bottom), 88, 89, 91 (top); photos William S. Keller: 97 (top), 99 (top); photo Fred Marig Jr.: p107; photos Hugo Skrastins: 32 (both); photos Cecil W. Stoughton: 67 (top), 68 (bottom), 69 (top), 97 (bottom); photo H. S. York: 113 (top).